LONE STAR MUSLIMS

D1520636

Lone Star Muslims

Transnational Lives and the South Asian Experience in Texas

Ahmed Afzal

NEW YORK UNIVERSITY PRESS
New York and London

NEW YORK UNIVERSITY PRESS
New York and London
www.nyupress.org

References to Internet websites (URLs) were accurate at the time of writing.
Neither the author nor New York University Press is responsible for URLs
that may have expired or changed since the manuscript was prepared.

ISBN: 978-1-4798-5534-6 (hardback)
ISBN: 978-1-4798-4480-7 (paperback)

For Library of Congress Cataloging-in-Publication data,
please contact the Library of Congress.

New York University Press books are printed on acid-free paper,
and their binding materials are chosen for strength and durability.
We strive to use environmentally responsible suppliers and materials
to the greatest extent possible in publishing our books.

Manufactured in the United States of America

10 9 8 7 6 5 4 3 2 1

Also available as an ebook

For my parents, Afzal and Sajida

CONTENTS

ACKNOWLEDGMENTS

During the last one decade, as I have worked on this research project, I have accumulated much intellectual debt thanks to the immense generosity of interlocutors along the way. This book bears my name as the author, but it is a collaborative effort with a number of people—both within and outside of the academy. I am sure to leave out some names, and I can in no way do justice to the generosity of those whose contributions continue to inspire, shape, and guide my scholarly endeavors. I am deeply indebted to my mentor, Kamari Clarke at Yale University, for her unflagging support, thoughtful guidance, and excellent scholarly advice. I remain extremely grateful to the intellectual and institutional support provided by George Marcus during my fifteen-month-long field research in Houston in 2001 and 2002. I am very appreciative of the opportunity to work with Thomas Blom Hansen during the initial stages of writing at Yale University.

At Yale University, from 1998 to 2006, I benefited greatly from the intellectual support and constructive feedback from the following colleagues: Arjun Appadurai, Bernard Bate, Faisal Devji, Joseph Errington, David Graeber, Kira Hall, William W. Kelly, Mary Liu, Patricia Pessar, Mridu Rai, Linda Anne Rehbun, Hal Scheffler, Helen Siu, David Watts, and Eric Worby. I am enormously thankful to members of a writing group at Yale University from 2003 to 2005: Karen Warner, Robert Clark, Tanya Hart, and Vladimir Gil for their excellent feedback, and most important, collegiality.

I would also like to thank Shemeem Abbas, Ping-Ann Addo, Safiya Aftab, Nina Bhatt, Nicholas de Genova, Richard Gioioso, Jason Harle, Chris Henke, Carolyn Hsu, Matthew Immergut, Naveeda Khan, Saba Khattak, Amitava Kumar, Nita Kumar, Prema Kurien, Meika Loe, Lisa Jean Moore, Mary Moran, Gaura Narayan, Hamid Naficy, Veronica

Perera, Nancy Reis, Eirik Saethre, Omid Safi, Deirdre Sato, Valencia Wallace, Agustin Zarzosa, Homayra Ziad, and Chitralekha Zutshi.

I have benefited immeasurably from the support, friendship, and encouragement of Carrie Lane, Tej Purewal, Simone Teelen, Jonathan Tindle, Johan Verly and Tiantian Zheng. I thank them for their deep intellectual roots, fellowship, and, above all, friendship. I am also thankful to Stanley Thangaraj, who read several chapters and offered detailed feedback. I owe an enormous amount of gratitude to my dear friend and collaborator, Mieka Ritsema, who went beyond the call of duty and read all chapters and provided detailed, thoughtful, and astute feedback. There is no way that I could have completed this project without her active engagement, and I remain forever in her debt.

As anyone who has arrived in a new city to begin ethnographic research will no doubt agree, the data we collect is often the result of the generosity and kindness of interlocutors. It is impossible for me to name here all of the hundreds of individuals I interviewed and built relationships with over the course of my fieldwork. Yet the stories that fill the pages of this book would be entirely lacking in substance and inspiration if not for their generosity and candor. I hope that they see a fragment or snapshot of their lives and stories reflected in the narratives and biographies that follow in the book. I interviewed more than two hundred Pakistani men and women and had informal conversations with several additional hundreds. I regret that many of the narratives that I had collected did not make it into the book, primarily because of constraints associated with the length of the book. Nonetheless, I hope that they know just how much I have learned from them.

I thank Jennifer Hammer at New York University Press for her unflagging support for this project. Her exemplary professionalism, skill, and incisive feedback have been critical in putting together this book. I am obliged to her along with Constance Grady and Dorothea Stillman Halliday and the whole staff at NYU Press. I also thank the anonymous readers whose detailed comments and critical engagement proved invaluable in revising the manuscript. I am also deeply grateful to Tapu Javeri for letting me use his beautiful artwork for the cover image.

My gratitude goes to my family in Pakistan, and especially my parents, Sajida and Afzal, who have ably anchored my journey from Pakistan to New Haven, Connecticut, to Houston, Texas, to Hamilton,

New York, to White Plains, New York. Certainly, the research became a "family project" with my family members pushing me to rethink my assumptions about the lived experience of Islam and being Muslim in a rapidly changing world. My sister, Fatimah, brother, Ali, and sister-in-law, Vaneeza, warrant a special thanks for their support and encouragement. My niece Noorulain Fatimah demonstrated great enthusiasm and excitement for this book and provided much inspiration to complete this project. Most memorably however, in spite of battling serious illness, my father read the entire manuscript and offered perceptive feedback. In a world increasingly affected by religious intolerance, prejudice, and discriminatory state surveillance on the basis of national origin and religion, my nieces, Noorulain Fatimah and Inaaya Jahan, offer me much hope and optimism for the future. They strengthen my faith that our interactions in our everyday lives may well contribute to empathy, mutual respect, and cross-cultural understanding. This book is dedicated to my parents for their life lessons in kindness, humility, empathy, and integrity that anchor all my journeys and endeavors.

Introduction

I had been in Houston for less than a week when I realized the difficulty in figuring out where cultural life took place for the interlocutors for my research: Pakistani Americans and Pakistani immigrants. Like many new immigrants in Houston, Pakistanis reside throughout Greater Houston. Even in the sections of southwest Houston along Hillcroft Avenue, Harwin Drive, and Bissonnet Street where Pakistani businesses and residential enclaves predominate, Pakistanis are a part of an ethnically and racially diverse landscape that also includes, among others, Afghani, Bangladeshi, Chinese, Ecuadorian, Indian, Japanese, Korean, Mexican, Nigerian, Palestinian, and Vietnamese businesses and residential communities. During this initial period of research, I could not discern a recognizable South Asian ethnic center that would not only anchor my research but also provide me with a sense of ethnic rootedness and belonging in an as yet unfamiliar city.

On one of my first exploratory visits, when I was wondering how, in a city as vast and populous as Houston, I would ever locate Pakistani interlocutors, I got into a cab to explore Hillcroft Avenue. The cab driver turned out to be a middle-aged Pakistani man named Wasim. As I learned during the ride, he had relocated with his family from New York City to Houston a few years earlier. "I wanted to be closer to my brother who lives here," he told me. "Besides, it's tough to raise a family in New York—life is so fast there. Houston is better that way."

While we continued our conversation, Wasim headed south on Hillcroft Avenue. I looked out the window and saw storefronts advertising Middle Eastern businesses in English and Arabic. Passing Harwin Drive, Arabic-language storefronts are replaced by South Asian and Latino businesses with storefronts in Urdu, Hindi, and Spanish. The blazing late summer sun and the oppressive humidity gave sidewalks and strip malls a deserted look. Commercial high-rises, large non-descript parking lots occupied by car dealerships, and roadways leading into gated communities gave way to open fields and prairie.

I was taking in the sights when Wasim asked me, "So, what brings you to Houston?"

"My research is on Pakistanis in Houston; you know, their cultural life here," I began to explain.

"You must listen to the radio then," he said as he turned up the volume of the car radio. A Pakistani folk song permeated the cab. A male radio programmer, speaking in Urdu, introduced the next song. Wasim continued: "There are so many Pakistani radio programs on 1150 AM—it is basically a Pakistani radio station. I always listen to it whenever I am driving—the programs are on all the time. You'll learn much about Pakistanis from listening to radio."

Wandering in a taxicab, on a quest to find interlocutors for my research, I was, thus, first introduced to Pakistani radio programs in Houston. Importantly, Wasim had not taken me to a spatially bound ethnic enclave or neighborhood, or pointed me to the institutional space of a mosque or a Pakistani or South Asian community-based organization. Instead, he had directed me to look for the Pakistani community through its participation in the airwaves of commercial radio. What is significant in Wasim's observation is the connection he made between radio and the production of a diasporic community in Houston. Indeed, during the course of my research, radio developed into an important field site for exploring mass mediated South Asian diasporic public cultures.

The multidimensional texture of diasporic public cultures such as radio represents an important facet of the Pakistani American experience that is often marginalized and only cursorily explored in scholarly studies of South Asians and Muslim Americans in the post-9/11 epoch. Certainly 9/11 is an integral part of the story told in this book. The terrorist attacks of September 11, 2001, took place when I was only a couple of months into my fieldwork in Houston. As the United States government quickly identified Osama bin Laden as the mastermind behind the attacks and began to characterize Pakistan as a "frontline state" in the U.S.-led global war against terrorism, Muslim Americans began to draw the sharp attention of law enforcement and intelligence services.

Several thousand Muslim men of South Asian and Middle Eastern descent were detained for months without being charged with crimes; many were deported for minor infractions. U.S. government agencies began targeting mosques, as well as South Asian and Middle Eastern charities, community centers and businesses based on the perception that these places propagate and nurture Islamic militancy, terrorism and anti-Americanism.

Much exemplary research has highlighted the damage to Muslim Americans in the context of post-9/11 government surveillance, Islamophobia, and racism, and rightly so.[1] Nonetheless, there remain other dimensions of people's lives within this broader context that call for further elaboration. This book argues that the everyday struggles Muslim Americans face are critical in shaping their ideas about identity, community, and citizenship. For some, these struggles take the form of living far from family or taking care of family responsibilities. Others are struggling to find and maintain employment. Still others are struggling to come to terms with their sexuality. They are not generally focused on the events of 9/11, but on more mundane everyday challenges relating to crafting their identities as Pakistani Muslim Americans. Indeed, in my interviews with Pakistani Muslims and during participant observation in Houston, 9/11 came up frequently in the months that followed, but then less so except when discussing particular issues such as the government surveillance of, or racism toward, Muslim Americans. Even though 9/11 provides one of the central lenses for understanding the Pakistani Muslim American and immigrant experience, I soon realized that this experience could not be reduced to or explained solely with reference to 9/11. In order to understand everyday life experiences of Pakistani Muslims in the United States, this book, therefore, examines a range of contexts, including Houston's South Asian ethnic economy, homeland politics and festive celebrations, ethnic media, transnational revivalist Islamic movements, and Muslim sectarian community formations, in addition to and in relation to the aftermath of 9/11.

To be sure, the events of September 11, 2001, had a profound influence on the lives of Muslim Americans. On the government level, the passage of the USA Patriot Act in the fall of 2001 expanded the authority of U.S. law enforcement agencies for the stated purpose of combating terrorism in the United States and abroad.[2] The Act also expanded the definition of terrorism to include domestic terrorism, thereby enlarging the number of activities to which the Act's expanded law enforcement powers could be applied. More than a decade later, these practices of surveillance, governmentality,[3] and control are now entrenched in U.S. statecraft and sustained by the ongoing U.S. geopolitical and militaristic engagements in the Gulf States, the Middle East and South Asia.[4] Representatives of the U.S. government argue that these laws and policies form an integral part of the U.S.-led global war on terrorism and are intended to keep the United States "safe." From the perspective of Muslim Americans, these laws and policies represent a state-sanctioned racism and criminalization of U.S. citizens and resident noncitizens on the basis of religion and country of origin. Moreover, post 9/11 policies homogenize Muslim populations as well as Islam itself, and render invisible the vociferous protests within Muslim American communities against religious militancy and terrorism—protests that, in fact, long preceded the attacks of 9/11.

On the everyday level, Muslim Americans throughout the United States became targets of nativist American attacks following 9/11 (Skitka 2006). The violence directed at Muslim Americans, especially Muslim men, was rationalized as falling into the category of "crimes of passion" committed in defense of the nation and as expressions of U.S. patriotism (M. Ahmed 2002). Indeed, the post-9/11 epoch has been marked by moments when it was deemed permissible to "say or do anything to Arabs and Muslims in the United States" (Cainkar 2009: 4). In Texas, where I carried out the research for this book, reports of harassment, arson attacks, and bias crimes appeared with regularity in the mainstream press. In Denton, for example, a mosque was firebombed. In Austin, an incendiary device was thrown at a Pakistani-owned gasoline station. Six bullets were fired through windows of a Dallas-area mosque. In Carrollton, a mosque had its windows shattered. In the border town of McAllen, the Muslim owner of a delicatessen reported that the phrase "Go Home" had been twice spray-painted on the main door of his Al-Madinah Market before an arson attack gutted the shop. In Houston's Montgomery County, the Ku Klux Klan sponsored a demonstration in front of a Pakistani-owned convenience store after an email circulated that employees at the store had allegedly ripped down American flags. The protest was eventually halted after the storeowner explained to the organizers that teenagers had removed the flags after being refused permission to purchase cigarettes without proper ID to verify their age.[5] As recently as the autumn of 2012, to protest the construction of mosques across the country, vandals left a slain pig in front of a mosque near Houston, indicating sustained hostility toward Muslim Americans that has persisted over a decade after 9/11.[6]

The fear of violent backlash and everyday hostility toward Muslim Americans has played a central role in the crisis over public self-presentations in Muslim communities. In Houston, several Muslim-owned businesses found it prudent to display the American flag and post large signs that read "God Bless America" and "We Support America" on storefronts and glass windows. A number of Muslim Americans began to display stickers of the American flag on cars and American flag pins on clothing. These symbolic gestures were intended to mediate the vulnerabilities resulting from government surveillance and the racializing of Muslims as foreigners at best and as anti-American Islamic militants and would-be terrorists at worst. One might read these acts as an affirmation of allegiance to the United States of America and inclusion in projects of U.S. nationalism, if they were not taking place in a climate of a pervasive and coercive state surveillance of Muslim citizens and resident noncitizens and thus motivated at least in part by fears of violence. The frustration and anger some of my interlocutors felt became evident when Sara, a young Pakistani American woman, a teacher at a public middle school in Houston, and a cohost of an arts-centered radio program on Pacifica Radio, remarked as we passed a patriotic sign on the glass window of a Pakistani restaurant, "I can't even look at these signs anymore. It makes me so angry that we are now obligated to display our American-ness. Does a sign make us more American? Will these signs change the way others think about us?"

The notion that Muslim individuals and business owners felt the need to publicly demonstrate their patriotism illustrates how emergent forms of U.S. nationalism are exacerbating vulnerabilities and marginalizing, if not entirely excluding, Muslim communities from an American imagined community. Writing about the vulnerabilities experienced by Detroit's Arab communities following 9/11, historian Sally Howell and cultural anthropologist Andrew Shryock note:

In the aftermath of 9/11, Arab and Muslim Americans have been com-
pelled, time and again, to apologize for acts they did not commit, to con-
demn acts they never condoned, and to openly profess loyalties that, for
most U.S. citizens, are merely assumed. Moreover, Arabs in Detroit have
been forced to distance themselves from Arab political movements, ideologies, causes, religious organizations, and points of view that are currently at odds with U.S. policy. (Howell and Shryock 2003: 444)

While the proliferation of literature on Muslim Americans has
greatly expanded our knowledge of the Muslim American experience,
as well as the myriad responses to 9/11, the scholarship has also, as sociologist Nazli Kibria argues, "flattened" understandings of Muslims,
obscuring the raced, classed and gendered heterogeneity of the Muslim
American experience. According to Kibria, "there has been a tendency
to homogenize Muslims, to present one-dimensional views of who they
are and how they organize and understand their place in the world and
the role of religion within it" (Kibria 2011: 3). Moreover, as Kibria states:

Much post-9/11 scholarship on Muslims has taken a top-down approach
toward its subject matter. Texts, official discourses, and the views of
Islamic leaders and elites have framed the dominant investigative window into the Muslim experience. Even when researchers have, in fact,
taken a broader and more inclusive approach, it has often been to study
those Muslims who are active participants in Islamic groups and organizations. The perspectives and experiences of those Muslims who are
marginal to these organized forums have received little attention. If
only in indirect ways, this too has nurtured the image of homogeneity.
(Ibid.: 3)

The flattening of the Muslim American experience has meant a relative absence of in-depth community-centered ethnographic analyses
of the Pakistani Muslim experience, especially those residing in southern states. Anthropologist Junaid Rana's (2011) examination of South
Asian labor flows and international studies scholar Adil Najam's (2006)
survey-based exploration of philanthropy in Pakistani American communities are among the few in-depth studies that explore the lives of
Pakistanis in the United States. This book contributes to the scholarship

on Muslim Americans through a community-centered ethnographic study of the Pakistani experience in Houston, tracking the community over a ten-year period, from 2001 to 2011.

Given the heightened U.S.-government surveillance and the racializing of Muslim Americans during the last decade, this book challenges commonly held perceptions regarding the complicity of Islam with global terrorism. Decentering dominant framings, such as "terrorist" on the one hand, or "model minority" on the other, that flatten understandings of Islam and Muslim Americans, it employs a cultural analysis to document the heterogeneity of the Pakistani American and the Pakistani immigrant experience. This book includes narratives that reflect the internal diversity of the Pakistani population and includes members of the highly skilled Shia Ismaili Muslim labor force employed in corporate America; Pakistani ethnic entrepreneurs, and the working class and the working poor employed in Pakistani ethnic businesses; gay Muslim American men of Pakistani descent; community activists; and radio program hosts. These narratives provide glimpses into the variety of lived experiences of Pakistani Americans and show how specificities of class, profession, religious sectarian affiliation, citizenship status, gender, and sexuality shape transnational identities, and mediate racism, marginalities and abjection.

Using a multisited approach (Marcus 1995) as a theoretical, in addition to a methodological, tool enabled me to dismantle the homogenizing impulse that characterizes most research on Muslim American communities. This book examines three different groups of people and two place-making processes in order to illuminate the complexity of the Muslim American experience and the category of "the Muslim." Chapters devoted to each of three groups—Shia Ismailis; gay Muslims; and entrepreneurs, working-class, and working-poor Muslims—demonstrate both broader patterns as well as specificities of experience in Pakistani Muslim communities in Houston. The focus on religious sectarianism, class, and sexuality emerged organically during the process of fieldwork and writing, and, under other circumstances, could well have included a range of other groupings. Indeed, more research is required, and future studies will further explore and document this heterogeneity, for example, through a greater consideration of the lives of women, especially lesbian Muslim Americans; Pakistani religious minority populations, notably, Hindu, Christian, Zoroastrian, and Ahmadiya communities; and activists involved in multiethnic and multireligious alliance and community building. The two place-making processes that are examined in detail, the Pakistani Independence Day Festival and the airwaves of a vibrant Pakistani radio programming landscape in Houston, demonstrate the diasporic public cultures within which Pakistanis are embedded in Houston.

This book argues that the homogeneity attributed to Muslim Americans and South Asians has obscured the increasingly important role of Islamic sectarian ideologies in shaping community formations in the West. Scholarly studies of Muslim Americans have focused primarily on Sunni Muslims and only tangentially explored other Muslim sectarian communities such as the Sufi orders, Shia, Ismaili, Druze, Ansaru Allah, and Ahmadiya communities, among others.[7] The homogenization of Muslim Americans obscures these variations in Islamic practice (Osella and Osella 2008). The professional life experiences of the highly skilled Shia Ismaili Muslims discussed in chapter 2 show appropriations of Ismaili forms of knowledge and transnational cultural histories during periods of crises such as unexpected unemployment in corporate America. An ethnographic analysis of Shia Ismaili Muslims employed in corporate America recasts educational achievement and professional success—commonly viewed as facets of American values in the model minority concept—as religious imperatives. Complicating the analysis further, the emphasis on education and professional success represents established strategies for negotiating racism, marginality, and discrimination experienced by Ismailis as minorities in several countries during the course of the twentieth century. The case of Shia Ismaili Muslim Americans in Houston therefore illustrates the complex alignment of the American dream, transnational sectarian ideologies, and broader historical experience that is obscured in conceptions of the Muslim American experience as a monolith without due consideration of sectarian specificities.

This book also argues against the presumed heterosexuality in South Asian and Muslim American population movements to the United States that renders invisible the experiences of gay and lesbian South Asian Muslim Americans. The construction of transnational identity among Muslim American gay men of Pakistani descent discussed in chapter 4 indicates complex negotiations of belonging to a transnational Muslim ummah, that is, "a transnational supra-geographical community of fellow Muslims that transcends nationality and other bases of community" (Kibria 2011: 4). These emergent transnational Muslim American same-sex sexual cultural formations disrupt hegemonic discourses in Islam that are centered on the criminalization of same-sex sexual love and relationships and instead reveal spaces of accommodation and inclusion.

Moreover, this book intervenes in the intellectual project that examines the intersections between Asian American, South Asian American, and Muslim American fields of study. As we will see, Pakistanis in the United States are well situated within genealogies of post-1965 Asian labor flows. As such, Pakistani Americans and immigrants may well be conceptualized within the rubric of Asian America. Historical and cultural convergences between Pakistanis and other South Asian nationality groups also enable a conception of Pakistanis within the analytical category of "South Asian diaspora." Indeed, I employ "South Asian" and "diaspora" to discuss the invocations of cultural epistemologies, idioms, and colonial, postcolonial and diasporic histories that transcend the boundaries of the South Asian nation-state and variously include nationality groups from all countries in the South Asian region.

At the same time, Pakistani Americans and immigrants also exceed Asian American or South Asian categorizations. For example, the central position of Islam in dominant Pakistani state ideologies of nationhood distinguishes Pakistani Americans from other Asian nationality groups. Pakistan is one of only two modern nation-states (the other being Israel) where religion was complexly the raison d'être in the creation of the nation and a critical component of ideologies of nationhood and community. The remapping of Pakistan within the Muslim world and the Greater Middle East in U.S. foreign policy and in post-9/11 practices of surveillance and U.S. imperialism racialized Pakistani Americans and immigrants in terms of religion (Rana 2011). The centrality of Islam in the everyday life of Pakistanis featured in this book draws attention to religious identifications. The alliances and sociality between Pakistani Muslims and Muslims from Asia, the Gulf States, the Middle East, Africa, and beyond further characterize reconfigurations of community within the rubric of Muslim America. This book explores the complexities and overlaps in Asian American, South Asian American, and Muslim American fields of study through the following set of interrelated questions: How and to what effect do Islam and South Asian diasporic histories shape the everyday life of Pakistanis in Houston? What explains the increasing centrality of Islam in mediating individual experiences of racism, marginality, and abjection on the one hand, and patterns of consumption and practices of capitalist production, such as within the South Asian ethnic economy, festive cultures, and mass media, on the other? And finally, how is Islam discursively produced in, and intertwined with, practices of diasporic nationhood and community formation?

The title of this book, *Lone Star Muslims,* acknowledges these complexities in categorizing Pakistani Americans and Pakistani immigrants. The multiple contextual categorizations of Texas, much like the varied contexts and the layers of identification that characterize the Pakistani experience in Houston—as new immigrants, as Houstonians, as Muslims, as Pakistanis, as Asians, and as South Asians and as variously classed, gendered, and racialized groups—exceed any singular heuristic and require multiple interpretive lenses. "Lone Star State," the nickname of the state of Texas, references the construction of an alleged statehood outside of the U.S. nation formed out of notions of conquest, manifest destiny, and white supremacy. Also, while Texas is geographically situated between the southern and southwestern United States and conceptualized as such in American area studies, it is also distinct from these categories because of specificities of historical experience.

On another level, the cojoining of the Lone Star State and Muslims highlights the embeddness of my interlocutors in raced, classed, and gendered genealogies of labor flows, and place-making practices in Houston. While most studies of transnational communities emphasize the transnational registers of identification, this book also explores the ways in which Pakistanis have claimed, and continue to claim, space as Houstonians. These claims are apparent in the establishment of residences and businesses in southwest Houston examined in chapter 1 as well as in discussions of the employment of Pakistani highly skilled labor in corporate America in chapter 2, and the transnational Muslim heritage economy in chapter 3. These claims are also evident in the reconfigurations of the Pakistan Independence Day celebrations as a practice of cultural citizenship and as a "Houston tradition" discussed in chapter 5. Finally, the involvement of Pakistanis in radio that is documented in chapter 6 also speaks to the specificities of local geographies, especially the significance of the car culture and automobile travel in a highway-dominated city, that make radio a vital space of connectivity for a community that is dispersed throughout the greater Houston metropolitan area. The Lone Star State is central in unpacking these myriad layers of Pakistani everyday life and experience in Houston.

Theorizing Transnationalism

The ethnographic study of the Pakistani American and the Pakistani immigrant experience provides a context for reexamining cultural analyses of globalization and transnationalism that emphasize porous and fluid national and cultural borders[8] and "flexible" notions of citizenship and belonging (Ong 1996). Theorizing around globalization and transnationalism emphasizes the accelerated movement of people and goods across national borders, facilitated by global neoliberalism (Harvey 2005). Citizenship, nationhood, and cultural belonging, in the contemporary period of globalization, are no longer bound within the territorial boundaries of the nation-state.[9] Theorists of globalization emphasize time-space compression characterized by increased flexibility in labor processes and markets, geographic mobility and shifts in consumption patterns (Harvey 1989). In his seminal work on globalization, anthropologist Arjun Appadurai argues that "global cultural flows" have replaced a single "imagined community" with "imagined worlds," that is, the "multiple worlds that are constituted by the historically situated imaginations of persons and groups" that transcend the borders of the nation-state (1996: 33). These theoretical interventions illuminate the formation of transnational belonging within shifting fields of power that link the local to the global[10] and reconfigure notions such as race, ethnicity, class, gender and sexuality.

Beginning in the early 1990s, scholars working with recent immigrant groups, noting the inadequacy of dominant conceptualizations of nationhood and belonging, offered "transnationalism" as a more appropriate conceptual framework for examining "the multiplicity of migrants' involvements in both the home and host societies" (Glick

Schiller, Basch, and Blanc-Szanton 1992: ix). In the 1990s and 2000s, anthropologists further developed the framework of transnationalism to examine negotiations of belonging to multiple nation-states and deterritorialized sources of power and authority in the context of new immigrant groups or transmigrants in the United States. These studies reveal the institutional structures, and every day practices and rituals through which transmigrants build financial and intellectual support for transnational projects and highlight the intersection of U.S.-based immigrant groups with individuals, infrastructure and institutions outside the geographical borders of the United States.[11] Immigrant communities living thousands of miles from their homeland are increasingly implicated in a wide range of cultural projects and practices that reconfigure their relationship with their homeland.[12] Ethnographic studies have examined the familial, socioeconomic, political, and communication networks and associations maintained by transmigrants in multiple nation-states.[13] They have also examined how certain "groups of immigrants fight against multiple techniques of subordination through claims that do not rely on citizenship" (Das Gupta 2006: 12) and instead use transnational institutional structures such as international human rights regimes, to claim rights, benefits, and privileges.[14]

As demonstrated in this book, countervailing trends, notably U.S. national security and global terrorism following 9/11, undermine transnational practices.[15] Moreover, the racialization of Muslim Americans following 9/11 shows how citizenship alone does not confer inclusion and belonging in projects of U.S. nationalism. The differential in access to citizenship-based civil, political, social, and economic rights is tied to schemes of classifying immigrants as illegal, legal but nonresident, legal and resident but noncitizens, naturalized citizens, and native born.[16] These schemes are important, as sociologist Monisha Das Gupta notes: "The legal nature of these distinctions normalizes the hierarchy, thereby making common sense the differential treatment of immigrants in these categories" (2006: 13). As is increasingly evident in the experiences of Muslim Americans documented in this book, U.S. government agencies deploy surveillance and the rhetoric of global security to discipline, criminalize, and persecute individuals whose engagements transcend national borders in diverse, multilayered patterns.[17]

Cognizant of the tensions between the nation-state and transnationalism (Appadurai 1996), this book intervenes in the theorizing around transnationalism through greater consideration of the intertwining of Islam with diasporic nationhood and belonging.[18] In spite of the proliferation of scholarly research on transnationalism, the intersection of transnationalism with religion begs greater analytical consideration. Indeed, as anthropologist Steven Vertovec has stated, "while attempts to theorize and topologize diaspora are certainly beginning to clarify a number of significant dimensions and developments surrounding today's globally dispersed populations, it is clear that their religious elements have received relatively far less attention" (2009: 133). Religious studies scholar Martin Baumann similarly argues that studies of transnational communities have "marginalized the factor of religion and relegated it to second place in favor of ethnicity and nationality" (1998: 95). Most scholarly analyses of religious transnationalism focus on a congregational model. These studies examine religious institutions established by Muslim immigrants in the United States and in the homeland, religious nationalism among diasporic communities, and alliance building centered on a global Muslim ummah.

This book examines Pakistani American and immigrant everyday life to illustrate how transnational religious revivalist movements intersect with practices of diasporic cultural production. In the case of Islam, transnational revivalist movements such as Wahhabism and the Jamaat-al-Tabligh emphasize the significance of Islam in all aspects of life.[19] These movements strive to "revive an original Islam based on literalist interpretations of the Qur'an as well as emulation of the recorded life of the Prophet and his Companions" (Kibria 2011: 3). They have found committed interlocutors among South Asian diasporic communities in the West, including the United States.

Religious orthodoxy in South Asian Hindu communities in the United States is similarly tied to "the politics of Hindu fundamentalism at home" (Appadurai 1996: 38) and is facilitated through the transnational flows of religious ideologies, personnel and capital.[20] In the case of right-wing Hindu revivalist movements, historian Vijay Prashad argues that "by the late 1980s organizations from South Asia were entering the United States to authorize syndicated forms of religiosity"

(Prashad 2000: 143). The ideologies of these revivalist movements are also contested by diasporic communities, notably gay and lesbian South Asians, as discussed in chapter 4.

Transnational revivalist movements in Islam have contributed to the formation of alliances and networks among Muslims from different countries of origin that transcend ethnicity and diaspora.[21] Universalizing Islam is mobilized to forge transnational protest movements to claim rights and entitlements locally and to mediate the relationship between the American state's regimes of control and surveillance and Muslim immigrant communities across race and country of origin.[22] These new alliances also reshape religious practice and, in the case of Muslim immigrant communities in the West, create a universalizing consciousness about practice in Islam.[23] Such developments are expressions of transnational public cultures—such as the Muslim World Day Parade and the Muslim Youth Day—and take place in major cities throughout the United States, creating space for building a pan-racial and pan-national religious community.

Greater attention to the place of transnational Islam in shaping the Pakistani Muslim American experience opens up the analysis to examining how transnational flows of religious ideologies reshape diasporic public cultures, notably festive celebrations and mass media, both undertheorized in studies of South Asian American and Muslim American experiences. In this book, the case study of the Pakistan Independence Day Festival in Houston illuminates the multiple and intersecting registers for making meaning of the Pakistani experience in the United States during the contemporary period of globalization and transnationalism. The Festival is a performance of long-distance Pakistani nationalism. It celebrates independence from Great Britain and the formation of a sovereign nation for Muslims of South Asia. The Festival also demonstrates a capacity to expand the parameters of community and long-distance nationalism through the inclusion of Muslim communities with ancestral affiliations to any country in South Asia. In recent years, Festival organizers have made concerted efforts to include Afghani, Indian, and Bangladeshi Muslims and reframed the Festival as a transnational Muslim celebration. This reframing suggests a creative deployment of festivals as practices to work through universalizing Islam, as well as colonial and postcolonial histories and experiences of war, religious disharmony, and national tensions among the various South Asian nationality groups.

The reframing of the Festival as a transnational Muslim celebration and public culture is further intertwined with and shaped by geopolitical contexts of subjectification. The recent reinvention of the Festival from an indoor event into a parade that is held at a venue associated with multicultural events situates the Festival and the Pakistani communities within specificities of the local milieu. This reinvention also exemplifies a second framing of the Festival: as a "Houston tradition." As a parade, the celebration mediates post-9/11 anxieties and vulnerability around racial hostilities toward Muslim Americans.[24] These transformations recast the Festival as a practice of cultural citizenship[25] and as a practice for making claims, rights, and entitlements as a racialized minority community.[26]

Advances in global media and communication technologies have created, and intensified the speed at which transnational Muslim communities can be forged.[27] Like the Pakistan Independence Day Festival, non-English language Pakistani radio programming also exemplifies a largely uncharted ethnographic register for documenting the Pakistani American and immigrant experience. Indeed, non-English language media production in the United States has been explored rather narrowly in theories of globalization and transnationalism. Analysts of transnationalism typically focus on the role of media produced in the homeland in the creation of "imaginary homelands" for diasporic communities and the formation of diasporic public spheres.[28] Recent literature also illuminates the role of transnational media, mostly movies and television programs produced in the homeland, in representing the relation between the diaspora and the homeland to people in both sites (Mankekar 1999).

Building on this scholarship, this book examines Pakistani radio in Houston as a historical and cultural product, a communicative and social practice, and an aesthetic form that participates in reconfigurations of transnational and cultural belonging. Much like the Pakistan Day Festival, the Pakistani radio programs discussed in chapter 6 are important public cultural formations for examining negotiations between transnational Islam, diasporic nationhood, and the global market economy. Pakistani radio provides a case study of the diversity of media practices that are only now beginning to be charted ethno-graphically (Ginsburg, Abu-Lughod, and Larkin 2002). Following re-cent scholarship in anthropology of mass media,[29] this book similarly conceives of media production as well as reception in the context of its embeddness in everyday life (Silverstone 1994). The circulation of non-English language radio programming in the contemporary United States presents an understudied aspect of transnational cultural flows that has been largely ignored in recent ethnographic studies of new immigrant communities in general and Asian Americans and Muslim Americans in particular.

Where the social importance of radio has been documented, as in Erik Barnouw's classic study of broadcasting in the United States (Bar-nouw 1968), or the more recent study of radio programming and genres in the United States during the twentieth century (Douglas 2004), scant attention has been paid to the role of Latinos, African Americans, and Asian Americans in the enterprise. Recent scholarship on radio has shown the centrality of radio in transnational flows that draw attention to the "urgent as well as the ordinary, the mundane alongside the meta-physical" (Bessire and Fisher 2012: 4). Scholarship has also explored the relationship between sound, technology, and power.[30] In spite of the growing scholarship on radio in the last one decade,[31] there is an absence of ethnographic research, especially reception studies, exam-ining the relationship between radio, transnationalism, and racialized community formations in the United States.

The literature on South Asian Americans and Muslim Americans has similarly largely ignored radio. In studies where radio is discussed, it is either in passing or as a descriptive fact of South Asian transnational life without any ethnographic richness. Historian Madhulika Khandelwal's (2002) ethnographic study of Indian immigrants in New York City, for example, provides a brief discussion of the first Indian radio program in New York, which began in 1975, in the context of her discussion of the Indian media environment in New York. Historian Padma Ranga-swamy's (2000) discussion of Indian radio in Chicago follows a similar representational trajectory, which has the effect of relegating radio to the margins of critical analysis without due consideration of its emer-gence as a historically situated development and as a meaningful cul-tural product, social and leisure activity, and communicative practice.

This book brings radio to the forefront of analysis of diasporic public cultures in the early twentieth century. The emphasis on radio is significant because it shows the tremendous enduring capacity of radio, a technology that is over a century old, in structuring cultural practices and everyday modes of leisure, sociality, and communication in Asian American and Muslim American communities. This is especially significant in Houston, where the Pakistani population is dispersed throughout Greater Houston, and automobiles are the principle mode of transport. In such spatialized geographies, radio provides a virtual medium for creating community that transcends boundaries of class, gender, generation and geography.

Pakistani radio programming in Houston locates listeners in wider constituencies such as national and religious communities and provides an important site for the discursive circulation of religion in transnational soundscapes and practices of "electronic" place-making (Browne 2008). In the case of Pakistani radio in Houston, radio is entangled with the everyday life, concerns, and aspirations of Pakistani Americans and Pakistani immigrants and intertwined with the transnational Muslim heritage economy in Houston. Instances of infighting among radio hosts, while a reflection of intense competition for sponsorship money, also index the loss of masculinity in the United States. The airing of grievances creates a space for Muslim Americans to recuperate their voice that has been increasingly marginalized in mainstream public spheres in the United States.

The case studies of the Pakistan Independence Day Festival and Pakistani radio programming in Houston also exemplify practices of place making in Asian American and Muslim American communities in the United States.[32] Research on place making and transnationality has examined the formation of religious institutions and infrastructure; the performance and observance of rituals such as funeral processions; congregational gatherings during Ashura among Shia communities (Fischer and Abedi 2002); religious festivals like Eid celebrations; the use of language to sacralize space and social interactions as religious (Metcalf 1996) and create a "global sacred geography" (Werbner 1996). The remaking of spaces of commerce by selling religious commodities and displaying religious symbols also indicates the intertwining of transnational religious place making with neoliberal capitalist economy.

These practices of place making in ethnic businesses such as restaurants serve to produce authenticity, invoke nostalgia, and create familiarity in ways that are distinctly different from "the anonymity of an ordinary restaurant" (Fischer and Mehdi 2002: 263).

The work presented in this book expands the scope of inquiry into place making by exploring everyday life at the intersection of transnational Islam, diasporic nationhood, and neoliberal capitalism in three sites. In the first site, the narratives of Shia Ismaili professionals offer an important corrective to the often-presumed incompatibility of Muslim lifestyle and the inapplicability of ethno-religious subjectifications with material pursuits and professional settings that are closely identified with the neoliberal capitalist economy (Deleuze and Guattari 1980). As evidenced from the experiences of Ismailis discussed in chapter 2, transnational religious forms of knowledge and authority not only structure spirituality but also provide the governing principles for professional life, achievements, and success in corporate America and in the pursuit of the American dream.

Ongoing transformations in the South Asian ethnic economies provide a second site for examining the intersections between transnational Islam, diasporic nationhood, and neoliberal capitalism. I argue that Pakistani ethnic enterprises are embedded in local, national, and transnational webs of financial and business networks and capital that are increasingly organized by Islamic values and beliefs. Indeed, the globalization of the halal food market showcases the growth of the transnational Muslim heritage economy as it intersects with a growing critical mass of Muslim communities in the west (I. A. Adams 2011). These ongoing transformations are situated between the globalization of Islamic revivalism, neoliberal capitalism, and consumer culture[33] and illustrate the emergence of "alternatives to what are seen as Western values, ideologies, and lifestyles" (J. Fischer 2005: 280) for Muslim communities residing in the West.

The narratives and everyday life experiences of Pakistani ethnic entrepreneurs, the working class, and the working poor provide a third site for exploring the intersections between transnational Islam, diasporic nationhood, and neoliberal capitalism. In spite of a considerable body of research on ethnic entrepreneurs, the working class, and the working poor in new immigrant communities,[34] few studies have focused on these demographics in Muslim American or South Asian American communities.[35] Such narratives are typically perceived as an inevitable rite of passage to "becoming American" and the attainment of the American dream that is commonly characterized as the seductive, relentless, and inspiring quest for success, prestige, and economic security in the United States.[36] The American dream is premised on individualism and the achievement of upward mobility, assimilation, and success.[37] An analytical consideration of the everyday life of Pakistani entrepreneurs, and the working class and the working poor who provide much of the labor for businesses in the transnational Muslim heritage economy problematizes the discourses around the American dream and raises several questions: How, for example, do Pakistani Muslim entrepreneurs and the working class negotiate U.S. regimes of surveillance of Muslims as they build lives in the United States? What are the sources of social capital deployed by these men and women to make meaning of their lives, struggles, and everyday experiences in Houston? What does an ethnographic focus on individual life experiences and biography of this grouping of Pakistani immigrants (ethnic entrepreneurs, the working class, and the working poor) tell us about the intersections of race, class, religion, and gender in shaping the experience of transnationality, diasporic belonging, and place making in spaces of commerce and economic activity? And finally, how are transnational Islamic ideologies implicated in practices of place making, consumption patterns and material life?

The book also explores the centrality of Islam in the formation of transnational Muslim American sexual cultures. In spite of the proliferation of ethnographic studies of transnational communities in the United States, there has been relatively little research on the gay and lesbian Muslim American experience. Indeed, as anthropologist Junaid Rana states, "queer sexual migration from Pakistan, a significant subculture, has mostly gone unstudied" (Rana 2011). Most of the "post-9/11 ethnographies" (Maira 2009) document the everyday life of gay and lesbian Muslim Americans only cursorily if at all. The relative absence of scholarship perpetuates erroneous understandings of the intenability of non-heteronormative accommodation in Islam and in Muslim communities, which are "teleologically read through the fanatic lens of Islamic fundamentalism" (Puar 2007: 16) and leave intact an assumed heterosexuality in Muslim American and South Asian population movements.

A few post-9/11 cultural analyses have addressed the topic of gay Muslims in the United States through the lens of regimes of governmentality and surveillance of Muslim Americans and immigrants in the country.[38] For example, in an important analysis of race, sexuality, and American citizenship, cultural theorist Chandan Reddy (2011) examines the contradictions of U.S. immigration law, which privilege heteronormative family structures and render queer sexuality subordinate to this heteronormativity. These regimes of oppression ironically coexist with "the liberal state's ideology of universal sexual freedom" (Reddy 2011: 164) at home for all subordinate groups including sexual minorities. In this contradictory location, "the figure of the gay Pakistani immigrant is both a symptom of globalization and the transnationalization of U.S. capital and a new formation developed in the interstices of the nation-state. This figure emerges in the breach between the nation-state and the political economy" (ibid.: 164).[39]

The rise of U.S. homonationalism (Puar 2007) provides another lens for examining LGBTQIA (lesbian, gay, bisexual, transgender, queer, intersex and asexual) Muslim Americans. In Jasbir Puar's astute analysis, the inclusion of some homosexualities within U.S. patriotism and nationalism is premised on the pacification and sanctioning of homosexuals, whereby "homosexuals embrace the us-versus-them rhetoric of U.S. patriotism and thus align themselves with this racist and homophobic production" (Puar 2007: 46). The confluence of U.S. nationalism and gendered, classed, and racialized homosexuality, or what historian Lisa Duggan has termed "homonormativity," creates a "demobilized gay constituency and a privatized, depoliticized gay culture anchored in domesticity and consumption" and embroiled in "a politics that does not contest dominant heteronormative forms but upholds and sustains them" (Duggan 2002: 179).

Building on this scholarship, I challenge Western epistemologies of monolithic gay identities[40] and disrupt the assumed heteronormativity in international population movements. As feminist and queer theorist Gayatri Gopinath notes,

The cartography of a queer diaspora tells a different story of how global capitalism impacts local sites by articulating other forms of subjectivity, culture, affect, kinship, and community that may not be visible or audible within standard mappings of nation, diaspora, or globalization. What emerges within this alternative cartography are subjects, communities, and practices that bear little resemblance to the universalized "gay" identity within a Eurocentric gay imaginary. (Gopinath 2005: 12)

The inquiry into Pakistani Muslim American gay men in this book follows scholarship that has examined the accommodation of vernacular cultures, group membership, and allegiances in transnational lives that traverse multiple geopolitical and epistemological systems.[41] Following anthropologist Richard Parker, such border crossings provide a starting point to grasp the "often messy reality of life in the contemporary, globalized or globalizing, late-modern or postmodern world—a world in which things often fail to fit neatly or hold coherently together, but in which a set of complex relationships does in fact exist and is marked by processes of social, cultural, economic, and political change that ultimately link both the West and the Rest as part of an interacting system" (Parker 1999: 7). Locating South Asian Muslim gay lives at the intersection of multiple geopolitical and epistemological systems provides insights into the changes taking place in the articulation of diverse sexualities in the contemporary epoch.

Methodologies, Data Collection, and Self-Reflexivity

I selected Houston, Texas, as the field site for this ethnographic study of Pakistani Americans and immigrants for several reasons. One, Houston is home to the fourth-largest and one of the most internally diverse South Asian Muslim populations of any major city in the United States. In recent decades, it has emerged as a primary gateway city for immigrants from South Asia. Two, South Asian cultural, religious, professional, and communication networks and infrastructure are particularly well established in Houston, in part due to the large number of Pakistani and Indian immigrants who have settled in Houston since the 1960s. And three, the presence of South Asian Muslims in all major occupational and professional categories and income levels, and from all major South Asian ethno-linguistic and Islamic religious sects (Williams 1988), provided an unparalleled opportunity to examine transnational identities at the intersection of race, religious sect, class and professional affiliations, and gender and sexuality.

The data for this study was collected during fifteen months of qualitative and archival research in Houston from July 2001 until September 2002, and then shorter follow-up research visits to Houston from 2003 until 2011. There were three key target areas for data collection: Pakistani immigrants and their families and relatives; Pakistani religious, civic, cultural, and media-based organizations; and Pakistani hosts and sponsors of Pakistani radio programs in Houston. I began the research process guided by the narratives, experiences, and suggestions of my interlocutors. For example, as I mention in the opening paragraphs of this introduction, only a few weeks into my research, as I rode in a cab driven by a Pakistani American, the cab driver started telling me about radio, and suggested that I listen to radio, which I did. Radio stations provided a vital field site to document mass mediations of transnationality. Listening to the radio also enabled me to build relationships with interlocutors—radio hosts/programmers, sponsors, and invited panelists—who are otherwise dispersed throughout the greater Houston area. Likewise, it was through a series of serendipitous encounters at a DVD and video store where I was carrying out participant observation that I was able to learn of social networks composed of highly skilled labor force members employed in the energy sector and engage them in my research. Finally, during the initial period of my research, when I wondered aloud what brought Pakistanis together in a city as large as Houston, a young Pakistani American student at the University of Houston, pointed me toward the Pakistan Independence Day Festival. These serendipitous encounters provided me with the starting points for research, but over time, these sites proved to be important spaces for charting the heterogeneity of practices and experiences that guided my research.

Ethnographic studies of new immigrants to the United States have shown the importance of individual narratives in understanding the specificities of homeland, immigration and migration, and multiple conceptions of identity and subjectification.[42] In following such research approaches, I conducted in-depth interviews with approximately two hundred men and women to document individual life histories, experiences of migration and immigration, and engagements with social, cultural, religious, and professional networks in Houston and globally.

Ethnographic research and qualitative interviews were combined with archival research to document the changes in the everyday religious, cultural, and social activities of Pakistanis in Houston over time. Recent ethnographic research on South Asian immigrants in the United States has utilized ethnic print media as an important source of historical data.[43] I similarly carried out research at the archives of Pakistani newspapers, along with documents available at Houston's city hall to chart a formal social history of Pakistani immigration to Houston and to situate the research historically within local and regional racial, socioeconomic, and political contexts.

During the entire duration of fieldwork, I resided in Hillcroft, the name of both a street and an area in southwest Houston that has a concentration of Pakistani retail outlets, restaurants, mosques, and residential settlements. This location provided an unparalleled opportunity to conduct ethnographic research at Pakistani organizations, form close relationships with Pakistani Americans and immigrants, and participate in their daily activities and engagements. It also enabled me to more fully understand the texture of Pakistani daily life and the range of religious, cultural, social, and professional relationships and networks within which Pakistanis are embedded in Houston.

Critiques of ethnography[44] have raised profound and still relevant questions regarding the predicament of cultural representations and the importance of increased self-reflexivity and experimentation in the project of writing culture. As a foreign anthropologist carrying out ethnographic research among his own nationality group in the United States, I was cognizant of the complex ways in which power relations shaped textual representations, and the situatedness of the anthropologist in the production of knowledge. In spite of my position as a Muslim, born and raised in an upper-middle-class family in Pakistan, the period of research was characterized by shifting positions—sometimes an outsider, and at other moments, as an insider.

As a Pakistani Muslim with complicated relationships to diasporic nationalist projects and transnational revivalist Islamic movements premised on literalist interpretations of the Qur'an, I had approached my fieldwork with some trepidation. I was overwhelmed by the generosity and candor of my interlocutors and the surprising ease with which I was able to enter the social scene and be included in the everyday and formal lives of Pakistani men and women from a wide range of professional, class, ethnolinguistic, and religious sectarian affiliations. Elders in the Pakistani community referred to me as *beta* (son), and younger male and female Pakistani interlocutors called me *bhai* (brother), inscribing me within the fabric of established Pakistani linguistic terminologies of kin relations. Shared ethnicity, national origin, and religion allowed ready access to a myriad of religious and Pakistani ethnic networks. For example, in a car-centered city like Houston, where I lived without a car, interlocutors and friends readily agreed to drive me to and from cultural events and gatherings and made sure to include me in wedding celebrations, birthday parties, family outings and picnics, and religious congregations.

This is not to state that the research that follows is a totalizing "insider's account." For one, as a single Pakistani male, I had greater access to men because of cultural and religious prohibitions regarding the interaction between sexes within certain segments of the Pakistani population in Houston. Having arrived in the United States as an undergraduate student in the late 1980s and having lived primarily on the East Coast, I lacked kinship relationships within the Pakistani communities in Houston that would have endowed me with status locally and, at least to a degree, mitigated gendered exclusions. I trained two female research assistants who helped collect oral life histories of Pakistani women and facilitated initial contact between Pakistani female interlocutors who observed the purdah (veil) and myself. When I first asked Amber, a young Pakistani American woman and subsequently one of the research assistants, about her interest in helping me collect data, she deferred making a final decision until after I had met with her father. Amber arranged for me to meet her father for lunch at a Lebanese restaurant. He agreed only after being satisfied with the authenticity of my research intentions.

Second, while my native fluency in Urdu and Punjabi greatly facilitated the fieldwork, it also marked me as Punjabi, the majority ethnolinguistic group in Pakistan. Punjabis are historically seen as the doubles for the hegemonic and dominant Pakistani statecraft and apparatus and are implicated in violent ethnolinguistic struggles for rights, entitlements, and benefits in Pakistan. That Punjabis form a minority within the Pakistani immigrant population in Houston, where the dominant group is Urdu-speaking from Karachi and Hyderabad, challenged me to build relationships given my identification as a Punjabi.

Third, being a Sunni Muslim marked me as an outsider during my fieldwork with interlocutors from the Shia, Ismaili, and Ahmadiya communities. While I freely interacted with Shia Muslims at their homes and at Pakistani events, I asked permission before attending ritualized Shia commemorations such as Ashura. Ashura, a day of mourning, commemorates the death of the Third Imam, Husain, the son of Ali and Fatima and the grandson of Prophet Muhammad, through affective passion plays at a Shia mosque and community center and a procession through downtown Houston.

I also spent a weekend at an Ahmadiya retreat and collected oral life histories of members of the Ahmadiya community. Ahmadiya Islam is a reformist movement founded in the nineteenth century by Mirza Ghulam Ahmad. Ahmadiya Muslims follow the teachings of Ahmad and believe him to be the messiah who is awaited by Muslims. This is a claim that is vociferously contested by the Pakistani state. It has led to an official classification of all Ahmadiya community members as non-Muslims. In Pakistan, the outcome of Ahmadiya claims to Muslim identity has been devastating and has contributed to the sustained persecution and vilification of Ahmadiyas. Indeed, within Sunni institutions in Houston, some commentators and leaders approach this issue with certitude, foreclosing the possibility of including Ahmadiyas within the Muslim ummah. A middle-aged Pakistani man who served on the board of a Sunni mosque and community center said to me on one occasion in unequivocal terms, "We are open to discussions on several issues, but a consideration of Ahmadiya community as Muslims is not one of them. There is a consensus among us that they are non-Muslims. It is just not open to discussion." Perhaps given such exclusions from the Muslim ummah, and the commitment among Ahmadiyas to protest them, a Pakistani radio personality who hosted an Ahmadiya Islam radio program in Houston encouraged me to attend the retreat.

Finally, my status, first as a foreign student, and subsequently, as a temporary worker on an H 1B visa, also shaped my position in the field, and as a researcher documenting the post 9/11 experiences of Pakistani Muslims. During the last decade, through the research and the writing of this book, I have experienced traumatizing racial profiling and encountered delays in the processing and renewal of my work permit that have severely disrupted my professional life, derailed research plans, and curtailed my mobility by restricting travel outside of the country for years on end. As I was about to assume to a teaching position in 2006, I learned that the processing of my work permit application had been delayed because of background security checks. No amount of intervention from the local state representative or the officials at the college where I had been hired helped with expediting the background security and clearance process. It took thirteen months for the work permit to come through. During this time, the immigration lawyers I consulted advised me not to return to Pakistan. Without a source of income and health insurance in the United States, I subsisted on small loans from family and friends and went from having a tenure-track teaching position to being ineligible for employment. When the work permit finally came through, the relief I experienced was short-lived and the anxiety of a renewal weighed on me. While I worked toward changing my immigration status, I encountered delays throughout the varied stages of the process. At the time of this writing, the process is still far from over.

These immigration-related experiences—the persistent stress and anxiety of a tenuous status in this country—coupled with the crisis of unemployment and downward economic mobility have undermined any effort to set roots, invest in long-term career planning, or build relationships in the United States. Furthermore, my kinship relations became fractured as I was unable to visit family members in Pakistan for several years. The racializing of Muslims that I document in this book resonates with the vulnerability and oppression that I have personally experienced and continue to experience. It is these situated negotiations of outsider/insider status that shaped the knowledge that is produced in this book. In the chapters that follow, I attempt to self-reflexively account for my shifting position and identification, guided by a desire to provide some semblance of transparency to the power relations and clarify the contexts of interactions between my interlocutors and myself.

Overview of Chapters

The chapters are organized around specific ethnographic sites that demonstrate the heterogeneity of Pakistani American and the Pakistani immigrant experience in Houston. In chapter 1, I set the geographic context for this book, attending to the intersections between patterns of urban development, the emergence of the energy sector, and racialized spatialities in relation to diasporic Pakistani and transnational Muslim place making in Houston. Although Pakistani communities are dispersed throughout the Greater Houston area, there is a preponderance of Pakistani businesses, residential communities, and religious infrastructure in parts of southwest Houston. In chapter 1, two localities, Hillcroft Avenue and Bissonnet Street in southwest Houston, and newer, affluent suburbs, notably Sugar Land, in the farther reaches of southwest Houston, exemplify two types of urban spaces within which Pakistani immigrants are embedded.

Chapter 2 turns to the narratives of upwardly mobile, highly skilled Shia Ismaili Muslims employed in corporate America as a case study of transnational Muslim sectarian community formations in Houston. Since the changes in the U.S. immigration laws in 1965, Houston's energy sector has served as a magnet for highly skilled Asian technical experts and professionals, as well as students pursuing higher education in the hard sciences. The collapse of Enron, an energy company based in Houston, in autumn 2001 resulted in massive layoffs. My Shia Ismaili Muslim interlocutors experienced rather unexpected unemployment. At this moment of crisis, they mobilized transnational Shia Ismaili networks to mitigate the impact of the loss of unemployment and rebuild their careers. The narratives and experiences of Shia Ismailis provide an important context for examining the intersection of transnational Islamic sectarian ideologies with racialized and classed regimes of U.S. labor flows, ideologies of the model minority, the neoliberal capitalist economy, and Pakistani nation building.

Chapter 3 continues to examine the intersections of transnational Islam with the neoliberal capitalist economy through an ethnographic analysis of the transformations in the South Asian ethnic economy, from its inception and development as a center of South Asian commerce in the 1980s to its twenty-first-century avatar as production and consumption nodes in what I term the "transnational Muslim heritage economy." The conjuncture of religious transnationalism, the realignment of Pakistani Muslim communities with coreligionists from other immigrant communities in Houston, and the transnational flow of capital and material commodities from Muslim countries to Houston has had the effect of transforming patterns of consumption and economic processes in Houston along the lines of religion and has contributed to the emergence of a transnational Muslim heritage economy.

I also relate these larger transformations in economic processes and practices of consumption to individuals embedded in ethnic spaces of commerce. The narratives and the everyday lives of Pakistani ethnic entrepreneurs who own and manage the businesses, and the working class and the working poor who provide much of the labor for these businesses, provide an important case study of the classed heterogeneity of the Pakistani Muslim community in Houston. Moreover, these narratives demonstrate the experience of marginality within ethnic spaces of commerce as well as within the larger American society. These narratives recast religion as a vital source of capital in mediating the experience of poverty and oppression.

Chapter 4, a case study of Muslim American gay men of Pakistani descent, illustrates the heterogeneity of the Pakistani population in Houston along the axis of sexuality. The narratives of my interlocutors center on everyday negotiations of religion and sexuality; they demonstrate deeply felt faith and spirituality and a desire to find acceptance in the Muslim ummah as gay Muslims. A cultural analysis of everyday negotiations of religion, race, sexuality, and transnationalism among gay Muslim Americans problematizes the exclusively heterosexual focus of research on transnational Muslim population movements and community formations in the United States in the early twenty-first century.

The complexities in negotiations of transnationality that are centered on the intersection of transnational Islam, South Asian cultural histories and diasporic nationhood, and racialized subjectification in the United States also find expression in Pakistani American festive celebrations, notably the Pakistan Independence Day Festival in Houston, the subject of chapter 5. I argue that the Festival belies the presumed secularity of ethnic festive cultures in the United States and provides an important case study for documenting the embeddedness of Islam in Pakistani diasporic festive cultural celebrations. Indeed, the centrality of Islam in performances of long-distance nationalism and diasporic nationhood position the Festival as a transnational Muslim celebration. At the same time, the post-9/11 framing of the Festival as a "Houston tradition" by the Festival organizers recasts it as a practice of cultural citizenship that is central in mediating the experience of surveillance of and racism toward Muslim communities, and in claiming space, rights, and privileges as Houstonians.

In chapter 6, Pakistani radio programming in Houston provides the final case study for examining the complex intertwining of transnational religious belonging with projects of diasporic nationhood. In Houston, Pakistani radio is central to mediated negotiations of transnational and diasporic community formations on the one hand and the exigencies of the global neoliberal market economy on the other. The chapter traces the development of Pakistani radio from the 1970s to the present as it was transformed from a community-centered initiative into a business enterprise. An examination of radio illustrates how Pakistani politics range from the airing of personal conflicts to the coverage of religion and homeland politics, especially the volatile relationship between India and Pakistan. These mass mediated engagements demonstrate the roles of diasporic nationhood and transnational Islam in the production and reception of Pakistani radio programming in Houston today.

The conclusion revisits some of the salient issues discussed in the book and emphasizes the critical importance, as an essential political project, of variegated alliance building between Pakistani Muslims and other ethnic, racial, and religious communities during the contemporary period of globalization and racialized U.S. regimes of surveillance.

1

Houston

Race, Class, Oil, and the Making of "America's Most Diverse City"

> Houston is a study in paradoxes. There are pines and palm trees, skyscrapers and sprawl; Tudor townhouses stop abruptly as cows and prairie take over. It deals in incredible extremes of wealth and culture. . . . Houston is all process and no plan. . . . One might say of Houston that one never gets there. It feels as if one is always on the way, always arriving, always looking for the place where everything comes together.
>
> —Ada Louise Huxtable, *Kicked a Building Lately?*

Why Houston? Pakistani immigrants in Houston typically respond to this question by stating one of the following reasons for why they choose to come to Houston. Many cite the presence of family—kin and biradari (the patrilineal kin group) already living in Houston. Others, especially those from the port city of Karachi in Pakistan, maintain that the climate of Houston is vividly reminiscent of Karachi's weather and is a significant factor in the decision to relocate to Houston. Yet others refer to the affordability of raising a family in Houston compared to say, New York City. Finally, the energy and medical sectors, the mainstays of Houston's economy, have made Houston a leading destination for students and skilled professionals with backgrounds and training in engineering, management, and medicine.

These explanations provide insight into why Houston,[1] along with New York City, Washington, DC, Chicago, and Los Angeles, ranks among the metropolitan areas with the largest Pakistani populations.[2] In terms of statewide distribution, Texas is home to the fourth-largest

Pakistani community in the United States, following New Jersey, New York, and California. The Pakistan embassy in Washington, DC estimates that there are currently half a million to a million Pakistanis in the United States.[3] At the time of my research between 2001 and 2002, there were 50,104 Pakistanis in Texas, including 26,981 foreign-born residents and citizens, 10,442 U.S.-born citizens, and 12,681 noncitizens of Pakistani descent.[4] One of the major Pakistani community organizations in Houston, however, doubles this estimate and places the total number at approximately 100,000.

Debates over the exact number of Pakistanis notwithstanding, and despite a relatively small percentage share of metropolitan Houston's population of over 5.95 million as of 2010,[5] Houston has emerged as a primary gateway city and destination for Pakistani immigrants, especially Pakistanis seeking employment in the energy and medical sectors. The inception of a Pakistan consulate in Houston in June 2004 and the ease of international air travel between Pakistan and Houston through direct and connecting flights on multiple airlines, including American Airlines, Emirates Airlines, and Pakistan International Airlines, further consolidate Houston's status as a significant gateway and destination for Pakistani immigrants.

What is remarkable, as well as instructive, about the relatively recent growth of the Pakistani population in Houston is the way in which Pakistanis, whether foreign-born or U.S.-born, have created a strong sense of place in Houston—a facet of the Pakistani experience that is abundantly evident from the narratives and experiences discussed throughout this book. From the settlement of middle-class Pakistanis in plush multiethnic planned suburban communities like Sugar Land, Pearland, and Missouri City to the establishment of multiuse localities that include mosques and Islamic schools, ethnic businesses, and residential areas like Hillcroft Avenue, and from the Pakistan Independence Day Festival to radio airwaves, Pakistanis have developed a vibrant community and public life with roots in Houston. A vast majority of the almost two hundred Pakistanis I formally interviewed, across class, professional, and sectarian affiliations, citizenship status, age, gender, and sexuality, as well as many more with whom I engaged during participant observation, were adamant about their rootedness in Houston and referred to Houston as "home." Locating the Pakistani community within this metropolis demonstrates how a transnational population at the turn of the twenty-first century claims a sense of place, home, and belonging to Houston.

This chapter begins with a brief genealogy of Pakistani population movements to Houston. I address the changes in U.S. immigration policies and laws in 1965 that facilitated the classed flows of highly skilled labor from Pakistan as well as from elsewhere in Asia. Next, I historicize patterns of racialized and classed urban development in Houston. I explore how Houston's oil-based economy has played a vital role in shaping urban spatialities within which Pakistanis are embedded. Although Pakistanis reside throughout the greater Houston area, concentrations of Pakistani immigrant populations have formed in several sections of southwest Houston outside of Interstate 610 (also termed "the Loop"), which circles around the older downtown sections of Houston. Pakistani settlements are concentrated outside the Loop in multiethnic neighborhoods in sections of southwest Houston such as Hillcroft Avenue and Bissonnet Street, and in the more affluent planned settlements such as Sugar Land. These localities exemplify geographical distance from the nineteenth and the early twentieth-century white, African American, and Latino urban settlements formed inside the Loop.

Settlement patterns in southwest Houston represent the more recent multiethnic localities that emerged with the conjunction of the real estate market collapse and the recession in the 1980s. The newly constructed gated communities and residential buildings had been designed with the professionals employed in the oil and gas sectors in mind. With massive layoffs and unemployment in these core industries, numerous buildings became vacant and available in the rental market for newly arriving professionals and service-sector laborers from countries like Pakistan. Established white residential areas in the northern and western sections inside the Loop maintained their demographic cohesion, limiting large-scale habitation by new immigrant communities in these areas. The close association between historically minority neighborhoods and the longstanding African American and Latino communities and businesses that they served created further incentive for new immigrant communities to set up house in newer developments in the southwest that were heretofore unmarked racially. My survey of two major localities, Hillcroft Avenue and Sugar Land, illustrates the ways in which Pakistanis are making claims to space in Houston.

Three overarching and intersecting themes characterize development in Houston and establish the larger urban contexts for situating the study of the Pakistani experience within local specificities. One is the nexus between corporate interests, political elites, and private real estate developers in shaping Houston's built environment; second is the centrality of economic imperatives in shaping patterns of urban growth; third is the racialized and classed production of space and locality that has led to the making of an exceptionally diverse but segregated metropolis. As I discuss subsequently in this chapter, pronouncements of Houston as the most ethnically and racially diverse city in the United States in the year 2013 are qualified by assertions of persistent racial segregation in residential patterns. Celebrating diversity in terms of ethnicity and cultural differences rather than race often cloaks persistent racial tensions; therefore, analyzing social and spatial divisions in Houston in terms of race, rather than ethnicity, makes visible historical categories of difference, experiences of injustice, and differential access to resources and opportunities. This chapter seeks to position Houston's Pakistani population within these broader historical, urban, and racialized contexts and developments, and set the stage for a consideration of the life experiences, economic processes, and mass-mediated engagements that appear in this book.

U.S. Immigration Policy and Pakistani Labor Flows

A genealogy of Pakistani migration to Houston provides an important starting point for locating Pakistani community formations with specificities of the local milieu. Pakistanis have been coming to Houston since the middle of the twentieth century, primarily as students. Between the years 1946 and 1965, the number of Pakistanis in Houston has been estimated at less than a hundred, mostly university and graduate students.[6] Relatively new entrants in the ethnic landscape in Houston, Pakistanis began arriving in large numbers following reforms in U.S. immigration law, notably the passage of the U.S. Immigration and Naturalization Act in 1965. Prior to 1965, immigration law had favored European immigration, severely restricting the immigration of Asians to the United States until after World War II.[7] The landmark Immigration and Naturalization Act of 1965 abandoned prior legislation that had set the national origins quota system based on the makeup of the United States population in 1890.[8] The 1965 act replaced the quotas with an annual limit of 170,000 immigrants (subsequently raised to 270,000) for countries outside the Western Hemisphere.

In the five years following the 1965 immigration reforms, over 30 percent of total immigrants came from outside of the Western Hemisphere (Williams 1988), and Asia became a major source of immigration to the United States.[9] Although Asians had constituted less than 4 percent of total U.S. immigration between 1921 and 1960, Asians made up 35 percent of legal immigration from 1971 to 1980, and 42 percent from 1981 to 1989. From 1971 to 1989, more than 4 million Asians, primarily from China, India, Korea, the Philippines, and Vietnam, immigrated to the United States (Ong and Liu 2000). From the mid-1960s until the late 1980s, the majority of Pakistanis in Houston were Western-educated and trained professionals in the medical, oil and gas, and energy sectors, and part of the Pakistani middle class and the elite (Najam 2006) who acquired capital, established kinship relations, and moved flexibly within and between multiple nations (Ong 1999).

The Immigration Reform and Control Act of 1986, which granted legal status to undocumented immigrants meeting specific requirements, along with the Immigration Act of 1990, which increased the numbers for family-based immigration, led to a significant increase in the Pakistani population in the 1990s. A pattern of chain migrations, whereby a first wave of recruited professionals in highly skilled labor is followed by a second wave that includes family members and kin working primarily in service and ethnic businesses, is found in cities throughout the United States, including Houston. In the 1990s, highly skilled Pakistani workers in Houston sponsored the immigration of relatives in the homeland as well as those who resided throughout the South Asian diaspora, notably in the Gulf States, the Middle East, Africa and Asia.[10] Following the Gulf War in 1991, for example, many semiskilled and unskilled South Asian workers based in the Gulf region immigrated to the United States as well as to Europe (Prashad 2000). A smaller group of immigrants consists of political refugees belonging to Pakistani religious minority groups and political groups who had come to the United States to escape persecution under the dictatorial regimes in Pakistan and reside in exile in Houston.

In addition to Pakistani immigrants from elsewhere in the world, Houston has witnessed an increase in the in-migration of Pakistani men and women from southern states other than Texas since the late 1990s. This has made Houston the South Asian hub of the southern and southwestern United States, akin to New York City in the Northeast and Chicago in the Midwest. For Pakistani students, professionals, and entrepreneurs in Florida, Alabama, Louisiana, Georgia, North Carolina, and South Carolina, Houston emerges as the preferred city of intended residence. Indeed, Houston's thriving South Asian ethnic economy offers employment opportunities for the working class and business opportunities for entrepreneurs. Houston also draws consumers looking for ethnic goods and services that may not be readily available in smaller towns and cities in neighboring states.

The steady increase in the Pakistani population in Houston over the last three decades has contributed to the presence of Pakistanis in all major income levels, occupations and professions. Pakistanis in Houston represent all major Pakistan ethnolinguistic and religious communities in Pakistan (Williams 1988). The presence of Pathan, Punjabi, Sindhi, Kashmiri, and Balochi ethnolinguistic groups, and of Ismaili, Shia, Sunni, and Ahmadiya Muslims, as well as of Zoroastrian, Christian, and Hindu Pakistanis, represents a microcosm of contemporary Pakistan. Despite the ethnolinguistic and religious differentiation and diversity within the Pakistani population, however, the majority of Pakistani immigrants and families in Houston are Sunni Muslims from Urdu-speaking communities in the port city of Karachi, the largest and most populous city in Pakistan. Shia communities are an important demographic force despite Sunni Muslims being the larger population, in large part because of their concentration as entrepreneurs and white-collar professionals employed in the energy and medical sectors.

The Making of a Racialized Metropolis

Houston's emergence as a global metropolis attracting immigrants from all over the world, including post-1965 waves of Pakistani skilled labor, began in the second half of the twentieth century. Houston originated in the nineteenth century, however, as a result of the Allen brothers' speculation on what was then swampland. Starting in the 1830s, the city "was sold aggressively to outsiders by the real estate developers who packaged the mosquito-infested swampland and called it Houston" (Shelton et al. 1989: 3). Private developers, not city planners, directed the dynamic growth that would come to characterize the greater Houston metropolitan area (Garreau 1992). By the late nineteenth century, Houston had become a major center for lumber, cotton, and grains attracting a blue-collar workforce made up of African Americans and Mexican immigrants, as well as a white-collar workforce that was almost exclusively white (McComb 1981). The agriculture-based economy led to the development of an infrastructure of railroads, warehouses, cotton gins, and banks, and by 1910, Houston was a railroad town servicing the Texas Gulf Coast and hinterlands (Fisher 1986).

Despite its origins in the nineteenth century, Houston owes its extraordinary growth as a metropolis in large part to the energy sector, and especially the discovery and extraction of oil, in the early twentieth century. Oil rapidly became the motor of Houston's booming growth. By the 1930s, oil-related industries contributed to more than half of all the jobs in Houston, attracting workers from rural and small-town Texas and beyond (Shelton et al. 1989). Continuing patterns begun in the nineteenth century, the growth in the industrial workforce was racialized: administrative and professional jobs were dominated by whites, and the blue-collar workforce was predominantly African American and Latino.

In the early twentieth century, as major oil companies consolidated their control over the Texas oil industry, automobile production in Detroit stimulated the need for crude oil production and raw materials produced in Houston, linking Detroit and Houston in the oil industry–automobile culture nexus that transformed urban life in Houston, as well as across the United States (McComb 1981). Oil replaced coal as the primary fuel for locomotives and industrial plants, embedding Houston within national economies and projects of industrialization and urbanization (Vojnovic 2003b). The rapid increase in automobile production led to the emergence of 1,200 oil companies and 300 oil supply houses in Houston, supported further by oil refineries and oil-related industrial facilities, oil equipment, and oil-services and port facilities

(Shelton et al. 1989). Although small oil companies controlled the oil fields through the 1930s, the balance of power shifted to large oil companies only a decade later in the 1940s. While the main offices were located in the northern states, oil companies maintained subsidiaries as well as oil facilities like refineries and office buildings in Houston that provided infrastructure for the oil boom.

Throughout the city's history, private developers, capitalists, and the political elite would play central roles in practices and processes of Houston's development.[11] Although Houston has a reputation for privatized development independent from government, an examination of Houston's political economy offers a more complex picture. Urban studies scholar Igor Vojnovic (2003b) argues that during the twentieth century a local growth coalition, composed of local business interests and local government officials, successfully lobbied for federal subsidies guided by the goal of building a shipping channel and port facilities to attract oil-related companies to Houston. In 1914, the Houston Ship Channel was completed after Buffalo Bayou was dredged to create a deepwater channel leading to the Port of Houston east of downtown (Shelton et al. 1989). Nearly a century later, this port would become the second-largest port in the United States in terms of total tonnage and first in terms of foreign tonnage.[12] Federal aid and capital were also used to construct public buildings, city hall, parks, monuments, schools, and roads, guided by the interests of Houston's private industrial and real estate corporations.

During World War II, the federal government provided further capital for private and joint private-public oil-related companies, including the petrochemical industry, aviation fuel, and synthetic rubber, all of which were necessary for the war economy (ibid. 1989). Following World War II, a rising demand for oil and oil products such as asphalt, jet fuel, plastics, and other petrochemicals received continued support, including tax subsidies from the federal government (Vojnovic 2003a). Federal money also supported road building, sewer facilities, and airport construction in Houston. The postwar boom contributed to the increase in transportation companies, including truck, pipeline, and shipping companies and a concurrent growth in steel, aluminum, metal fabrication, oil-tool, and construction companies (Shelton et al. 1989).

By the 1970s, the oil industry had restructured, shifting its major operations and subsidiaries, including production, consumer, and marketing operations, to Houston. The consolidation of the oil industry in Houston also included geological firms, petroleum engineering firms, drilling contractors, geophysical contractors, supply and transportation companies, law firms, and accounting firms embedded in Houston's expanding and diversified oil and gas sectors (ibid. 1989). In fact, the energy crises during the 1970s were a boon for Houston's growing economy as the price of oil climbed. The discovery of oil in the North Sea, the Gulf States, and in Malaysia and Indonesia in the 1960s and the 1970s embedded Houston's oil and gas economies within international networks (ibid. 1989).

In contrast to its experience during earlier periods of depression and recession nationwide, Houston was impacted greatly by the recession of the 1980s. Developments in the international oil market and the decrease in oil prices by the Organization of the Petroleum Producing Countries (OPEC) impacted economic activity in Houston and led to large-scale layoffs in the oil and gas sectors. Domestic oil production also decreased, further impacting Houston-based oil and petrochemical industries. Economic activity, notably industrial production, decreased. Unemployment rose to almost 15 percent in 1986 (ibid. 1989).

Oil and gas companies headquartered in Houston have at some point included Marathon Oil, Phillips 66, ConocoPhillips, Texaco, Enterprise Products Partners, Plains All American Pipeline, and Exxon Mobil (formerly Humble Oil) in nearby Irving, among numerous others. Historically the oil and gas sectors have played central roles in shaping Houston's cityscape. Today, aerospace including NASA's Johnson Space Center, information technology, and the biomedical sector, including the Texas Medical Center, are additional mainstays of Houston's increasingly diversified economy (Vojnovic 2003a). In all of these areas of activity, Houston belies its mythical reputation as a fiercely and uniquely independent city that has resisted governmental intervention and dependency on the outside world. Evidence suggests that "Houston businesses, and their workers, are heavily dependent on energy markets whose prices are controlled in such places as New York and Saudi Arabia" (Shelton et al. 1989: 123). For example, Enron, an energy, commodities, and services company based in Houston before its collapse in autumn 2001, included offices and operations globally and played a central role in the design and implementation of energy policies in several countries (Bradley 2009a; 2009b). Moreover, Enron and other Houston-based energy sector companies have served as the magnet for the highly skilled professionals drawn from new immigrant communities, including the Shia Ismaili Muslims I discuss in the next chapter. The emergence of information technologies and high-tech industries in the late twentieth century is just as dependent on the outside—stimulated by highly skilled transnational labor flows and firms based elsewhere in the United States, as well as in Asia and beyond.

NASA's arrival in Houston, similar to the oil and gas industry, demonstrates three interrelated aspects of Houston's economic and urban development: first, the intersection of local politics with federal and transnational contexts; second, the pattern of pursuing federal money for economic development while disavowing public interference in issues of social development and reform; and third, the development of NASA as "a historically white and male aerospace sector" (McQuaid 2007: 406). On land donated by what was then Humble Oil (now Exxon), NASA's Johnson Space Center was built during the Cold War, signaling new priorities and geopolitical exigencies marked by the repositioning of the United States as the leader of the free world. As in the oil and gas sectors, African Americans and Latinos were represented primarily in semiskilled and unskilled labor positions such as janitors, and clerical staff at NASA (Northrup 1968).[13] Women were similarly relegated to low-tier positions as clerks and typists. NASA's institutional culture, focused on missions and not personnel-related issues, undermined efforts to hire women and minorities. Even by the 1990s, NASA had remained primarily white and male, and it continues to exemplify one of the largest gender gaps for science and technology organizations in the United States (McQuaid 2007). NASA justified such exclusions on the grounds that the industry required specialized skills acquired through higher education in engineering and the physical sciences and that a pool of qualified minorities and women was largely absent. NASA's rationale obscured structural barriers such as segregation in education, including institutions of higher education, as well as the historical experience of poverty and racism that had limited opportunities for people of color to acquire the financial capital neces-sary for higher education.[14]

On the other end of the workforce spectrum, the city itself has been built by African Americans and Latinos. According to Beth Anne Shel-ton and colleagues,

> From the slave labor of the mid-nineteenth century to the more recent undocumented Mexican and Central American immigrants, the city's large black and Hispanic labor pools provided much of the unskilled labor that constructed bridges, water systems, factories, railroads, high-ways, office buildings, and houses. Stereotyped, discriminated against, exploited, and abused, black and Hispanic workers have done much of the daily construction, especially the "dirty work" that has built Houston. The image of independence, prosperity, and glitter often associated with the city's growth has obscured not only a basic dependence on outside corporations and governmental aid but also the substantial dependence on these cohorts of workers. (1989: 70)

During most of the twentieth century, as Houston's economy experi-enced growth, job creation has continued to be racialized and classed. For example, African Americans, residing near the downtown, tend to have greater access to a high concentration of employment opportuni-ties; however, a vast majority of these jobs in knowledge centers such as the downtown office complexes, medical centers, and universities are low-paying, blue-collar jobs (Cohn and Fossett 1996: 565). According to Cohn and Fossett:

> Medical centers and universities employ many physical plant workers, drivers, security agents, food-service workers, and cleaning-service workers. Downtown office complexes employ many physical plant workers (both janitors and repair workers) and transportation workers (notably truck drivers, cab drivers, and delivery workers). The demand for food service is augmented by the high concentration of restau-rants. Downtown hotels also create concentrations of food-service and cleaning-service workers. Consequently, the distribution of unskilled and entry-level jobs closely parallels that of civilian employment in gen-eral. (1996: 564)

Despite the availability of more jobs for African Americans in and near the downtown, these jobs suggest classed and racialized occupations rather than opportunities for upward economic mobility. In addition to racial discrimination, "structural change in the form of declining aggregate demand for unskilled labor driven by deindustrialization and changes in the occupational mix toward jobs with higher educational requirements is also likely to be relevant" (ibid.: 572). Likewise, the general pattern for employment for the Latino population has included lower-status manual jobs and white-collar sales and clerical positions (Shelton et al. 1989). Educational attainment levels have been among the lowest for Latino communities residing in Houston, in large part because of the lack of bilingual education as well as limitations in English-language teaching programs (Fix and Zimmermann 1993).

African Americans and Latinos became especially vulnerable as Houston transitioned from a manufacturing and industrial economy to a more diversified business-service economy in the 1990s. This economic restructuring contributed to the racializing of newer waves of Latino semiskilled and unskilled workers as the primary labor for low-wage, nonunion jobs, including residential building attendants and laborers for a range of mainstream and ethnic businesses including Pakistani restaurants in southwest Houston. Low-income and low-skilled blue-collar jobs continue to be concentrated near areas and localities in which minority communities predominate, such as the southwest corridor (Cohn and Fossett 1996). Indeed, as Shelton and colleagues argue: "Houston employers have come to depend more and more on the immigrant workers of the area's Hispanic labor force. Thus, to a considerable extent, the Houston economy draws low-wage labor from a transnational labor market—one that extends deep into Mexico and areas of Central America" (Shelton et al. 1989: 118).

Car ownership, or at least access to a car, and spatial mobility have also proven to be classed and racialized phenomenon that are mapped onto patterns of employment among low-income and blue-collar populations. In a car-centric city, limited access to automobiles that would enable efficient travel to places of work in the suburbs is a significant variable in limiting access to jobs. Even with access to reliable transportation and opportunities for jobs farther away from historically African American and Latino residential areas inside the Loop, Cohn and Fossett (1996) found that most blue-collar workers (racialized as primarily African American and Latino workers) typically find employment near their place of residence, or, when given a choice, prefer job opportunities closer to home than those that are geographically more distant.

A similar dynamic is apparent for working-class Pakistanis in Houston who are employed in South Asian businesses located near their place of residence in southwest Houston. The vast majority of the working-class Pakistanis I interviewed and engaged with during the course of my research and who worked at Pakistani businesses in Hillcroft Avenue and Bissonnet Street, did not own a car. They lived within walking distance of or a short bus ride to their place of residence. The presence of residential buildings and mosques within a few-mile radius in these localities and places of work enabled the working class and the working poor to negotiate limited financial resources that in other circumstances would permit them to afford a car and work at businesses based elsewhere in the greater Houston metropolitan area.

Racialized Spacialities

The oil and gas industries have shaped the social and spatial geography of the city, creating racialized and classed segregation not only in employment opportunities and sectors of employment but equally in residential settlement patterns and business activity. It is important to review this history in some detail so as to understand the racialized spacialities that exemplify the urban milieu in which new immigrants found themselves. Long-established patterns of social and spatial segregation continue today in Houston, as in many other U.S. cities. However, the configuration of power brokers discussed in the preceding section made Houston the only major city in the United States without zoning laws that would restrict certain types of building activities to specific areas and localities (McDonald 1995). In the place of zoning laws, deed restrictions and civic and homeowners associations have served as the primary mechanism to restrict and direct development in specific localities (ibid.). These associations have been most effective in affluent and primarily white neighborhoods, enabling white communities to have a degree of control over development of industry and service sector businesses. However, these associations have had less power in historically African American and Latino neighborhoods inside the Loop surrounding the downtown area.

At the beginning of the twentieth century, the small downtown area included "low-rise office buildings and shops, railings to tie horses, and extensive railroad yards, and repair facilities north of the downtown area" (Shelton et al. 1989: 21). Most residential areas were within a mile of the downtown. White residential areas located downtown were ringed by African American and Mexican residential areas on the city's perimeter. By the 1940s, spearheaded by business and government partnerships, oil-related industrial facilities such as oil refineries had developed southeast of downtown (McComb 1981). Low-income residential developments emerged to the east, near the refineries and the petrochemical industry developing along the Houston Ship Channel. White-collar residential localities, such as the area called West University, developed to the west of the downtown and housed scientists and technicians employed in the oil and gas sector and related companies.

After World War II, Houston's expansion was shaped in large part by the construction of major highways north, south, and west from the city and an emphasis on an automobile-centered cityscape, buttressed by the nexus between oil and automobile production. As Shelton and colleagues observe: "These highways, together with an absence of any commitment to a significant mass transit system, meant that Houston was clearly a car dominated city. . . . Given this highway-centered transportation system, Houston's real estate development has radiated out along this grid in a decentralized pattern" (Shelton et al. 1989: 21–22). Over time, Houston developed one of the most extensive roadway networks of any city in the United States, with the goal of facilitating access to all parts of the city and its outlaying areas. Office and shopping sites sprawled beyond the Loop and were connected through highway networks. Since the 1950s, offices, shopping centers and residential developments have expanded in south, southwest, and southeast Houston near NASA.

The construction of high- and mid-rises in central Houston and the development of suburbs and multiuse localities, including hundreds of new office towers and massive shopping centers such as the Houston Galleria, can be attributed to growing demands from oil- and gas-related industries (Garreau 1992). By the 1980s, several business-activity centers had developed, extending outward from downtown, and they included commercial real estate development. As Shelton and colleagues conceptualize the growth in the real estate: "In a short period, a polynucleate city has been built up, with only a modest portion of the city's construction dating from before the 1940s. . . . The expansion of the city has been so rapid that there are large vacant areas within the city available for future development" (1989: 23). In some sections of the downtown, pre–World War II office buildings and department stores were replaced by new office buildings, both high- and mid-rises.

The absence of zoning, along with a highly decentralized, oil-centric pattern of urban development contributed to excessive construction in the 1970s and early 1980s. Indeed, nearly 80 percent of the buildings in Houston were constructed during the 1970s and the 1980s; these included 485 structures that provided administrative offices for white-collar workers in the oil and gas corporations and related businesses and firms (ibid.). In southwest Houston, for example, there are more office buildings, shopping centers, single-family residences, and apartment buildings than in the entire downtown.

Joel Garreau (1992) describes the mushrooming suburban centers that developed in metropolitan areas along highway routes as "edge cities." In this urban formation, automobiles dominate. Garreau writes:

> Automobile is the finest expression of transportation-individualism ever devised. Edge Cities never succeed financially without accommodating the automobile. However, parking lots spread buildings apart. The farther apart buildings are, the less willing people are to walk between them. The fewer people there are within walking distance of any one place, the less able that place is to support civilization as measured by the existence of restaurants and bookstores. Therefore, individualism in the form of the automobile fights the formation of society and community and civilization. (1992: 245)

In the early 1980s, investments in construction of middle-class housing and amenities were made anticipating a continued boom; by 1983, however, economic recession socked Houston, resulting in massive employee layoffs and numerous vacant apartment buildings and office spaces. Parts of Houston, including the southwest, were littered with empty mid-rise buildings. The 1980s recession had mixed consequences for the housing market. Master-planned and primarily white residential developments like the Woodlands, located inside the Loop, continued to experience stability and growth. Concurrently, the recession contributed to the emergence of ethnic neighborhoods in newer settlements located mostly, but not exclusively, outside the Loop. In southwest Houston, for example, South Asian immigrants began moving into the housing stock outside the Loop that had been built for middle-class residency. Priced low as a result of the recession, this housing stock, which included gated communities with amenities such as swimming pools, gym facilities, business centers, and convenience stores, became available to semiskilled laborers, the working class, and entrepreneurs. Vacant strip malls nearby were rapidly filled with ethnic businesses.

> Houston was a bargain for immigrants in the 1980s. Cheap place to buy a house, buy an office building, start a business. Now that the place has bottomed out and is turning around, you find a plethora of diverse shops. Peel off the Southwest Freeway at Hillcroft, outside Loop 610, and there's a discount warehouse sari emporium. (Garreau 1992: 255)

It is important to recognize that the availability of newly built middle-class housing with low rents occurred during a period when new immigrants were making their way to Houston in increasing numbers as a result of changes to federal immigration policy in 1965. Thanks to Houston's construction boom and then economic recession, South Asian working-class and other financially struggling immigrants had unexpected access to inexpensive residential and business opportunities in newer parts of the city. They chose to build communities here instead of joining historically working-class and poor neighborhoods with lower rents, which were primarily African American and Latino.

Urban Neighborhood Development, Environmental Racism, and Urban Sprawl

The racialized workforce in the oil and gas sectors and racialized patterns of urban development played a key role in the formation of racially segregated and largely self-contained neighborhoods. As urban sociologist Jan Lin argues, "Race and ethnic neighborhoods in the early part of the twentieth century were largely 'invisible' to the Anglo middle classes and elite . . . since they generally inhabited unwanted land adjacent to downtown and on the industrial side of the city" (1995: 633). It is not so much that the affluent white communities were unaware of these spaces but more that these localities were not part of the landscape affluent white communities experienced on a regular basis traveling through the city.

Historically, African American neighborhoods developed on the perimeter of downtown, notably the Third Ward to the southeast, the Fourth Ward to the west, and the Fifth Ward to the northeast.[15] Following the end of the Civil War in 1865, Houston's first African American neighborhood, the Fourth Ward, also known as Freedmen's Town, was settled by freed slaves who migrated to Houston to take advantage of jobs in the growing economy (Meeks 2011). Freedmen's Town developed as an important and vibrant center for African American economic, religious, and public life. By the mid-twentieth century, however, urban development projects enforced through eminent domain were undermining the cohesion of the neighborhood. Those projects included an all-white housing project for World War II veterans in the center of the Fourth Ward as well as the construction of the Interstate 45, which sliced through the Fourth Ward.[16] The building of the interstate highway system in the late 1950s "privileged interests of middle-class Anglo suburbanization at the cost of near-city minority neighborhoods, which did not have the political clout to contest these land-use decisions" (Lin 1995: 634) and contributed to a decentralization of Houston's urban development. By the turn of the twenty-first century, the Fourth Ward, originally built on the edge of downtown, had become valuable real estate inside the Loop in a city that sprawled in every direction. Affluent, predominantly white residents seeking to live inside the Loop rather than suburbs further displaced poorer African American residents during processes of gentrification.[17]

El Segundo Barrio (the Second Ward), Denver Harbor, and Magnolia Park are among the oldest Mexican American neighborhoods in Houston. From the city's inception, Mexican workers were critical for Houston's development into a center of agricultural production as well as railway and, later, oil-centered industries (Shelton et al. 1989). In the early 1900s, a Mexican community developed in El Segundo Barrio, east of downtown Houston, with the Our Lady of Guadalupe Church as the community's nucleus. By the 1920s, a Mexican American neighborhood called Magnolia Park, east of Houston near the Houston Ship Channel, could be characterized as "a city in itself, affording numerous job opportunities" and residential buildings (ibid.: 94). Community and cultural life included churches, ethnic businesses, Spanish-language newspapers, Mexican national festivals, and cultural societies and associations (Trevino 2006).

Institutionalized racism has meant that people of color, primarily Mexican and African Americans, were subject to the systematic policies and practices of prejudice and discrimination typical of American society during most of the twentieth century. They were formally excluded from Houston's political life, which was dominated by the white middle class and elite—mostly industrialists and business tycoons with interests in oil and gas, real estate, construction, and banking.[18] While Houston experienced rapid population growth, state laws and ordinances racially segregated schools, parks, and railroads, as well as authorizing segregation on street cars and in hotels, restaurants, and theaters. Anti-miscegenation laws outlawed interracial marriages and habitation.

Nonetheless, African American and Mexican communities actively protested Jim Crow laws and practices that restricted mobility, curtailed civil liberties, and limited opportunities for professional advancement. Catholic religious networks and institutions played central roles in mediating economic exploitation and social inequities of Jim Crow laws (Trevino 1994; 2003); developing Mexican American political activism and participating in the 1960s civil rights movement (Kreneck 1985); initiating school integration projects (Miguel 2005); and participating in processes and modalities of cultural citizenship (Mayer 2000). Research on African American communities in Houston shows a similar involvement of churches throughout the early decades of the twentieth century as a resource for mediating exclusion from mainstream political and economic society.[19]

Periods of economic growth and prosperity that have provided benefits and upward mobility to the city's white population have not benefited African Americans or Latinos to nearly the same extent. As

Shelton and colleagues argue: "Discrimination remains an impediment to employment, housing, and education equality for Houston's black and Hispanic citizens. Prosperity for some white Houstonians has meant little advance for minority Houstonians, who have had to cope with decades of racial discrimination and neglect" (1989: 71). This remains the case in the early twenty-first century, as borne out by a recent study that extols the diversity of Houston today but shows the persistence of differential educational achievement levels of whites, African Americans and Latinos in Houston (Emerson et al. 2013).

The historical experience of racism has contributed to deterioration in the quality of life in low-income and minority neighborhoods and made these localities and communities especially vulnerable to severe environmental problems and crises. As sociologist Robert D. Bullard states in his seminal book on environmental racism, *Dumping in Dixie: Race, Class, and Environmental Quality*:

> Houston, Texas, the nation's fourth largest city, is a classic example of an area where race has played an integral part in land-use outcomes and municipal service delivery. As late as 1982, there were neighborhoods in Houston that still did not have paved streets, gas and sewer connections, running water, regular garbage service, and street markers. Black and Hispanic neighborhoods were far more likely to have service deficiencies than their white counterparts. (Bullard 1990: 6)

In a city that lacks comprehensive zoning, the establishment of hazardous facilities such as petrochemical factories, refineries, incinerators, and landfills has predominantly affected poor neighborhoods. The conjuncture of poor people, who are predominantly people of color disproportionately affected by environmental hazards such as air pollution, characterizes environmental racism in Houston.[20] For example, Bullard's (1987; 1990) scholarship on the siting of solid waste disposal facilities demonstrates how macrolevel industrial projects disproportionately impact African American and low-income communities. Of the nine waste disposal facility site locations assessed, Bullard (1990) found that seven were located in predominantly African American neighborhoods, one in a predominantly Latino barrio, and one in a white neighborhood.

Furthermore, Houston's eastward sprawl is replete with petrochemical industries that follow the Houston Ship Channel to the Gulf of Mexico. This complex of heavy industry has had damaging health consequences for neighboring populations, specifically low-income, African American, and Latino populations.[21] A task force funded by the city and the Center for Disease Control (CDC) examined air pollution and found "a 56 percent increased risk of acute lymphocytic leukemia among children living within two miles of the HSC [Houston Ship Channel] compared with children living more than 10 miles from the HSC."[22] Although the city government has addressed air pollution by engaging a research team to study the issue, the long-term implications remain to be seen.

Histories of institutionalized racial discrimination, evident in the disparities in distribution of wealth, jobs, housing, and environmental problems in Houston, illustrate the linkages between race, class, and place (Peterson and Krivo 2009). During the boom in real estate construction in the 1970s, most development took place in the suburbs rather than in lower-income and minority neighborhoods. As middle-income white families took advantage of the housing boom of the 1970s and relocated in the suburban enclaves, African Americans lacked the equity capital to make down payments or take bank loans and came to occupy previously white localities, especially in southeast and northeast Houston neighborhoods. In spite of the Federal Fair Housing Act of 1968 and Houston's Fair Housing Ordinance, which made racial discrimination in housing illegal, African Americans have been largely disadvantaged in their access to bank loans and routes to home ownership, reflecting racialized practices in the real estate market nationally. As Shelton and colleagues state: "The practices of refusing to sell or lease housing to blacks, coding records and applications to indicate racial preferences of landlords, selective advertising, redlining, racial steering, and threats or acts of intimidation continue to limit the housing alternatives available to black families" (Shelton et al. 1989: 78).

Latino communities have experienced mobility by moving to suburbs in southwest Houston, even though historically Latino localities are predominantly in center city Houston. However, many suburbs, such as sections of Hillcroft Avenue in southwest Houston, which hosts Latino as well as Asian and African new immigrant communities, are not sites of affluence and upward mobility but are in fact largely blue collar in composition, shaped by the decrease in rental prices following the real estate bust in the 1980s.

Similar to the initial development of African American and Latino neighborhoods surrounding downtown Houston, it was through the expansion of Houston that new immigrant communities, such as Pakistani immigrants, established residences and negotiated exclusion from historically white-dominated neighborhoods and localities. Patterns of racialized segregation begun in the nineteenth century have persisted in residential patterns as new populations, including Pakistanis, have entered the cityscape. Although Pakistani communities reside throughout the greater Houston area, it is southwest Houston, around Hillcroft Avenue and Bissonnet Street, where Pakistani residences and businesses predominate. The emergence of Pakistani residences and businesses in largely newer settlements in Houston illustrates historically contingent practices of urban development and city life that precluded the integration of new immigrant and minority communities into largely white residential localities such as the Woodlands inside the Loop. Additionally, upwardly mobile Pakistanis have established communities that include residences, mosques, community centers, and businesses in "ethnoburbs" (Li 1998; 2009), that is, suburbs with residential and business concentrations of ethnic minority communities. Suburbs with high concentrations of Pakistanis include Sugar Land, Missouri City, and Pearland.

Diversity and Segregation in America's Most Diverse City

In 2013, Houston was heralded as the most ethnically and racially diverse city in the United States, narrowly beating New York City, in a research report by Rice University's Kinder Institute for Urban Research and the Hobby Center for the Study of Texas (Emerson et al. 2013). Comparing the ten largest U.S. metropolitan areas, the report asserted that Houston outranked all cities as the one with the most equitable distribution of major racial and ethnic groups as classified in the census: Asian, Latino/Hispanic, white, and African American/Black. As the fourth-largest U.S. city, the population of Houston's metropolitan area of 5.95 million as of 2010 more than doubles the population of the city of Houston.[23] In the Houston metropolitan area, which is made up of several counties, Fort Bend is the most diverse, followed by Harris County, Brazoria, Galveston County, and Montgomery County. Harris County, which includes much of central Houston, emerges as the only county where Latinos constitute the largest group (40.8 percent of the population), followed by whites (33.0 percent), African Americans (18.4 percent), and Asians (6.1 percent). Among those under the age of thirty, 78 percent of the population of Harris County consists of people of color.

Some of the key demographic findings of the Kinder Institute study bear reiteration and discussion here. From 1990 until 2010, the white population represents a declining share of the total population. The white population decreased from 57.9 percent of the total population of the Houston metropolitan area in 1990 to less than half (48.2 percent) in 2000 and to 39.7 percent by 2010. During the same period, the Latino population increased from 20.8 percent in 1990 to 35.3 percent of the total population in 2010, indicating a metropolis in which Latinos stand to emerge as the majority in the near future.[24] Asians marked a steady increase over the twenty-year period, from 3.4 percent in 1990 to 4.8 in 2000 to 6.5 percent of the population in 2010. African Americans remained relatively constant, from 17.5 percent in 1990 to 16.8 with 1.3 percent self-identifying as multiracial in 2010 (Emerson et al. 2013).

While there are increasing levels of diversity in other major cities in Texas such as Dallas-Fort Worth and Austin, both of these metropolitan areas are predominantly white, with other racial/ethnic groups constituting much smaller shares of the total metropolitan population compared to Houston. Similarly, New York City's white population constitutes almost half of the total population (48.9 percent). Miami and Los Angeles similarly rank high on diversity, but Latino populations in both cities are larger than other ethnic/racial groups, and other groups are less well represented in the overall population figures in both cities. The ethnic and racial heterogeneity of Houston is in part due to the immigration of African American, Mexican, and Chinese, as well as European immigrants. During the late nineteenth and the early and mid-twentieth century, for example, German, Irish, English, French, and Jewish immigrant populations settled in Houston and established distinct ethnic communities and neighborhoods (von der Mehden 1984).

Still, it is the post-1965 waves of new immigrant communities from Central and South America, South and East Asia, and Africa that affirm Houston's status as a primary gateway and global city and consolidate its status as the most diverse city in the United States.[25]

Although Mexicans historically constituted the majority of the Latino population in Houston, the Latino population has diversified and includes immigrants from throughout the Americas, notably Salvadorians, Guatemalans, Hondurans, Nicaraguans, and Costa Ricans. These populations reside in multiethnic neighborhoods, including historically Mexican neighborhoods such as El Segundo Barrio and Magnolia Park, but the Latinadad in Houston is not monolithic. Restaurants and other ethnic businesses differentiated by nationality, culture, and region point to internal diversity within the Latino population in Houston.

In spite of affirmative assessments of the city's diversity, Houston remains one of the most segregated metropolitan areas in the United States; cleavages of race and ethnicity, class, educational attainment, and income levels continue to spatially divide the city. While suburban localities in southwest Houston such as Pearland, Sugar Land, and Missouri City are multiethnic and multireligious, segregation is the highest in the central city of Houston: "Houston . . . has older, more established neighborhoods and a disproportionate share of the region's poverty. Both of these factors are associated with greater segregation between racial/ethnic groups" (Emerson et al. 2013: 14). Recent scholarship on ethnic formations in Houston has used the trope of "multiple cities within a city" to underscore the historically racialized and classed segregation of Houston that persists to varying degrees today, in spite of the growth of multiethnic suburbs and newer settlements.[26]

The Kinder Institute report found that segregation between African Americans and whites saw only "modest or moderate declines" (Emerson et al. 2013: 12). According to the report: "Recent experimental research has also found that holding other factors about neighborhoods constant—such as housing values, educational quality, and crime rates—Whites in the Houston area are less likely to say they would buy homes as the percentage of Blacks or Latinos in the neighborhood increases" (ibid.: 13). Levels of segregation between Asians and whites are lower, suggesting both the incorporation of Asians into high-income and high-skilled labor force in Houston and the historical ambiguity regarding Asian racial classifications in the United States that I discuss in the next chapter.

The experience of Hurricane Katrina evacuees provides an important case study in understanding the modalities for racial antagonism in the early twenty-first century, where racism is masked in the belief of a color-blind society (Bonilla-Silva 2006). In 2005, following Katrina's unprecedented damage to coastal areas in Alabama, Mississippi, and Louisiana, a significant number of evacuees, including a disproportionately high number of African Americans and poor people, relocated to Houston. The approximately 150,000 evacuees added upwards of 3 percent to the city's population (J. Shelton and Coleman 2009). Local communities in Houston initially came together in the immediate aftermath of the Hurricane to participate in high numbers in rehabilitation efforts (Klineberg 2008). Public perception shifted over time, however. Evacuees started to be perceived as a social problem in terms of the city's inability to provide all evacuees with housing, employment, and enrollment in public schools (J. Shelton and Coleman 2009).

Studies found that even though the evacuees were displaced communities or refugees, many city residents did not differentiate between the Katrina evacuees and other non-U.S. citizens and noncitizens who immigrate to Houston (ibid.). In a place commonly conceptualized as the gateway city for undocumented and documented immigrants, the evacuee population became framed in terms of race, class, and immigration.[27] Ironically, in spite of the unexpected increase in the local labor supply, the evacuees did not impact local market opportunities for Houstonians.[28] Studies have shown that over time, whites were more hostile toward evacuees, followed by Latinos and African Americans. African Americans and whites who had the same opportunities remained antagonistic toward the evacuees, demonstrating the complex intersection of class, race and status in constructions of color-blind racism (ibid.). As Shelton and Coleman lament: "The sad truth is that many local residents viewed the mostly poor, mostly black new arrivals from New Orleans in the same apprehensive light that they viewed noncitizens seeking entry into the United States" (ibid.: 494). This also illustrates how concerns over the "immigration peril" are discursively produced in conceptions of native-born migrants from elsewhere in the United States.

Hillcroft Avenue: Place Making in a Translocality

The 2013 Kinder Institute study reports that "suburban areas have much newer housing and neighborhoods with no historical tradition of belonging to one racial/ethnic group or another" (Emerson et al. 2013: 14). That absence of historical tradition has perhaps allowed new immigrant communities to develop their own traditions in this growing city. Toward that end, the establishment of religious infrastructure has been important to processes of place-making and practices of cultural production among new immigrant communities in Houston.[29] The construction of places of worship is particularly significant in a city in which the economic and political elite have largely framed the terms of urban development, because places of worship create important community nodes within the cityscape.

Ethnographic and historical analyses of Muslim and South Asian immigrants across the United States attest to the privileged position of religion in building community in the West (Williams 1988). Pakistani immigrants in Houston developed religious institutions and infrastructure during the early 1970s when the local South Asian Muslim population began to grow. In 1972, the first mosque in Houston, and in fact the first in the southern United States, opened and was housed for a short time in a chapel at the University of Houston and then in the Rothko Chapel before moving into an independent space (ibid. 1988). The first mosque in downtown Houston opened its doors in 2002. The Islamic Da'wah Center, supported by Houston Rockets basketball player Hakeem Olajuwon, was constructed in the renovated Houston National Bank building, originally built in 1928 by Ross Sterling, a former Texas governor as well as founder of Humble Oil.[30] Attesting to the growth and diversity of the city's Muslim population, Greater Houston now hosts more than forty mosques according to Ihsan Bagby's *The American Mosque 2011*.[31] Yet, violence perpetuated against the often-stigmatized and stereotyped population of South Asian Muslims following 9/11 has not left Houston unscathed. In 2011, an arson attack targeted an Islamic school and mosque just off Hillcroft in Southwest Houston.[32] Founded in 1989, this mosque maintains the largest Islamic school in Houston and anchors a sizable South Asian population.

Given the presence of residential as well as a broader South Asian ethno-religious environment, Hillcroft Avenue may well be characterized as an edge city (Garreau 1992), that is, a post–World War II high-density, mixed-use urban area that developed outside the traditional downtown.[33] As is characteristic of edge cities, Hillcroft Avenue is marked by mid-rise office towers and skyscrapers interspersed with parking lots and open spaces, a higher population density, and a concentration of jobs, businesses, shopping areas, and private residences. Hillcroft Avenue is located between Beltway 8 and Westheimer Road, and its development and growth are in large part due to its accessibility from highways and major roadways established by automobile-centered patterns of urban development.

The Metro, a light-rail line, commenced operations in 2004 after several decades of delay and opposition that favored improvement and expansion of the highway system. Proposed expansion of the light-rail will serve Hillcroft Avenue. Following national trends, these developments are intended to create communities where people can live closer to where they work and shop; they are seen as the best long-term solution to solving traffic problems in the city. However, in 2010, the section of Hillcroft Avenue between Bellaire Boulevard and the Southwest Freeway (U.S. 59) was widened from six lanes to eight lanes indicating the continued privileging of automobiles over railways and sustained classed and racialized patterns of development in Houston.

Houstonians typically divide the city and differentiate between areas of the city that are inside or outside the Loop, referring to the 610 Highway Loop that encircles the oldest and central area of the city. Interestingly, the hundreds of Pakistanis of all backgrounds that I spoke with rarely made this distinction, which is perhaps explained by their recent history in Houston. The majority of South Asians came to Houston at a time when their institutions and communities developed outside the Loop. Since the majority have always lived outside the Loop, the terminology did not seem to hold significant meaning for many of my interlocutors. Pakistanis instead differentiated places through the use of specific names—Hillcroft, Bissonnet, Sugar Land, the Astrodome, Woodlands, and so on—calling all of these areas "Houston" without distinguishing between central city and suburbs, and reflecting in many ways how Pakistanis move through the city.

As a Pakistani space, Hillcroft Avenue and its arterial and minor roadways connect Pakistani immigrants residing in mid-rise apartment complexes and gated communities with ethnic businesses and enterprises, community centers, and places of worship. Hillcroft in many ways represents a balance between self-containment and intertwinement and interconnectedness to the larger city, as well as local, national, and transnational financial, ethnic, and religious nodes and networks. As upwardly mobile Pakistani professionals moved to suburbs such as Sugar Land, Missouri City and Pearland, ethnic entrepreneurs, the working class, and the working poor began to dominate the Pakistani ethnic environment in southwest Houston. Often lacking language, professional, or educational capital to enter mainstream society and economy, these individuals turned to ethnic businesses for employment and to the Pakistani civic organizations for leadership positions that eluded them in the mainstream. It is indicative of the salience of the Pakistani ethnic environment in the lives of the more recent Pakistani immigrants in Houston that a twenty-eight-year-old Punjabi chef at a Pakistani restaurant exclaimed to me with discernible pride: "Houston is the only city in America where one can live and die without ever having to speak English or encounter an American. The apartment buildings, the restaurants, travel agencies, mosques, and Indian movie theatres are all owned by Pakistanis—you can do everything in Urdu. You don't need to know English to live here."

Like most localities in Houston, much of Hillcroft does not have the kind of high-density development that typically promotes pedestrian usage. Instead, most Houstonians navigate the length of Hillcroft Avenue via some form of transportation, typically car or bus. The Hillcroft Transit Center (a bus station and park-and-ride facility), located near the northern end of Hillcroft Avenue, serves mostly working-class people who do not own cars and use the bus to travel for work, shopping, eating, and services. Living near the transit hub and using it daily during fieldwork, I was surprised to find a relative absence of South Asians riding the bus. After several months of fieldwork, I began to recognize that while entrepreneurs and middle-class Pakistanis blended into Houston's car culture, working-class Pakistanis lived, worked, and attended mosque within a smaller three- to four-block area of Hillcroft, and they generally walked.

At first glance, Hillcroft appears similar to localities in many American cities: non-descript parking lots, strip malls, and open lots. However, further investigation reveals the transnational character of this area. Indeed, the experience of place in Hillcroft is one of "translocality" (Leichty 1996) in which locality is demarcated as a physical space of social interaction and the identity of the place emerges through the multiple imaginations and experiences of of the place that transcend national geographical boundaries (Greiner and Sakdapolrak 2013). In a strip mall near the originating north end of Hillcroft, for example, a Persian and Iranian grocery store and supermarket, founded in 1979, provides a wide range of food and goods. Freshly made Middle Eastern pastries and pita bread, prepared at the in-house bakery, combine with DVDs, audiocassettes, and CDs from the Middle East as well as a jewelry section to create an eclectic business establishment. This store caters to Muslim customers from throughout the greater Houston area looking for halal food and other products. A restaurant section, added in 1988, offers an affordable Middle Eastern buffet and sandwiches; it is especially busy during lunch hours, catering to workers from nearby strip malls and mid-rises. In the next strip mall moving south on Hillcroft, a Guatemalan restaurant, much like the other ethnic restaurants throughout Hillcroft, is a cornucopia for the senses that represents cultural heritage not only through food but also decoratively. Landscape photographs of Guatemala adorn the restaurant walls, and a headless mannequin wearing a traditional Guatemalan dress hangs next to the restaurant's bar. Guatemalan clothing, fabric, and rugs available for sale are stacked high on a table near the bar. Colorful tablecloths and stylized utensils on each table attempt to confer authenticity within the confines of the restaurant, as also noted in the case of Iranian carpet stores in Houston (M. Fischer and Abedi 2002).

Further south, but still toward the northern end of Hillcroft, another strip mall consists primarily of Indian and Pakistani businesses, including the following: a halal kabob restaurant; nine ethnic clothing boutiques specializing in saris, shalwar and kameez for men and women, and accessories; three salons and spas; a juice and beverage bar; a travel agency; an academy that offers classes in salsa, samba, belly dancing, bachata, hip hop, and ballroom; an upscale bar and lounge; and an Indian jewelry store. Nearby, a mosque and Muslim community center provide daily prayer services and offer Arabic language and Qur'anic study classes as well as community outreach activities such as dinners for low-income people. Roads neighboring this strip mall lead to unde-veloped open spaces and to apartment complexes that house many South Asians.

In 2010, this stretch of Hillcroft Avenue north of Highway 59 was designated as Mahatma Gandhi District, following initiatives of the India Culture Center and several South Asian businesses based along Hillcroft Avenue. Signage indicating the name of the district, accom-panied by a photo of Gandhi, appeared more than thirty times on Hill-croft Avenue and its intersections at Harwin Avenue, Fondren Road, and Westpark Drive. The renaming of this section of Hillcroft Avenue reveals the negotiations of place making in a locality where several different ethnic and racial communities and groups share space and resources. According to a news report, non-Indian business owners resisted the initial plan to change the name of the street from Hillcroft to Gandhi, claiming that it privileged one nationality group over others and might cause confusion among visitors, tourists, and customers.[34] The plan to rename the area, rather than the street, was then approved. The renaming suggests that Hillcroft Avenue is a translocality where the imagination, experience, and history of a place are variously con-structed by different communities and groups.

Continuing south on Hillcroft, a multi-ethnic configuration of busi-nesses and community establishments dots the landscape. A Pakistani-owned video and DVD store in another multiethnic strip mall next to Highway 59 serves South Asians looking for an alternative to Western media and popular culture through DVDs of newly released and classic Indian movies and CDs of Indian and Pakistani music and songs. More than just a business catering to a niche market, this store represents a node in the transnational Muslim heritage economy, as well as a site for transnational community building in Houston. As a researcher, I spent months learning about the Pakistani community in Houston by carry-ing out participant observation in this store, where customers would spend an hour or more browsing the titles and initiating conversations with the thirty-something owners, Ali and Nadia. I explore their expe-riences as ethnic entrepreneurs further in chapter 3.

Following Hillcroft south after passing beneath Highway 59, called "59" by Houstonians, one comes to the Alliance for Multicultural Community Services, a multiethnic community space that serves a number of new immigrant and refugee communities. The location of the Alliance within this multiethnic neighborhood speaks to the cosmopolitan makeup of southwest Houston. The Alliance provides services in more than seventy languages to refugees, new immigrants, and low-income communities in Houston. The Alliance's extraordinary range of services includes resettlement, employment assistance, counseling, health education, and assistance navigating public services such as schools, food stamps, transportation, social security, and Medicaid.[35] Hillcroft's mix of parking lots, strip malls, and mid-rise buildings continues as one heads south, although there are fewer and fewer South Asian shops. Street signage is in Mandarin, indicating the predominance of Chinese businesses and enterprises. Chinese shops, restaurants, and cultural centers share blocks with Indian, Pakistani, Middle Eastern, South American, and Central American markets and businesses. Farther south of 59, a nondescript building surrounded by vacant land on a street adjoining Hillcroft houses a major radio station for Pakistani radio programs. The radio station provides a mediated anchor and an auditory imagined community for the Pakistani communities dispersed throughout the greater Houston metropolitan area. These programs, which permeate the soundscape and public life of the Pakistani community, are explored in chapter 6.

Sugar Land: A Twenty-First-Century "Ethnoburb"

Like Hillcroft, Sugar Land represents a center for Pakistani immigrant life. It also continues racialized patterns of urban development by locating new immigrants farther from the city center, given the limited opportunities for new immigrant communities to purchase homes within the Loop. Like Hillcroft, Sugar Land is characterized by mixed land use development that includes residential settlements and service-sector businesses like restaurants, malls, and offices of lawyers, accountants, and real estate agents. Also, like Hillcroft, Sugar Land is also connected with the rest of Houston through the highway network. In spite of these convergences with the existing southwestern suburban developments, Sugar Land exemplifies newer multiethnic and multireligious developments that are anchored by an upwardly mobile, highly skilled and educated workforce employed largely in the energy sector. Indeed, it is the classed composition of Sugar Land that most distinguishes its residents from those in Hillcroft. Moreover, the wide array of associated infrastructure, notably mosques, Islamic schools, community centers, and restaurants, suggest the development of an increasingly variegated ethno-religious environment that caters to white-collar South Asians. In this spatialized configuration, Sugar Land 1990s may be characterized as an ethnoburb (Li 1998; 2009), that is, a suburban area that is characterized by a residential and business concentration of an ethnic group or groups.

Sugar Land, named after the Imperial Sugar Company, the nation's oldest and one of its largest sugar-manufacturing plants, is today an affluent suburb (officially classified as annexed city) and the largest city in Fort Bend County in the southwestern reaches of the greater Houston metropolitan area. In the nineteenth century, Sugar Land began as a plantation for growing and processing sugar. By the early twentieth century, the lands and refinaries were consolidated into a company town for the Imperial Sugar Company. Until the middle of the twentieth century, Sugar Land included the company offices as well as housing and associated infrastructure such as schools, hospitals, and business centers that provided services for company employees. While the Imperial Sugar Company has long since ceased growing sugarcane and stopped refining sugar, its corporate headquarters remain in Sugar Land.

Today, master-planned communities with large brick houses, immaculately landscaped lawns, lush greenery on either side of the main roads, parks and open play grounds, and recreational development like golf courses and country clubs distinguish Sugar Land from the uneven and ad hoc urban development that characterizes Houston's downtown, as well as sections of southwestern Houston such as Hillcroft. Sugar Land is home to the headquarters of energy companies and offices of software, engineering, and petroleum exploration companies and refineries. The city is dominated by white-collar residents, mostly employed in the energy sector, and connected to the rest of Greater Houston via two major intersecting highways, Highway 6 and Highway 59.

Unlike the suburbs that developed after World War II and were dominated by whites, newer suburbs of Houston like Sugar Land are distinguished by high levels of ethnic and religious diversity. For example, Woodlands inside the Loop is historically and remains predominantly white, but the cluster of newer suburbs like Sugar Land, Missouri City, and Pearland is currently the most diverse, with higher percentages of Asians than any other locality in the Houston metropolitan area. In fact, Pearland, one of Houston's least diverse localities in 1990, ranked among the most diverse twenty years later (Emerson et al. 2013). Asians represent 12 percent of the population in Pearland, 16 percent of the population in Missouri City, and 35 percent of the population in Sugar Land.

Sugar Land boasts the highest concentration of Asians in Texas and is consistently ranked among the top neighborhoods in the state on the basis of educational opportunities, low crime rates, high employment, housing data, and diversity. *Forbes* magazine rated Sugar Land among the top ten suburbs in the United States.[36] The public school system, which is considered one of the finest in the Greater Houston area, is a major reason why upwardly mobile, college-educated professionals representing a wide breadth of ethnic and religious communities and affiliations have relocated to Sugar Land. Pakistani and Indian professionals are among those who have relocated en masse, taking advantage of the expanding real estate market in Sugar Land and the neighboring suburb of Missouri City. Sugar Land and Missouri City are largely inaccessible via public transportation—buses do not run through or to Sugar Land—and the need for a car to visit marks this suburb as an exclusive community of upwardly mobile middle- and upper-middle class white-collar professionals.

Without exception, all of my research interlocutors who lived in Sugar Land spoke of it with discernible pride. For many of my Pakistani interlocutors employed in the energy sector, notably the Shia Ismaili men and women discussed in chapter 2, home ownership in Sugar Land is a marker of their attainment of the American dream and a testament to their success in the United States. Pakistani immigrants, along with Muslim communities from other countries in South Asia and elsewhere, have also been able to participate in the planned development of Sugar Land in ways that are different from the ad hoc planning and development that characterizes older centers of Pakistani life in Houston. Sunni and Shia mosques and community centers, along with with the sprawling Sugar Land jamat khana (prayer hall) and center on 11.5 acres of property that caters to the Shia Ismaili community, reflect the multisectarian Islamic infrastructure in Sugar Land. Zoroastrian, Hindu, and Sikh communities have also claimed large properties to construct temples and gurdwara, suggesting the salience of religion in practices of place making in Sugar Land.

Conclusion

Variously conceptualized as Magnolia City, Freeway City, Mobile City, High-Tech City, Space City, Spectacular City, Strip City, Oil Town, Cowboy City, and "Shining Buckle of the Sunbelt," Houston is, as it has been argued, "a provincial oil capital reaching for nationally minded sophistication" (Lin 1995: 633). The feeling of being "always on the way, always arriving, always looking for the place where everything comes together" (Huxtable 1976: 144) is exemplified in the decentralized and unregulated urban planning and the fragmented ethnic neighborhoods that are dispersed on unwanted land, open prairie, and woodland adjacent to downtown, the industrial east side of the city, and in the far reaches of southwest Houston.

In spite of being the fourth-largest city in the United States, Houston has resisted public regulation and land use zoning, making it one of the only cities of its size that follows a traditional free market philosophy of minimal public involvement in local and urban development issues (Vojnovic 2003a). In the absence of sustained urban planning, Houston became characterized by urban anonymity—nondescript commercial strips, parking lots, shopping malls and an uneven mix of industrial, commercial and residential land use. Public involvement in urban development historically privileged the white elite and corporate interests and marginalized the interests of ethnic minorities in Houston. For example, during the period of urban renewal in the United States in the 1950s, African American and Latino neighborhoods in Houston were demolished to make way for highways and other urban development projects. These projects of renewal and similar projects that have followed have had the devastating effect of eroding the cohesion and unity of ethnic neighborhoods and localities, and fragmenting the city.

Pakistanis are relatively new entrants to Houston, arriving in large numbers in the decades following the changes in U.S. immigration policies and laws in 1965. As new immigrant communities, Pakistanis have had to negotiate racialized and classed spatialities in Houston, in practices of place making. This chapter's survey of Houston's growth and development into a global city points to the centrality of the energy sector in shaping the city's geography, creating racialized settlement patterns and a labor force within which Pakistanis are embedded. Although Pakistanis reside throughout the greater Houston metropolitan area, Pakistanis are a distinctly visible presence in sections of southwest Houston where they have created infrastructure and institutions to support their working, religious, public and private lives. The survey of two major localities, Hillcroft Avenue and Sugar Land indicates the centrality of Islam in practices of Pakistani place making and constructions of identity and community as Houstonians.

2

"A Dream Come True"

Shia Ismaili Experiences in Corporate America

In the winter of 2001, a financial scandal emanating from Houston exploded onto the international scene. Enron Corporation, one of the largest multinational energy, commodities, and services companies based in Houston, had become embroiled in a financial scandal centered on unprecedented levels of corporate corruption, greed, and mismanagement of funds and appropriations.[1] Enron filed for Chapter 11 protection, sued rival Dynegy Inc. for $10 billion, and initiated widespread layoffs that significantly impacted its 7,500 employees in Houston (Bradley 2009a). Within a year, Enron's twelve remaining core assets, natural gas pipelines, and electric utilities were auctioned (Fox 2003). Enron's rapid fall and eventual bankruptcy challenged mythologies of unbridled freedom of opportunity and success in America's neoliberal capitalist economy.[2] Enron's collapse also tested conventional wisdom about the vitality of Houston's energy sector.[3] As I discussed in chapter 1, Houston's economy, driven by a concentration of the oil and gas sectors, had shown remarkable resilience and longevity, including recovery following the recession during the 1980s, in large part because of the presence of energy giants such as Enron.

The collapse of Enron found scarcely any interlocutors in Houston's South Asian civic and cultural organizations, Pakistani and Indian radio programs, and Urdu- and English-language Pakistani newspapers. I found that I had to listen very hard for commentary or even a passing reference on the topic in the South Asian diasporic public sphere. A Pakistani radio program that specializes in replays of Pakistani and Indian pop music and soundtracks of current Indian movies provided one such fleeting moment. A listener had called in to request a song from a recently released Bollywood film. The following on-air interaction between a Pakistani American radio host/programmer and an Indian male listener ensued:

RADIO PROGRAMMER/HOST: So what kind of work do you do?
CALLER: I am an engineer.
RADIO PROGRAMMER/HOST: Great, man. Where do you work?
CALLER: Well, I am originally from Mumbai and just moved from Atlanta.
    . . . I am looking for a job.
RADIO PROGRAMMER/HOST: You aren't applying to Enron, are you?
CALLER: What? Eh, no.
RADIO PROGRAMMER/HOST: Good, because I don't think they are hiring!
    (The programmer, the studio staff, and the caller laugh). All right
    man, here's your song. All the best!

Aside from such passing references intended to elicit an easy laugh, it took me several serendipitous encounters to identify the Pakistani professionals impacted by the Enron crisis. It was through a chance encounter at a Pakistani-owned and -managed DVD and video store on Hillcroft Avenue where I had been carrying out participant observation for several months that I met Amjad, a thirty-three-year-old Pakistani male. Like most customers, Amjad's interest in Indian cinema gravitated toward classics from the 1970s or newly released big-budget Bollywood blockbusters. Amjad had come to the store on a slow weekday and had rented five DVDs, a high number even for the most diehard fans of Bollywood. "I have a lot of time on my hands these days," he said, smiling slightly, before continuing, "You see, I was laid off from Enron."

Over the next few weeks, I got to know Amjad during his increasingly frequent visits to the DVD store. It was through Amjad that I learned of his Pakistani and Indian friends who had also been laid off from Enron and other energy companies such as Reliant Energy. I ran into Amjad on several occasions and subsequently friended him and a few of his friends on Facebook.

Given the importance of the Houston-based energy sector in driving the immigration of Pakistani skilled labor to the metropolis, the lack of sustained discourse on the Enron crisis within the South Asian ethno-religious environment misses an important opportunity to criti-cally examine the experiences of Pakistani skilled labor in corporate America. In this chapter, I examine the conjuncture of access to edu-cation and employment opportunities in corporate America; deploy-ment of transnational religion as cultural capital; and the specificities of historical experience in shaping the professional life trajectories and experiences of Pakistani skilled labor employed in the energy sector in Houston.

The passage of the U.S. Immigration and Naturalization Act of 1965 opened immigration to Asians after decades of exclusionary and racially restrictive policies (Prashad 2000) and provided opportunities for education and employment in the United States. The immigration reforms created a highly skilled labor force, the majority of whom were trained in the sciences, engineering, and medicine and represented middle-class and elite backgrounds in their countries of origin in South Asia.[4] In Houston, the absorption of highly skilled Asian labor in the energy-centered economy affirmed the city's status as a primary des-tination for highly skilled Pakistani immigrants (Williams 1988). The city's population grew by 30 percent during the 1970s and the 1980s, an increase that is explained in large part by the in-migration of a highly skilled workforce (Feagin 1985).

The immigration reforms of 1965 intersected with the emergence of the "model minority" concept in the mainstream U.S. press and pub-lic policy.[5] The model minority concept served to promote the United States as the leader of the free world, the land of opportunity, and a colorblind multicultural society grounded in meritocracy. In the 1960s and the 1980s, for example, media reports referred to the achievements of Japanese and Chinese entrepreneurs, extolling Asian values and the ability to overcome histories and experiences of racism in the United States as explanations for success.[6] Public policy and mass media char-acterized respect for parents and authority, a reverence for learning, and proclivity for hard work as cultural capital (Bourdieu 1984)[7] that enabled Asian immigrants to overcome racism and achieve individual success, and assimilate into American society—all with limited govern-ment assistance. In the case of South Asians, the model minority con-cept attributes success to "the supposed value that South Asian cultures place on education, discipline, and respect for authority and hierarchy" (Das Gupta 2006: 77).[8]

Pakistani Muslim professionals discussed in this chapter may be characterized as the model minority, but they also complicate this notion. Shia Ismaili Muslims, who constitute the largest branch within the Shia Muslim sect, are an important component of the highly skilled Pakistani labor force. I argue that for my Shia Ismaili interlocutors, seeking higher education in the U.S. and employment at Enron, a Fortune 500 company, is not simply a product of American values, capitalism, and modernity, but, importantly, a religious imperative. Indeed, in conversations on the topic, my interlocutors readily attribute their desire to pursue higher education at elite universities and seek employment at high-profile energy companies such as Enron as religious imperatives grounded in Ismaili ideologies centered on success and individual achievement.

As I discuss later in this chapter, the importance placed on education and professional achievement and sustained engagements in religious community is not an innate Ismaili characteristic as presumed in mythologies around the model minority, but a product of Ismaili cultural histories and experiences during the twentieth century. Indeed, as Vijay Prashad has argued: "The implication is that the high proportion of Asians in the technical fields says something about Asians' nature rather than about their recent cultural history" (Prashad 2000: 70). Similar to the case of my interlocutors, transnational Ismaili community formations in Africa, the Gulf States, the Middle East, South Asia, and North America have been characterized by high levels of entrepreneurship, professional achievement, and success (Coleman 1990). However, such achievements emerge as religiously sanctioned strategies that mediate the experience of marginality, discrimination, and racism experienced by Ismaili entrepreneurs and businessmen and women in a variety of national and cultural settings. These achievements are not simply premised on individualism but acquire meaning in the context of fulfilling obligations to family and kin groups and as members of a transnational religious community.

The centrality of Ismaili ideologies in structuring professional lives is intertwined with variegated civic engagements in the Ismaili community at local and global levels. Finding themselves unexpectedly laid off, my Ismaili interlocutors received little support from mainstream employment agencies and career advisory services. During this period, these professionals created ad hoc networks of Ismaili professionals that were forged in the corridors of energy companies like Enron and at Ismaili community centers and mosques. These upwardly mobile and affluent men and women provided each other with emotional support and career counseling, collaborated in business ventures, and sought out coreligionists for job leads, referrals, and as clientele for their post-Enron business ventures.

The emphasis on education in the sciences and professional achievement intersects with another transnational register, notably ideologies and practices of nation building and modernization in South Asia.[9] Following Pakistan's creation in 1947, ideas of progress, modernity, and development became intertwined with the need for an educated workforce and bureaucracy trained in the fields of engineering, medicine, and public administration that could create and strengthen public institutions and infrastructure. Since the 1950s, strategic alliances with the United States have provided opportunities for Pakistani students to travel to the United States for higher education. The emphasis on higher education then is recast as a historical development—as a facet of nation building in South Asia.

In this chapter, a case-study focus on Ismaili Muslims provides insights into the professional life experiences of highly skilled Pakistani labor in the United States. It ruptures dominant understandings of Islam and Muslim American communities as a monolith and illuminates Islamic sectarian ideologies and forms of knowledge in shaping the Muslim American experience. Deconstructing notions of success, achievement, and excellence in education and professional life through the lens of sectarian Islamic religious ideologies as well as practices of nation building in South Asia illuminates transnational registers for a critical reading of the American dream propagated by successive American government regimes through changes in immigration laws and inclusion in corporate America.[10]

1965 Immigration Reform and South Asian Labor Flows

The landmark Immigration and Naturalization Act of 1965 opened American doors to Asian immigration and abandoned legislation that had used race as the basis of immigration to the United States. The Chinese Exclusion Act of 1882 prohibited the admission of unskilled Chinese labor; the 1917 Immigration Act, also termed the Asiatic Barred Zone Act, denied admission to Asian Indians; the 1924 Immigration Act banned the admission of persons ineligible for citizenship, a category that included Chinese, Japanese, Koreans, and Asian Indians; and the Immigration Act of 1952 restricted Asians through an annual quota of only one hundred from each Asian country.[11] The 1965 landmark legislation abandoned the national origins quota system that had favored European immigration and severely restricted the immigration of Asians to the United States until after World War II.[12] Following the passage of the 1965 Act, Asia became a major source of immigration to the United States.[13]

The opening up of immigration is a critical component in the mythologizing of U.S. ideologies of freedom and open access to opportunity in a meritocracy-driven colorblind society. In spite of the broader discourse of freedom of access to opportunities for career advancement and achievement, these reforms did not lead to immigration for all; rather, they created classed, gendered, and racialized classificatory schemes and hierarchies of immigrants (Malick 2010). Although the immigration reforms of 1965 had made admission to the United States more available to Asian nationality groups, it was the middle-class and the elite, and mostly men, who benefited from the changes in immigration law and constituted the majority of the South Asian labor flows to the United States (Prashad 2000). The classed and gendered hierarchy of South Asia labor flows selected for technical experts and students in the sciences, turning education and access to financing into forms of cultural capital in U.S. immigration policies.

By the early 1990s, Indian immigration represented a record 4.44 percent of all immigration to the United States (Rangaswamy 2000). These professionals included physicians, engineers, and executives employed in corporate America.[14] In addition, the Nursing Immigration Relief Act of 1989 and the Immigration Act of 1991 created preference criteria for the immigration of nurses and professionals to meet U.S. economic and labor shortfalls through skilled Asian labor.

The mythology of the American dream obscures domestic and global factors that made it imperative for the United States to liberalize its immigration laws. According to scholars Paul Ong and John M. Liu, "the civil rights movement made state-supported racism less tenable then before. While the movement fought for the extension of political rights and later economic rights, the attack on de jure discrimination logically extended to the immigration arena" (2000: 155). Economic prosperity, low unemployment levels in the 1960s, and the gains made by the civil rights movement converged with the emergence of the United States as the leader of the free world. While consolidating its global standing, it became untenable for the United States to justify exclusionary and racialized immigration policies. Consequently, it became politically expedient to "adopt immigrant policies congruous with democracy's fight against fascism" (ibid.: 157). These domestic and global contexts shaped immigration reform and intersected with the emergence of notions such as the model minority in the 1960s.[15]

Shia Ismaili Skilled Labor and Assertions of the Model Minority

The model minority concept emphasizes the capacity of Asian immigrant communities to overcome experiences of racism and achieve material success.[16] Educational and occupational achievement "without government support, by relying on their family" (Shankar 2008: 13) is a central component in constructions of the model minority. In promoting the concept of the model minority, mainstream U.S. media and public policy referred to selective empirical data that emphasized the educational and occupational achievements of some members of the Japanese and Chinese American communities. As an ideology, the concept calls attention to culture, positioning respect for parents and authority, a reverence for learning, and proclivity for hard work as innate Asian cultural values and as explanations for excellence in education and professional lives (Shankar 2008). Residential settlement patterns, the emphasis on education, the pursuit of excellence in professional lives, and an unwavering belief in neoliberalism and corporate

America exemplify assertions of the model minority among South Asian communities (Bhatia 2007).

Residential Settlement Patterns

I first traveled to Sugar Land to visit Amjad and his friends, Salim and Feroz. These men had been laid off from Enron in the winter of 2001. We were meeting at Amjad's house, where Feroz and Salim had also gathered to speak with me at length about their experience working at Enron and their life following the layoffs. Amjad and his wife, Saima had recently purchased the house in Sugar Land. As we sat down in his beautifully decorated living room, Amjad pointed to the large backyard and said to me: "We were going to install a swimming pool there. Of course, now we don't even know if we can afford to live here. My wife is also working again. I don't think we can maintain this place unless I start earning again."

Ismaili Muslim Americans laid off from Enron may be characterized as flexible citizens (Ong 1999), in the sense that they navigate the ups and downs of life in the corporate sector with the knowledge that their employment options are not constrained by geography. However, the narratives of my Ismaili interlocutors run counter to notions of flexible citizenship, which are premised on the absence of deep connections to locality among highly skilled labor to specific labor markets.[17] What is significant in their narratives is the fact that in spite of the existence of familial, religious and business networks across multiple nation-states and the acquisition of skills and professional experiences that are transferable and marketable in any number of labor markets globally, these professionals remain deeply invested in their lives as Houstonians. Take for example, Zeenat, a thirty-one-year-old Ismaili Muslim woman, who was born and raised in Houston and left to attend law school in Dallas. Zeenat returned to Houston in 1999 after working for a few years at a large law firm in Dallas. "I decided to come back to Houston because it is my home. My parents, brother, and relatives are all here." Zeenat laughed as she continued: "You can never get away from Houston. If you leave, you always come back."

Much like Zeenat, other Ismaili interlocutors, like Salim and Amjad, both management graduates, also emphasize that their roots are in

Houston. In order to be close to his family, Amjad explored job opportunities in Houston after completing his MBA on the East Coast.
Amjad's brother was already living in Houston, and Amjad's wife's
family was based in Houston as well. Upon receiving a job offer from
Enron, Amjad relocated to Houston, where he has lived since. As he
said to me: "For me, it was really a question about being in Houston,
close to my family." When I ask Salim and Amjad about the possibility
of relocating to another state, their responses suggest a desire to stay in
Houston, in large part because of home ownership, the existence of religious and familial relationships, and their appreciation for the quality
of life afforded to them in Houston.

> AHMED AFZAL (AA): Did any one of you think about relocating to another
> city or another state where you might have better career options?
> SALIM: For me, moving is not really an option. Moving is not desirable
> but I had done that before so I was open to it. . . . So I had talked to
> companies in Atlanta initially—the first fifteen-day period—and also
> in New York and a couple of companies on the West Coast. However,
> my roots are here—my family and extended family are here. I have
> a strong network and support base here, so moving was never a real
> option. . . . Let's say, if I did not find a job here but found one outside
> of Houston, I still would have leaned toward staying here and done
> something on my own. I would want to stay in Houston.
> AMJAD: I am not excited about moving at all. I have just purchased a house
> and my son is just getting settled in school, and I just did not want to
> uproot us again. But again, understanding the harsh realities of lim-
> ited professional opportunities in Houston, we have given ourselves
> more time. That is when I would have expanded my job search and
> looked for jobs outside of Houston.

Residential settlement in exclusive and wealthy gated communities, suburbs, and neighborhoods such as Sugar Land demonstrates the
investment South Asian professionals make in grounding themselves
within specific status-laden localities in the United States that position
them within the mythology of the American dream, where success is
symbolized by home ownership.[18] The emphasis on home ownership
in suburbs and "wealthy neighborhoods with Whites and other Asian

Americans [who] send their children to high performing schools" (Shankar 2008: 12) indicates appropriations and assertions of the model minority. It also points to the investments these new immigrants have made in establishing lives in Houston as revealed in their characterization of themselves as Houstonians. Indeed, all of the interlocutors referenced in this chapter stated to me that they could not imagine leaving Houston for another city, and that they would contemplate the move only because of extreme financial necessity.

Educational and Professional Excellence

Ismaili Muslim professionals also embody the model minority concept through their pursuit of higher education and professional achievement and success. For many Pakistani professionals employed in the energy sector in Houston, working at Enron, an elite energy company that had ranked consistently in the top ten among Fortune 500 companies *is* the American dream. Founded in the mid-1980s, Enron was widely regarded within the energy industry as being at the cutting edge of energy solutions (Henderson et al. 2009). Within just a decade, Enron emerged as a leader in the energy sector globally, with high-profile projects and collaborations with governments in Asia, the Middle East, South America, and Europe (Bradley 2009b). By 2001, Enron had become a conglomerate that owned and operated "gas pipelines, electricity plants, pulp and paper plants, broadband assets and water plants internationally and traded extensively in financial markets for the same products and services" (Healy and Palepu 2003: 5). The company grew to several thousand employees, and its influence in public policy, both in the United States and abroad, was, by all accounts, enormous.[19]

Enron's reputation as a leading energy giant attracted a labor force educated at top-tier colleges and universities and converged with the emphasis on education in middle-class Pakistani families like those of my interlocutors. Amjad had attended an Ivy League university, where he had pursued graduate education in business administration. In an ethnographic study of South Asians in the high-tech industry in the Silicon Valley, anthropologist Shalini Shankar (2008) notes the significance of education in upper-middle class households. According to Shankar:

At home, upper-middle-class parents emphasize the importance of earning high grades and test scores from elementary school onward. They prioritize schoolwork and draw on their own educational background to help their children with homework and school assignments. It is not unusual for Desi parents of this class background to push their children to perform academically and emphasize education over leisure. These parents also have the financial means to ply their children with spending money and urge them to focus on school assignments and pursue internships that will embellish their resumes. (2008: 147)

Enron's reputation was a motivating factor not only for Amjad but also for his friends whom I met. Salim, almost a decade older than Amjad and Feroz, was the sole breadwinner in his family and financially responsible for his wife and seven-year-old son. Salim had grown up in India, where he was a private entrepreneur for about ten years before he came to the United States to pursue his graduate education. Like Amjad, after he completed business school at a top-tier university on the East Coast, Salim received a job offer from Enron. He moved to Houston in 1997. Enron was Salim's first exposure to corporate America. Rather enthusiastically, Salim recounted when he was hired by Enron:

Enron had a tremendous reputation on campus at my business school. They had recruited on campus in the past few years. In the year before me, they had hired six people. From my class, fourteen of us ended up at Enron. In fact, I had three other offers on the table, but once I heard from Enron, I basically turned everybody else down.

The collective admiration Amjad and his friends Salim and Feroz expressed for the company can be attributed to Enron's reputation as well as an affirmation of their own educational and professional achievements. In some sense, their emphasis on individual success and hard work echoes the qualities admired by people who are employed at high-profile energy companies. According to Amjad:

As I explored my options and learned more about Enron, I found that it was one of the more innovative companies in the industry. I think for any graduate of a bachelor's or a master's program in [business administration], working at Enron was a dream come true . . . in the sense that Enron had a go-getter attitude. You are basically part of a team that conquers the world. . . . When I was working at Enron Middle East, the attitude was that other companies couldn't get this done. That is why Enron is here. . . . Enron brought governments together... No one else could have taken the risk to get into a country like India where the laws are ill defined but we made it happen. Enron had the most, in my experience, aggressive bunch of professionals. You could just imagine anything and make it happen.

Amjad's friend Feroz, who had also been laid off from Enron, continued:

I would say that whether it was someone at the associate's level or the managerial level, we knew that we were working with the best of the best.

Salim, who had worked at Enron for four years, echoed the thought:

Enron was a company with a vision, a sense of destiny. People were very hardworking and the rewards were tremendous. There were people there whom I identified with as role models. These people were experts in their own businesses. . . . So very clearly, it was an assembly of people who were leaders in their own right.

Their collective enthusiasm for hard work at Enron was coupled with an appreciation for networking and collaboration at the company, suggesting again an understanding of the rituals associated with a go-getting attitude and the drive for success in corporate America. According to Feroz:

Enron was the kind of place where networking was almost a prerequisite. To do well at Enron, you had to know people, you had to be able to pick up the phone and call colleagues in different divisions, take their advice. . . . From the perspective of communication between colleagues, Enron was awesome. We had tools that no other company had . . . we had amazing technology to facilitate greater communication. Lunch was an important part of the day . . . every day we set up lunch dates with someone just so that you could know people and know what they are doing . . . also that internal movement within groups was so high that if someone did not network, I don't think they could have survived there.

Feroz's enthusiasm for Enron was not diminished by the company's downward spiral and eventual collapse. In spite of being laid off from Enron, my interlocutors continued to believe in the company's potential, held it in high esteem, and termed their exposure as "awesome." For Amjad, Enron had provided an excellent first job out of business school. His contacts, beyond those forged with fellow Ismaili colleagues, persisted during the post-Enron job search. Indeed, Amjad proudly listed his employment experience at Enron on his résumé, believing it to be an asset that, in fact, gave him greater credibility in the job market. In spite of their layoff and the collapse of Enron, their tenure at the company continued to serve them well as it had provided skills that were readily transferable and marketable in a variety of professional settings. Enron's reputation as a leading energy company provided these upwardly mobile, highly skilled, and well-educated professionals the capital with which to profess a high level of competency and intelligence even after their termination, as Feroz and Amjad discuss.

> FEROZ: Everybody acknowledged that Enron had the smartest people. . . .
> But let me tell you that when we started our own business, I think
> for the most part, being at Enron enhanced our credibility. A lot of
> people we approached for business knew that since we had been
> working at Enron, we had to be smart or we wouldn't have gotten
> there in the first place.
> AMJAD: Absolutely. . . . Coming from Enron, not only in our minds but
> also in the minds of the general industry, positioned us as the smartest. The top guys did not really do well but the lower and middle
> level—we were at the middle level moving up slowly and steadily—I
> would say certainly, it was an asset to have worked at Enron.
> FEROZ: If you talk to people in the energy industry, they are pretty sure
> what Enron was and how Enron defined the industry, [and] how
> Enron opened up markets. So, I think the energy industry very much
> looks upon Enron experience as an asset.

The massive layoffs following the collapse of Enron had not made any of my interlocutors rethink a career in corporate America. Rather, the belief in corporate America suggests a neoliberal assimilationist trajectory of "full incorporation into the economic and social mainstream simply through integration into dominant institutions and reliance on ethnic capital" (Dhingra 2012: 13). The following vignette from my conversation with Amjad, Salim, and Feroz illustrates their persistent belief in corporate America, despite negotiating professional setbacks and financial loss.

> AMJAD: Financially, we all lost out. We all took a hit individually. Personally, I think I was the least affected because I was with Enron for only a little over two years. My wife was working with another company, so financially speaking it was not as burdensome for us as it was for some other families. In my case, it was an awesome experience over all. I think I got the skills I was looking for; it just worked out really well for me. Yes, there is some inconvenience now, but we've moved on to better things.
>
> SALIM: Things were just awesome. We loved our jobs; we were having a lot of fun, we were learning a lot. The only regret is that I wish Enron had survived. Even if I were not a part of it, I wish the company had survived. At least we are at an age when we can begin again.

Salim and Amjad express their certainty that there will continue to be opportunities as they move on from Enron. Here it is important to consider both American and Ismaili understandings of professional success in corporate America. Their belief in corporate America is not only a result of their experiences at Enron but also a facet of Ismaili ideologies of assimilation and success that I discuss later in this chapter. In the model minority concept, culture is deployed to reaffirm the American dream and its attendant concepts of a colorblind meritocracy, individual achievement, and fairness. The model minority stereotype places Asian Americans in a position of having to meet and maintain high standards associated with being a model minority.[20] It certainly resonates in the conception of success and the achievement held by my Ismaili interlocutors, but it also raises complicated issue of race in the attainment of the mythical American dream.[21]

The Model Minority and U.S. Race Regimes

The projection of culture to explain the success of some members of a minority community elides experiences of poverty, unemployment, homelessness, or the elusiveness of the American dream by other members of Asian immigrant communities as well as other racial minorities.[22] The model minority concept has been critiqued for obscuring entrenched racialized and classed differences in access to opportunities (Ong 1996) and undermining alliance building between Asians, Latinos, and African Americans.[23] As Shankar argues, by praising "the success of some minorities, these reports indirectly blamed others for not advancing in what was touted as an open society. The racist dynamics that govern structures of opportunity were neither acknowledged nor taken into account" (2008: 13).

South Asian communities in the United States may confound the myth of the model minority.[24] The racialization of South Asians, especially in relation to whites, African Americans, and Latinos, suggests a complicated and ambiguous positioning within U.S. racial hierarchies.[25] In terms of the residential settlement patterns, educational attainment levels, professional achievements, and perceptions of corporate America, the interlocutors I discuss in this chapter embody the model minority. Yet these modes of integration are complicated by a strategic racialized positioning that distances South Asian professionals from other minority communities, notably African Americans and Latinos.

Some scholars have argued that South Asians largely have not identified with the struggles of African Americans and Latinos, building few alliances across racialized borders. As sociologist Monisha Das Gupta states, "for South Asians . . . racism toward Blacks and Latinos has long been a rite of passage into model minority citizenship. This rite of passage is complemented by disinterest in the economic disenfranchisement and the struggles against police brutality of African American communities" (Das Gupta 2006: 133). Moreover, as historian Vijay Prashad has noted:

> The entry of desis in large numbers after the passage of the Civil Rights
> Act not only brought them into the model minority category but also set
> the terms for the desi view of Black Liberation. It did not take long for

the media to add desis to the model minority category. Here was a community with phenomenal demographic data: Almost everyone had an advanced degree, and almost all the migrants imbibed bourgeois values of education and a work ethic. . . . This was the cream of the bourgeois South Asian crop, and it was certainly going to make an impact despite its small numbers. (2000: 169)

Assertions and appropriations as a model minority have meant appealing to dominant and predominantly white societal norms, rather than identifying with other people of color. Critics of the model minority concept frame it as a class-based racially divisive project that constructs good and bad racial subjects. Scholars of Asian Indian communities acknowledge racism, sexism, and class-based inequalities and elisions but fall short of terming experiences of glass ceiling and differential access to rights, entitlements, and privileges in the neoliberal economy as discrimination.[26] Critiquing the model minority concept from a feminist and anti-racist perspective, Monisha Das Gupta (2006) states that "the enthusiasm with which the South Asian mainstream embraces the model minority image is reprehensible not only because it accepts anti-Black and anti-Latino racism but also because this acceptance is tied to patriarchal oppression and compulsory heterosexuality in the name of culture" (59).

Indeed, Ismaili men like Amjad and his friends filter whiteness through the lens of neoliberal ideologies to illustrate what ethnic studies scholar Jasbir Puar has termed "fitness-within-capitalism" and the promise of incorporation that "always appears almost on the verge of fulfillment, but is never quite satisfied" (2007: 26). There is then a disavowal of racism so that it is less real, and "the seduction by global capital is conducted through racial amnesia, among other forms of forgetting" (ibid.). Reflecting this, Salim once said to me: "If the company had continued, we would have seen many non-whites at the highest level at Enron." Likewise, when I ask Amjad whether he had experienced any discrimination at Enron because of his religion, race, or nationality, he was quick in his defense of Enron:

Enron awarded merits and guts and visions. Race was never an issue. If I had stayed there, I could see myself as a senior executive. . . . My personal experience was that at the level of associates or managers, glass ceiling did not exist. Enron was the type of company where I would have wanted to be, twenty years from now. Perhaps in the future, I might have felt a glass ceiling.

Amjad and Salim, however, more readily acknowledge a glass ceiling and barriers for upward mobility for women in corporate America. According to Amjad:

> The energy industry is driven by traders. It is an industry driven by experts in the energy field, and if you look at these traders or experts, more often it is men. Traders are extremely aggressive, extremely cut throat, and mostly male. . . . It was a very macho kind of an environment that might turn off women . . . but racially, there was no issue.

Certainly the "aggressive" and "macho kind of environment" referenced by my interlocutors suggests gendered constructions of professional achievement and success that reward men more than women. The appropriation of such gendered explanations for success in corporate America shapes Amjad and Salim's observations and assertions and suggests a gendered "ascendancy to whiteness" (Puar 2007) and management of racial difference and sameness. This is in spite of research findings that indicate that Asians are, in fact, not advancing despite high academic and professional qualifications, and that Asian Americans are paid less than whites across a variety of sectors of employments (Shankar 2008). This ascendancy produces heteronormative and bourgeois notions of family that are deployed to consolidate privilege. The disavowal of racism may be premised on a disidentification with disenfranchised populations "in favor of consolidation with axes of privilege" (Puar 2007: 28). Moreover, model minority discourses depend on a "deferred or deflected gratification . . . gender and sexual normativity and the reproduction of the hybrid multicultural body politic in exchange for lucrative possibilities within the global economy" (ibid.: 27).

This configuration of privilege may require a lack of investment in progressive politics (Das Gupta 2006) and interracial and interclass coalition building. Alternatively, racial marginalization may be one of scale. As sociologist Pawan Dhingra (2012) suggests, "[R]acism may not be so significant to them that they form hostilities against whites. . . . Race and ethnicity continue to matter; the only question is how much. The more they matter, the stronger are the ethnic and pan-ethnic boundaries and the weaker the integration" (13). Further, the seeming homogeneity of South Asian professional labor flows and complicity in racial regimes is complicated in the post-9/11 epoch in which some South Asian communities have become "invested in separating themselves from others who may be mistaken for enemies of the state" (Shankar 2008: 15).

Among the underlying currents, I argue that the disavowal of racism finds continuities with the past, especially the ambiguities around racial classifications of South Asians in the United States and shifting understandings and constructions of whiteness.[27] At various times in the twentieth century, South Asians have been classified as Caucasian, Hindoo [sic], Asian (other), Asian Indian, and Asian or Pacific Islander. As recently as the year 2000, 25 percent of second-generation South Asian Americans checked "white" as a racial category of self-identification in census reporting. Referring to the persistence of such ambiguities in census reporting, anthropologist Alison Brooks and colleagues (2004) note, "Anthropology departments sometimes receive desperate calls from parents: 'I am from Pakistan. Should I check 'White' or 'Asian'?" (156).

Revisiting the historical archive here reveals racial exclusions as well as the ambiguities around racial classification that were codified in law and premised on faulty scientific theorizing around race. In the late nineteenth and the early twentieth centuries, South Asian immigrants consisted of men who settled on the West Coast of North America (Leonard 1992). During the late 1800s, about seven hundred people came to the United States from Punjab in British colonial India (Rangaswamy 2000). Although most were Sikhs, with smaller percentages of Hindus and Muslims, all the immigrants were racialized as "Hindoo" (Song 1998). The population grew in the early twentieth century when over 6,000 immigrants from British India entered the United States (Hess 1976).

These men worked in agriculture as well as in the timber industry and were the objects of systematic racism and discrimination. The 1909

Federal Immigration Commission and the 1920 California State Board of Control, for example, labeled "the Indian" as "the most undesirable immigrant in the state. His lack of professional cleanliness, his low morals, and his blind adherence to theories and teaching so entirely repugnant to American principles make him unfit for association with American people" (Leonard 1992: 24). At the same time, these men also protested such state-sanctioned racism. Vijay Prashad notes, "Run out of Bellingham, Washington, in September 1907, reviled by Samuel Gompers's American Federation of Labor, and denounced by the Asiatic Exclusion League, the Punjabis married Mexicans, formed the revolutionary Ghadar Party, and challenged white supremacy at every opportunity" (Prashad 2000: 72). Punjabi immigrants also protested racially exclusionary laws such as the 1913 Alien Land Laws, which legally compromised the rights of these men to farm ownership.

In the 1920s, a series of U.S. Supreme Court rulings intervened in the racialization of Asian immigrants. In the oft-cited *Ozawa v. United States* in 1922, the Supreme Court ruled to deny citizenship to Japanese people on the basis of their inability to scientifically demonstrate Aryan and therefore Caucasian ancestry. Having noted the significance of self-representations as white in making claims of citizenship, a Punjabi immigrant, Bhagat Singh Thind built an argument based on racialized science at the time that claimed Indians shared the same Aryan heritage as Americans of northern and western European origin and were therefore white.[28] Contradicting its ruling in *Ozawa*, the Supreme Court ruled that in spite of the validity of these claims, "brown skin tone and other phenotypic features precluded [Indians] from blending in with whites" (Shankar 2008: 35) and could not be used to substantiate claims of whiteness. The results of this ruling were devastating. As Shankar states: "Laws now prohibited Hindoos from sponsoring spouses or brides for immigration, owning land, or marrying Whites" (ibid.: 35). Although the laws have changed in the ensuing years, the ambiguity of racial and census classification remains to some extent.

In spite of such histories of ambiguities in racial categorizations, assertions and assignations as a model minority (Bhatia 2007) during the contemporary period is not necessarily premised on a disinvestment in progressive politics or coalition building or a negation of racism of Muslims within the larger U.S. society. On the contrary, the investment in building mosques and religious infrastructure I described in chapter 1 has been central in creating multiracial places of worship that are inclusive of African Americans and Latinos. The same extends to religious proselytizing and outreach in correctional facilities to members of all racial minorities. The investment in civic engagements similarly includes outreach to Muslims across race and country of national origin. For example, Zeenat, an Ismaili Muslim American and lawyer by profession, routinely organizes legal clinics and seminars in the fields of immigration, family law, and business transactions. As a Pakistani American woman who had been actively involved in the Ismaili community center, Zeenat's training in immigration law made her well positioned to provide counsel in immigration-related cases that affected Muslims across race, class, Muslim sectarian affiliations, and immigration status. Zeenat's sense of responsibility to the broader Muslim community is echoed by Amjad and Salim, as discussed later in this chapter. It points to the intertwining of civic engagements with individual achievement and success, and an acknowledgement of racism toward Muslims in U.S. society.

Shia Ismaili Religious Ideologies and Approaches to Education and Work

Islam is divided into several different sects, with the primary split between Sunni and Shia Muslims. The Sunni-Shia split is premised in large part on disputes over succession to Imamate following the death of the Prophet Mohammad. While Sunnis contend that leadership is elective, Shias believe in the centrality of patrilineal descent through Prophet Ali, the son-in-law of Prophet Mohammad in determining succession. The Ismailis[29] constitute the second-largest branch of Shia Muslims with presence in more than twenty countries throughout the world (Kadende-Kaiser and Kaiser 1998). Historically, Ismailis originated in Gujarat and Punjab, which in the present day are split between India and Pakistan; hence the importance of transnational religious identification and community formations over ancestral affiliations to a single nation-state. Since their origins in the eighth century, Ismailis have represented "the most important revolutionary wing of Shi'aism" (Daftary 1990: 1). Ismailis emerged from obscurity in the ninth century to found the Fatimid dynasty in North Africa in 909. Extending their power via conquest of Egypt in 969, the Ismailis then experienced a decline in North Africa but spread throughout South Asia, notably India and Pakistan, Africa, Europe, and North America (Daftary 1998).

In addition to the Qur'an and the hadiths, that is, sayings attributed to the Prophet Mohammad, Ismailis also follow a living and known spiritual leader, the Aga Khan. Ismailis recognize the Aga Khan as their Imam, or spiritual leader, and are distinguished as the only Shia sect that believes in a revealed Imam, "still walking among them" (Morris 1957: 198). As Robert J. Bocock argues, "[T]he existence of a living Imam has meant that Ismailis have been more flexible in adjusting to changing conditions in the last 100 years or so . . . [because they] have been able to refer to another authority in addition to the Qur'an and the Hadith canons—a living person" (Bocock 1971: 366).

The importance of combining religion and work as a community imperative is illustrated in the sayings of the Aga Khan III (November 2, 1877–July 11, 1957) and provides a transnational register for understanding the emphasis on education and assimilation in the mainstream society of the country in which Ismailis reside. The emphasis on modernizing Ismaili Islam through education has been articulated by the Aga Khan III who, in several pronouncements, has encouraged the Ismailis to acquire specialized and technical skills. The Aga Khan III also provided numerous scholarships for eligible students to attend institutions of higher education in the West (Kaiser 1996).[30] During his long imamate, the Aga Khan III devoted much of his time and financial resources to consolidating and organizing the Ismaili community. According to Farhad Daftary, a noted scholar of Ismaili history, the Aga Khan III was particularly concerned with introducing socioeconomic reforms that would transform his Shia Muslim followers into a modern, self-sufficient community with high standards of education and welfare. For example, the Aga Khan III "created and maintained a network of schools, vocational institutions, libraries, sports and recreational clubs, hospitals and dispensaries for the benefit of his followers in East Africa, India and Pakistan" (1990: 526).

An interlocutor in my research, Jamil, a young Indian American Ismaili male, brought home this emphasis on education as a religious imperative when he said to me:

I am very much influenced by the Ismaili ideology about education. In fact, I did not even apply to a non–Ivy League school. If I had not gotten accepted into an Ivy League school then I would have just kept applying until I was accepted. . . . Just having an MBA degree is not going to accomplish anything. *And that was because of His Highness's guidance to us* [emphasis added].

Jamil's emphasis on the Aga Khan's instruction conceptualizes success and achievement through the lens of transnational religious ideologies. As such, it begs a radical rethinking of the American dream, shifting the focus from the individual to larger collectives such as family, kin groups, and religious community. That education and professional lives are intertwined with religious imperative might, at first, appear to invoke Weber's thesis on the Protestant ethic and the spirit of capitalism (Weber 1905). However, as evident from the preceding discussion, the Ismaili approach to work and success is different. It is centered less on the individual and more on contributions and service to one's community. At the same time, the validation of rationality, modernity, and capitalist enterprise in Ismaili ideology allows Ismaili men and women to envision material success as a morally sanctioned career aspiration. That the Ismaili approach overlaps the values embedded in the American dream goes some way in locating Ismailis skilled labor within American ideologies of the model minority on the one hand and specificities of transnational Muslim community formations and religious forms of knowledge on the other.

Education and Practices of Pakistani Nation Building

In addition to transnational Ismaili Muslim ideologies that emphasize the importance of higher education and professional achievement, Pakistani nation building provides another important transnational register that decenters the salience of education as either an intrinsic Asian cultural trait or even an assimilated American value embedded in notions of the model minority. Pakistanis first came to Houston as students to pursue higher education in engineering, medicine, and education in the 1940s and the 1950s under severely restrictive American immigration laws. Between 1946 until 1965 nearly six thousand Indian immigrants (classified as Asian "other"), mostly students, business-men, refugees, and twice migrants, moved to the United States (Hess 1976).[31] Almost 34 percent of these students came from families who had migrated from India to Pakistan in the years following the partition of British Colonial India into two sovereign nations, India and Paki-stan, in 1947. For most of these students, education in the United States constituted the second in a series of prolonged transnational popula-tion movements.

Pakistan achieved independence from British colonial rule amid unparalleled communal violence and formed as the sovereign nation-state for Muslims of South Asia in 1947. It then faced a plethora of problems, including an influx of millions of refugees into West Paki-stan, a war with India over the territory of Kashmir, and hunger, dis-ease, and poverty.[32] Pakistan found itself lacking severely in industry, institutions of governance and higher education, and communications networks. Moreover, the civil bureaucracy and the military were "des-perately short of skilled manpower and the requisite infrastructure" (Jalal 1995: 54).

Given such deficiencies, an emphasis on higher education and train-ing in engineering, medicine, and management sciences became central in Pakistani ideologies and projects of nation building, modernity, and progress.[33] Indeed, following the Indo-Pakistan War of 1965 over the disputed territory of Kashmir, which both India and Pakistan claim as a part of their sovereign territory, education, patriotism, nationalism, and dogma became synonymous. In Pakistan, the emphasis on the sci-ences illustrated the infrastructural, industrial, and economic growth models followed in newly independent nation-states in Asia that des-perately needed professionals to build industry and institutions.

For the United States, building variegated alliances with a newly formed Pakistan was guided by Cold War imperatives. Pakistan's geo-strategic location in Asia, neighboring China and the former Soviet Union, made it an ideally suited ally to contain the potential spread of communism in the region. According to a retired U.S. Foreign Service officer, from the military point of view, each Asian country with which the United States signed a military agreement would "become little anti-Communist bastions, prepared to resist a Communist assault" (U.S. Congress 1959: 24).

During the post-independence period in Pakistan, strategic alliances with the United States provided technical assistance and expertise, as well as scholarship opportunities for the education of Pakistan's emerging bureaucratic elite and the military. The alliances between Pakistan and the United States materialized through military agreements, financial assistance for economic and social development, bilateral initiatives to promote the higher education of Pakistanis through the development of educational institutes in Pakistan, and the training and education of Pakistanis (almost all of them men) in the United States. For Pakistan, these alliances were motivated primarily by the exigencies of nation building, and specifically the creation of industries, social services and education sectors.[34] These opportunities were intended to create an elite group of Pakistanis who would return and play important roles in economic, social, and industrial development in Pakistan.

By the 1960s, government departments, universities, and private institutions in Pakistan included administrators, bureaucrats, and specialists who had been trained either at American universities or by American specialists in residence at Pakistani institutions. For example, University of Pennsylvania established the Institute of Public and Business Administration (IPBA) in Karachi. At the Institute, Pakistani students were educated and trained using models of education from American business schools, and the "MBAs not only formed the skilled cadre for Pakistan's comprador bourgeoisie but they also became articulate spokesmen for the efficiency of American methods and advocates of free enterprise" (Waterston 1963: 36).

Pakistan's emphasis on American education reflected the perception that "American colleges had more to offer in the [student's] field of interest and were geared to practical education rather than just theory alone" (Rathore 1957: 14). According to a report on the experience of Pakistani students in the United States in the 1940s and the 1950s (Rathore 1957), several of the students stated that education in the United States would confer distinction in Pakistani society. According to the same report, almost all Pakistani students who were interviewed felt "that Pakistan would benefit from his personal foreign study or training and that the Government of Pakistan would welcome him on his return" (ibid.: 13).

Discourses centered on higher education in Pakistan and its diaspora continue to be dominated by the hard sciences, technical fields, and medicine. For example, the growth in the U.S. economy in the 1990s provided the highly skilled South Asian labor force, including Ismaili Muslim professionals employed at Enron, with the possibility of upward economic mobility and prosperity through careers in science, technology, and medicine. These occupations are understood to be "widely valorized and coveted in South Asia and among diasporic desis" (Shankar 2008: 47) in large part due to the emphasis of the sciences during the period of nation building in South Asia.

The emphasis on education in the hard sciences and professional achievement is also an outcome of the specificities of the twentieth-century Ismaili experience. A survey of the cultural politics and ideology of the Ismaili Shia Muslim experience in the twentieth century shows a concerted emphasis on assimilation and accommodation in all regions of the world where Ismailis live as minority populations.[35]

Shia Ismaili Cultural Histories and Historical Experience

The centrality of the assimilation narrative in twentieth-century Ismaili histories speaks to Ismailis' minority status in all countries of residence and reflects a belief that assimilation would in fact provide greater freedom to practice religion. Indeed, Ismailis maintain the principle of *taqiyya*, "a precautionary dissimulation of their faith in a hostile environment, in practicing their beliefs, thereby preserving their religious literature and safeguarding their identity" (Emadi 1998: 103).

In his memoirs, the Aga Khan III, emphasizing the importance of integration of the Ismaili communities in East Africa, states that his followers "would suffer real disabilities in East Africa if they retained Indian habits and an Indian pattern of life, and he has undoubtedly helped them to organize themselves in this manner so that they can participate fully in the new societies" (Morris 1957: 202). In African nations such as Uganda and Tanzania, community service and engagement have been central in interracial alliance building between Asians (read Ismaili) and black African communities (Kadende-Kaiser and Kaiser 1998: 468). In 1914, the Aga Khan III traveled to Burma and "advised his followers there to adopt measures, such as giving up their Indo-Muslim names and habits that would facilitate their sociocultural assimilation in Burma. In later years, the Aga Khan III recommended similar assimilatory measures to his followers in other parts of the world; a policy designed to reduce the local difficulties of the Ismaili who lived as minorities in many countries" (Daftary 1990: 521).

Ismaili approaches to assimilation, education, and work intersect with and extend to networking and investment in community. This investment is evident in the elaborate transnational networks of committees that focus on trade and finances, political representation, health, education, legal assistance, and civic engagement among others (Morris 1957). These transnational networks enable Ismailis, "who are minorities in every country where they reside, to negotiate successfully the politics of their diverse places of residence and to ensure that their religious, social, and economic needs are addressed" (Kadende-Kaiser and Kaiser 1998: 463). Indeed, networking within the religious community is the norm rather than an exception.

These transnational networks operate through community centers in major cities with substantial Ismaili populations such as Houston. According to the Constitution of the Shia Imami Ismaili Muslims, these networks provide guidelines that are intended to "make a valid and meaningful contribution to the improvement of the quality of life of the Ummah and the societies in which they live" (Constitution 1987: 5). In the case of my interlocutors in Houston, these transnational affiliations and structures have created opportunities for networking and collaboration and mediated failure and crisis in the neoliberal economy.

I return to vignettes from my conversation with my Ismaili interlocutors to illustrate the intersection of transnational religious ideology and Ismaili social history in framing experiences in corporate America. Amjad, Feroz, and I were sitting at a Starbucks cafe on Westheimer Avenue when the conversation turned to their job search following the layoffs from Enron. I asked Amjad if Enron had actively assisted laid-off employees with potential job leads and career advisory service. According to Amjad:

> Enron did have a career services on the web but I never really got any responses from that. They had a career fair that my friends along with four thousand other people attended . . . I mean, everybody was laid off and there were actually some non-Enron people there as well. Most of the employers were like, "here is our website address, go check out our

website." That's it. It was a bad time for hiring. It was December, and no one was hiring. Plus there was a glut of this so-called talent. I don't think at my level, I could utilize contacts at Enron at that time. I did get some leads from the online Enron message boards. These were unofficial message boards. I did send out resumes but never heard back.

In the apparent absence of any career advisory services at Enron or mainstream resources, my interlocutors tapped into the Ismaili community networks for job leads and support. Networking, the same skill they had deployed successfully while employees of Enron, was the skill that aided them during their period of unemployment. One former Enron employee, also a member of the Ismaili community, had put together an e-mail list of forty Ismaili men and women who worked at Enron and other major energy companies in Houston and used this list to arrange informal social gatherings. Once laid off, these professionals used the same e-mail list to arrange networking events to share résumés and potential job leads. As word of this group spread in the community, members of the Ismaili community came forward to offer moral support, and job leads that in fact materialized into real jobs and consultancy assignments. Amjad eagerly discussed the importance of the Ismaili community:

> We had a lot of support from our friends and the Ismaili community network also both in terms of fleshing out ideas and [having] brainstorming sessions about what we could do and what we couldn't do. Our friends who were already working at other energy companies and technology companies provided a lot of support.

Although Amjad and Salim had been colleagues at Enron, their association with each other went back three generations. Amjad and Salim's grandfathers were businessmen in Gujarat in British India. In 1947, as the British left a fractured colonial India divided into two nation-states—India and Pakistan—Salim's family had stayed in Ahmadabad in Gujarat, India, while Amjad's family migrated to Karachi in Pakistan. Amjad's father grew up in Pakistan hearing tales of his father's friend and business associate in India. A generation passed without any contact between the two families divided by national borders and boundaries created at the time of Partition. It was in the corridors of Enron and at the Ismaili jamat khana in Houston more than fifty years later that Amjad and Salim met, connected the dots regarding the friendship between their paternal grandfathers, and rekindled familial ties. Amjad and Salim became close friends, and their friendship extended to their involvement with the Ismaili jamat khana. Amjad elaborated on his ongoing active engagements within the Ismaili community.

> AMJAD: People knew of us within the community. We serve in various capacities as volunteers . . . if someone wanted to open up a clinic, we would do the financial model. You know, they need this kind of support and you have got to do that. There are a few projects for kids in our community to make sure that they go to the right schools and stuff; so individually we were already working on various things.

The friendship and association forged through ancestral relationships, professional interests, religious affiliation, and active involvement in the Ismaili community center's activities contributed to plans for a business partnership, indicating another theme in twentieth-century Ismaili history: self-reliance and self-sufficiency. As Amjad said to me:

> My father was an entrepreneur . . . my grandfather was an entrepreneur . . . so I come from very strong entrepreneurial roots. My uncles, everyone is in business. They have done very well for themselves. It just made sense to bridge over into running our own business. And this seems like a perfect setup because these guys are also my good friends.

Combining their educational background in business administration and management, professional expertise in energy management and solutions, and contacts in the Ismaili community in Houston, the three friends decided to start their own business as independent energy consultants. As Salim explained:

> We are in the energy services business. We help medium and small size businesses with their total energy management needs. We negotiate energy contracts on their behalf and receive a percentage of the savings. We provide our clients with energy technology solutions that allow them

to manage their energy almost instantaneously. They save by reducing their energy consumption.

Salim recounted their entry into the world of independent energy consultancy via a project for an Ismaili-owned convenience store, a sector dominated in Houston by Ismaili entrepreneurs:

> We were looking at the retail energy and then, very interestingly, our Ismaili community association approached us . . . within our community, there are hundreds of convenience stores and gas stations. [The community organization] approached Amjad and Feroz, [who] are very active in the community and asked for their help in negotiating an energy contract. . . . This is what we were thinking of doing . . . and serendipitously, it just came about. . . . We said, let's help them negotiate the deal, save them loads of money and you know, we can make a business out of it.

In large part because of their shared religious affiliation, active engagement, and contacts within the Ismaili Muslim community, and also because of the high market share of Ismaili Muslims in convenience stores, gas stations, and grocery stores in Houston, the three friends targeted the South Asian business community as their primary clientele. According to Salim:

> We are starting off with that but are going to be utilizing our expertise in the small and medium size businesses and taking it to other non–South Asian businesses. Our focus and platform is built on the South Asian community today.

Amjad elaborated:

> They respect our experience. They understand that we are professionals from the industry. We are South Asians, so we have a heavier moral connection because we see the same people in the mosque and the jamat khanas. So there is a stronger sense of ownership. We are using our community associations as a launching pad that would launch us into the mainstream. But this is a perfect base to start from.

The same characteristics that these men valued at Enron—best educated, smartest, hardworking—were the characteristics long valued by their transnational community. The layoffs at Enron provided an important opportunity to utilize community-based ties and relationships and translated into strategies for mediating crisis and risk in the neoliberal economy. A decade later, by 2011, my interlocutors had consolidated their businesses and reentered corporate America, having successfully navigated the ups and downs of their professional lives, in large part thanks to the availability of cultural capital grounded in transnational Ismaili religious ideologies.

Conclusion

The mocking and casual references to the Enron crisis on Pakistani radio in Houston with which I began this chapter reflect perhaps a certain uneasiness and inability to critique mythologies of the American dream, and the precariousness of success in corporate America. The model minority concept posits innate cultural values that predispose some minority communities toward education and professional success and achievements. Such conceptions render invisible the role of U.S. racial regimes (Mohanty 1991) in creating hierarchies in transnational labor flows along the axis of education, class, gender, religion, and nationality (Prashad 2000). As I have argued in this chapter, U.S. immigration policies also illustrate that Asian success stories are not simply about rewarding individual efforts and a fair system. Rather, these success stories speak to the bias in immigration policies that preselects highly skilled professionals in labor flows to the United States.

Certainly, my Shia Ismaili Muslim interlocutors demonstrate resilience and self-reliance that is used to substantiate the success of Asian immigrants. Yet, as I have shown in this chapter, part of the story here is the central role of transnational religious ideologies and networks in mediating periods of risk, crisis, and uncertainty. South Asian professionals assert model minority status, as evidenced in Ismaili approaches to education and career in corporate America, and patterns of residential settlement. Even as Enron became an important case study in the failure of corporate governance, it did not disrupt the belief in the

American dream, in part because of mediation by professionally based transnational religious networks and affiliations. The individuals whose narratives appear in this chapter draw on Ismaili religious edict and morality as cultural capital in making meaning of professional life and experiences in corporate America. Additionally, transnational religious networks prove to be critically important in providing support, anchoring the layoff period and facilitating reentry in the U.S. corporate sector.

An ethnographic inquiry into the professional life trajectories of highly skilled Ismaili Muslims in Houston disrupts the conception of Muslim Americans as a monolith and instead illuminates transnational Muslim sectarian community formations in the United States. For Ismaili Muslim professionals like Amjad who were laid off from Enron, Ismaili ideologies constitute a vital knowledge system and provide an important case study of the interaction between religious ideology and historical conjuncture (Asad 2003) and the embodiment of this interaction in everyday and professional life. "The structure of the conjuncture" (Sahlins 1981) here reveals a confluence of historical contingencies such as ideologies and practices of Pakistani nation building, Ismaili social histories, and socioeconomic contexts of opportunity and privilege in economies of late capitalism in the production of upward mobility and success.[36]

3

"It's Allah's Will"

The Transnational Muslim Heritage Economy

For several months during the course of my ethnographic research, I carried out fieldwork at a South Asian video and DVD sale and rental store located in a strip mall on Hillcroft Avenue. This particular strip mall, a couple of blocks south of the Mahatma Gandhi District, overlooking Highway 59, was within walking distance to several predominantly Pakistani and Indian residential buildings and gated communities as well as a mosque. The strip mall included Middle Eastern and Indian grocery stores, an Indian ethnic jewelry shop, a photocopy and printing center, a South Indian vegetarian restaurant, a travel agency specializing in travel to South Asia, a Middle Eastern bakery, and a Mexican-owned and-managed deli. Most businesses were family-run enterprises. The video and DVD store, for instance, was owned and managed by a young Pakistani couple, Ali and Nadia, who had resided in Houston since 1999.

The business catered to a South Asian population. The store specialized in South Asian ethnic entertainment and offered an extensive collection of DVDs and video cassettes of Hindi language films and television programs produced in India and Urdu-language television programs produced in Pakistan. In addition to the several hundred alphabetically arranged videotapes and DVDs, the store also carried an enviable array of audiotapes and CDs of Indian and Pakistani film soundtracks, folk, and classical music that were visible through glass countertops that spanned the length of the brightly lit, rectangular-shaped store. In one corner of the shop, colorful and vibrant displays of imported Pakistani ethnic jewelry adorned the glass counter and wooden shelves. During the long day, Ali and Nadia would take turns napping on a two-seat couch in an eight-by-four-foot room at the back of the store. It would not be inaccurate to state that the business also doubled as Nadia and Ali's home. Although they maintained an apartment nearby, Nadia and Ali spent almost all their waking hours at their store.

Every morning, Ali and Nadia picked me up from my apartment in a gated community only a few blocks north of the strip mall near the intersection of Hillcroft Avenue and Westheimer Road. A typical day consisted of a series of routines and rituals. On the way to the store, Ali would stop at a cafe to pick up coffee and breakfast sandwiches for the three of us. Soon after opening the store, Nadia would begin dusting the glass countertops. I would reshelve the DVDs and videos that had been returned the previous day. Ali worked the cash register when he was not traveling to meet wholesalers to purchase videos and DVDs.

In a day filled with routine activities, the most important one took place as soon as Ali unlocked the front door and turned on the lights. Ali would turn on the stereo behind the cash register and play recitations from the Qur'an in Arabic. "I like to begin each business day with the Qur'an recital. I believe it makes each day auspicious for business," Ali said to me. His explanation of the daily ritual emphasized an auditory and symbolic sanctification of his business as well as expectations of barkat or baraka (blessings) from Allah.

As Ali and Nadia's store flourished, they began to expand the business. They started selling CDs and DVDs of Qur'an recitals, and lectures and sermons by prominent Muslim leaders on various aspects of Islamic history and heritage. Only a few, if any, were produced locally. Most had been produced for initial broadcast on television in India or Pakistan. Within a couple of months, Ali added beautifully woven Islamic prayer mats and rugs, prayer beads, incense, stickers, key chains, holiday cards, scholarly books on Islamic history and heritage, and decorative wall hangings with Islamic calligraphy. "It makes business sense to do this. People want to buy these things. Besides, I am Muslim, so why shouldn't I use my business to promote Islam," Ali said rather casually when I asked him about the additions to the store.

As this ethnographic vignette shows, Islam increasingly foregrounds patterns of consumption and economic processes within which Pakistani immigrant lives and businesses are embedded in Houston. The ongoing transformations in the South Asian ethnic economy in Houston that I explore in this chapter are centered on the mass circulation and sale of Islamic religious commodities in the West, the increasing centrality of Islam in structuring consumption patterns among transnational Pakistani Muslims, and assertions of belonging to a global Muslim ummah.

An analytic and ethnographic focus on such transformations is an important intervention in theorizing the relationship between U.S.-based ethnic economies and patterns of consumption among new immigrant communities. Indeed, Nadia and Ali were not alone in inscribing places of commerce with religious markers such as audio recordings of Qur'anic verses or diversifying their business by selling mass-produced religious commodities. As I learned through the course of my fieldwork, several Pakistani businesses had begun to sell mass-produced "religious commodities." As Gregory Starret notes: "What characterizes these diverse items as religious is either a direct association with acts of worship, as with prayer beads, or, more commonly, their bearing of sacred images or writing, often only the single word 'Allah' or 'Muhammad'" (1995: 53). Pakistani supermarkets in Houston sell copies of the Qur'ans, prayer beads, skullcaps, rugs, bumper stickers, key chains, posters, framed Qur'anic verses, greeting cards, decorative items, paper models of mosques, and miniature plates with Qur'anic verses. Several Pakistani fashion boutiques carry a wide variety of hijab along with other staple South Asian ethnic clothing and fashion accessories. Pakistani grocery stores offer halal frozen food items, and oils and herbal medicines and syrups such as black seed and caraway oil that are mentioned in the Prophet Mohammad's hadiths (sayings).[1] Pakistani-owned and-managed travel agencies routinely organize seminars as part of the "Hajj package" for individuals and families traveling to Mecca in Saudi Arabia for the annual pilgrimage. Pakistani restaurants serve only halal food and maintain cordoned-off areas for prayers and separate dining sections for women and families.

The ethnographic focus on ethnic economies in this chapter offers a lens for examining the lived experience of ethnic entrepreneurs who facilitate such transformations, and the working-class and the working poor who provide the labor for these business establishments. In this chapter, I first chart the ongoing transformations in the South Asian ethnic economy in Houston from its inception and development as a center of South Asian commerce in the 1980s to its twenty-first-century incarnation as a node of production and consumption in what I have elsewhere called a "transnational Muslim heritage economy" (Afzal 2010). In the 1960s and the 1970s, consumption patterns and constructions of community among Pakistani Muslim immigrants privileged the shared cultural histories and heritage that united South Asian immigrants across nationality and religious traditions: Buddhism, Christianity, Hinduism, Islam, Sikhism, and Zoroastrianism. By the 1990s, the confluence of several factors radicalized community formation, contributed to assertions of difference based on religion, and transformed patterns of consumption. These factors included the dramatic increase in the Pakistani Muslim population in Houston, the rapid growth of Muslim infrastructure and business enterprises locally and internationally; increasing interactions between Pakistani Muslim immigrants and coreligionists from India, the Middle East, Asia, Africa, and beyond and the influence of militaristic and political tensions between India and Pakistan in diasporic communities in Houston.

Following an analysis of the transformations in the South Asian ethnic economy, I relate such larger transformations to the lives of individuals embedded in ethnic spaces of commerce. For the Muslim entrepreneurs, the working class, and the working poor discussed in this chapter, variegated engagements in the transnational Muslim heritage economy are critical in understanding the often-harsh conditions of their lives. Muslim identity serves as an anchor in contexts of abjection and oppression in U.S. raced, classed, and gendered regimes of governmentality following 9/11. Islam also anchors experiences of marginality and exploitation in the transnational Muslim heritage economy. The absence of paid leave, job security, health insurance, reasonable work hours, and possibilities for upward mobility in most of the Pakistani businesses, for example, greatly limit integration into mainstream U.S. economic society.[2] As Pawan Dhingra notes in a study of Indian moteliers, ethnic businesses "often work with limited or no staff, struggle to make ends meet, go without health care for themselves and their workers, and lack social prestige in their local community even while the ethnic group as a whole is praised" (2012: 7). A consideration of such sidelined narratives enables consideration of "tenuous position [of the working class and the working poor] within the hierarchies of capitalism, race, gender, economic and political opportunity, and culture" (ibid.: 6–7).[3] In addition, such experiences offer a valuable and complex counterpoint to the model minority examples represented in chapter 2.

Two caveats are in order before progressing further into the chapter. One, although South Asian businesses have emerged in several suburbs in southwest Houston and north Houston, the discussion in this chapter focuses primarily on businesses based in Hillcroft Avenue and Bissonnet Street, the two major centers of South Asian ethnic businesses in Houston. The transformations and issues highlighted here may be generalized to other South Asian business centers undergoing similar transformations in Houston and other American cities with large Pakistani populations.

Two, although I focus on Pakistani ethnic entrepreneurs, the working class, and the working poor, my intention is not to negate the fluidity of classed identities as individuals experience upward and downward mobility at various times in their lives. Indeed, a number of Pakistani ethnic entrepreneurs with whom I interacted had previously worked in corporate America. Following Houston's economic downturn in the 1980s and massive layoffs, several Pakistanis started businesses that catered to a niche South Asian population. Likewise, while I term the blue-collar workers employed in menial jobs in ethnic businesses as the working class, I recognize that "working class" and the "working poor" are contextual categorizations that vary across time and space. Members of the working class often accrue middle-class status in Pakistan given their educational capital and accumulation of financial capital.[4] Grouping together ethnic entrepreneurs and those employed in menial jobs in ethnic businesses underscores their embeddedness and overlapping engagements in the transnational Muslim heritage economy in ways that distinguish them from, say, the upwardly mobile professionals who visit ethnic businesses primarily as consumers of ethnic goods and services.

The Making of a Transnational Muslim Heritage Economy

In the 1970s, as a South Asian immigrant population was starting to emerge in Houston, South Asian spaces of commerce were limited to a couple of Indian grocery stores. Although data regarding the state of the South Asian business environment during this period is scarce, anecdotal accounts culled from conversations and formal interviews with Pakistanis and Indians who had resided in Houston during the 1970s point to a virtual absence of South Asian economic activity and infrastructure.

A robust South Asian ethnic economy developed in Houston in the 1980s. South Asian ethnic businesses became concentrated in sections of southwest Houston, primarily along Hillcroft Avenue, because of the availability of inexpensive commercial real estate and open spaces for new construction south of the downtown (B. Shelton et al. 1989). By the 1980s, the southwest corridor had "more office building and shopping center space than the entire area of downtown Houston [and] many residential subdivisions and apartment buildings were subsequently built" (ibid.: 22). Growth slowed during the recession from 1981 to 1983, and unemployment rose to nearly 15 percent by 1986; housing became more readily available to low- and middle-income new immigrant communities. Sections of southwest Houston then began to evolve into multi-ethnic residential and commercial spaces in a process that has contributed to the city's continued spatially segregated development along race and class as discussed in chapter 1.

Pakistani and Indian restaurants, grocery stores, convenience stores, and gas stations are concentrated in low-density blocks near the north end of Hillcroft Avenue, peppered with open ground, vacant parking lots, residential buildings and gated communities. Other businesses that developed over time included family-run video and DVD stores specializing in Hindi language films produced in India and television soap operas produced in Pakistan, boutiques for women, jewelry stores featuring traditional jewelry exported from South Asia, and travel agencies specializing in air travel to South Asia, the Middle East, and the Gulf States. The emergence of a South Asian ethnic economy also coincided with the establishment of mosques in Houston during the 1970s and the early 1980s. By the 1990s, the presence of mosques, Islamic community centers and schools, the offices of Pakistani and Indian professionals—doctors, lawyers, real estate brokers, and social service workers—and multiplex theaters featuring first-run Hindi-language movies created a thriving South Asian ethnoreligious environment around Hillcroft Avenue, with newer South Asian business and residential concentrations developing further southwest on Bissonnet Street. Most strip malls with Pakistani businesses are multiethnic in composition, reflecting the racial and ethnic diversity of southwest Houston.

The proliferation of Pakistani restaurants, boutiques, ethnic video, and DVD stores, grocery stores, and super markets coincided with the development of the transnational Muslim heritage economy. This characterization foregrounds the importance of Islam in organizing ethnic businesses as well as flows of capital within neoliberal regimes. Belying characterization of ethnic economies as transitional spaces of consumption and at the fringes of the mainstream U.S. economy, this transnational economy consists of a variety of institutions, goods, and services with production and consumption nodes in major cities such as Houston in North America, as well as in Asia, Europe, the Middle East and the Gulf States.[5] Indeed, the data presented in this chapter emphasize significant possibilities for growth as well as the embeddedness of Pakistani ethnic businesses and spaces of commerce within local, national, and transnational webs of financial and business networks and capital. The ways in which these vast networks are increasingly organized by Islamic values and beliefs demonstrates local growth intertwined with global expansion.

On a local and regional scale, this means that South Asian ethnic entrepreneurs based in smaller cities in Texas and neighboring states routinely visit Houston to purchase ethnic commodities. Since the 1990s, Houston has emerged as a South Asian ethnic hub in the south and southwestern United States. South Asian families and individuals from Dallas, Austin, and San Antonio in Texas, and from neighboring states travel regularly to Houston to purchase South Asian ethnic products and to participate in cultural and religious events organized by Pakistani and Indian businesses and entrepreneurs. As the center for South Asian Ahmadiya, Ismaili, and Shia congregations and gatherings, Houston also attracts South Asian visitors from throughout the United States.

The globalization of the halal food market is central in the transnational Muslim heritage economy that I document in this chapter. It is in large part, a result of a growing critical mass of Muslim communities in the West "and the stimulatory effect of this growth on halal exports" (I. Adams 2011: 129) from Muslim countries to the West. The Islamic observance of halal food refers to food that is permitted and lawful based on the Qur'an and the *Sunna* (the life, actions, and teaching of the Prophet Mohammad). It also refers to ritual slaughtering requirements that ensure that the animal be killed in the name of Allah by making a fatal incision across the throat. It also includes the processing and preparation of all consumable items and ingredients according to the same precepts. In Houston, halal food items, including spices and fruits, and a wide variety of other consumer goods are imported through international business networks composed of coreligionists.

The global-export-oriented halal industry, pioneered in countries such as Malaysia, Singapore, and Brunei (I. Adams 2011) today encompasses countries throughout the Muslim world and the West. Halal monitoring agencies regulate and standardize halal practices, further indicating the growing global importance of the halal industry. This industry extends far beyond just the food and beverages that can be consumed by Muslims (Chua 2010). Indeed,

> The international halal industry comprises goods and services as diverse as pharmaceuticals, finance, logistics and bio-tech. It is more than just how livestock is prepared; it is the integration of many separate industries linked by a unique set of Islamic-based guidelines. This growing awareness of halal is creating new commercial possibilities. (Chua 2010: 10)

For Muslim communities residing in the West, these ongoing developments are situated between the globalization of Islamic revivalism, neoliberal capitalism, and consumer culture.[6] The mass production of religious commodities in the late twentieth century is in large part a product of the global neoliberal economy, which is built on notions of a global consumer base and market and supported by a desire among some Muslim immigrants in the West to lead a life within the confines of an exclusive religious economy. The emergence of a transnational

Muslim heritage economy then illustrates the emergence of "alternatives to what are seen as Western values, ideologies, and lifestyles" (J. Fischer 2005: 280). The incorporation of Islam in public and everyday life, the inscription of public places of business with religious meanings, and the mass circulation of religious commodities indicate the significant cultural transformations that are taking place in the practice of Islam globally.[7]

The emergent transnational Muslim heritage economy also reveals the intersection of neoliberal global capitalism, historically contingent affiliations to religious and ancestral communities, and global geopolitics. In the 1990s, as a transnational Muslim heritage economy began to emerge in Houston, it overlapped with a prolonged period of heightened and volatile political tensions between India (read: Hindu) and Pakistan (read: Muslim) that escalated to militaristic attacks by both nuclear-armed nations. In 1998, a clandestine warfare and military action erupted in the disputed territory of Kashmir that both India and Pakistan claim as part of their territory. The Kargil War, named after the Kashmiri village of Kargil where part of the military action and warfare took place, coupled with nuclear tests by both India and Pakistan during the summer of 1998, served to politicize all facets of Indian-Pakistani sociality and interaction in the homeland as well as the diaspora.

The rise of right-wing Hindu nationalist politics in India and Islamic revivalism in Pakistan since the late 1980s found interlocutors within the Indian and Pakistani immigrant populations in the West and also implicated popular cultural forms such as Hindi-language films and associated Indian entertainment and media. As discussed further in chapter 6, several Pakistani community leaders appeared on Urdu-language Pakistani radio programs in Houston to advocate a voluntary boycott of all Indian media and popular cultural industries, and businesses locally. That, combined with vociferous support by several local Indian ethnic businesses for Indian military action in Kashmir, provided a watershed moment in creating fissures between Indians and Pakistanis in Houston. These geopolitical contexts demonstrate how place making and economic activity in Houston are intertwined with flows of religious capital in the global neoliberal economy. Moreover, the emergent ubiquity of halal food products in Muslim businesses and the commodification of Islam in the sale of a wide range of consumer products suggest the Islamizing of commerce and consumption and belie the assumed secularity of ethnic businesses and enterprises.

Everyday Life in the Transnational Muslim Heritage Economy

These transformations also beg a consideration of the lived experience of entrepreneurs who own small ethnic businesses, and the working class and the working poor who provide the labor force for these businesses. In the 1990s, the increase in the in-migration of semiskilled and unskilled Pakistanis and kin relations contributed to the rapid growth of the Pakistani population in Houston. As a result, "increasing numbers of South Asians . . . joined the ranks of the U.S. working class and petty bourgeoisie" (Prashad 2000: 78), having arrived with varying levels of education ranging from some high school to postsecondary degrees and varying levels of fluency in English. The differences among immigrants are also gendered, with more men than women arriving in general and with men arriving with relatively higher educational levels and competencies in spoken and written English (Shankar 2008). Lacking English-language skills and the requisite educational background to gain employment in the mainstream economy in Houston, a significant number of these new immigrants have found menial and low-paying jobs in Pakistani and Indian restaurants, convenience stores, grocery shops, and other ethnic businesses.

Extended family members and single men constitute the majority of the working poor. A vast majority of young Pakistani men and women not only support themselves but also contribute financially to family and kin networks in Pakistan and elsewhere in the diaspora. The residential concentration of the Pakistani working class and the working poor in parts of southwest Houston has contributed to the emergence of primarily working-class multiethnic residential buildings and gated communities, in some of which these new entrants constitute the majority of the residents. Within walking distance to mosques, Pakistani restaurants, grocery stores and super markets, barbershops, travel agencies, and boutiques, these residential buildings and gated communities are well suited for Pakistani immigrants with limited financial resources or access to automobiles to travel long distances in a car-centered city like Houston.

Pakistani residents near Hillcroft Avenue and sections of Bissonnet Street include extended and nuclear families as well several other types of households. There are households made up of single men or married men who have immigrated alone and do not have any family in Houston. Vacancies are advertised through word of mouth or handwritten notices on the bulletin boards in South Asian restaurants, barbershops, grocery stores, and ethnic video and DVD rental outlets. For example, a recently arrived Pakistani immigrant might utilize existing contacts to find accommodation in a two-bedroom apartment that is shared by six or more men. Most of the gated residences are managed and owned by non-Pakistanis, and management often ignores violations regarding the permissible number of occupants. Occupants negotiate the limited living space by carefully choosing working and sleeping hours in order to accommodate all housemates. In such productions of "migrant subjectivities" (Rana 2011), many migrants, especially men, who are away from their families in Pakistan for extended periods, develop "familial and residential arrangements that are outside of elite notions of the bourgeois family" (ibid.: 119). Nayan Shah (2001) describes such residential arrangements, partly an outcome of U.S. labor laws, as "queer domesticity" (2001) that produce migrant homosocialities and nonheteronormative social relationships and sexuality that reference "racial and classed abjection" (Rana 2011: 119).

It is within such specificities that I explore everyday life within the transnational Muslim heritage economy in Houston. The following biographies and narratives complicate a positive assessment of ethnic entrepreneurs as a model minority who will overcome white male capitalist privilege (Glenn 2002) and integrate over time as they are able to "take advantage of economic and educational opportunities and adopt useful parts of mainstream culture while also relying on resources within their ethnic group" (Dhingra 2012: 9–10). Moreover, attention to the lived experiences disrupts conceptions of Muslim immigrants who share ancestral affiliations as a monolithic community and instead highlights the heterogeneity of Pakistani Muslim community formations in the United States at the intersection of class, citizenship status, and differential access to capital and resources.

*Nadia and Ali: "We'll Struggle Now So My Children
Can Have a Better Life"*

During the course of my field research in Houston, Ali and Nadia, who owned a South Asian DVD and video store in a strip mall on Hillcroft Avenue, became a surrogate family to me. In between working long hours side by side, we would often just sit together and laugh and chat about anything and everything. I helped Ali and Nadia catalog their video and DVD collections, prepare posters for sales and promotions, and manage the cash register. I saw their struggle first hand, and could only marvel at Ali and Nadia's ability to persevere while raising two young children in a demanding work environment.

Ali was born in Karachi and had migrated with his family to Toronto in 1970 when he was four years old. He completed his high school and college education in Toronto. As a young child, Ali was religious, actively participating in youth clubs at the Muslim community center. As an adult, Ali become a practicing Muslim and followed all prohibitions—refraining from drinking alcohol, fasting during Ramadan, and praying five times during the day. "I am much more Muslim than I am Canadian or American. I think I am becoming more religious as I grow older," Ali laughingly said to me once on our way to the mosque for the Friday afternoon prayers.

Ali was still a teenager when his mother passed away. His father died the following year, leaving Ali in the care of his older brother and sister. Ali's sister had since married and remained in Canada. Ali's brother had also married and resided within walking distance of his sister's house. Over the years, most of Ali's relatives emigrated from Pakistan and also settled in Toronto. One of his paternal uncles and his family, however, chose to immigrate to the United States and had lived in Houston since the early 1990s.

Ali was twenty-seven years old when he visited Pakistan for the first time since immigrating to Canada. He had returned to Pakistan for an arranged marriage to a distant cousin, Nadia, a vivacious twenty-year-old, whom he had never met. Once, as she showed me photographs from her wedding album, Nadia said to me: "I trusted my family to arrange my marriage to the 'right' person. I really didn't worry too much that I hadn't met Ali before our marriage. I had seen his picture, of course, but yes, I met him for the first time at our marriage." Nadia concluded, "Ali is truly my best friend," as she closed the album and carefully placed it in a drawer underneath the glass countertop. Ali returned to Canada soon after his marriage, and Nadia followed once she received her immigration papers. At the time, Ali worked as support personnel at an information technology firm. A year after their marriage, Nadia became pregnant with a daughter. A son followed three years later. "We never planned on having a family right away, but when it happened—it was Allah's will," Ali said to me one evening as we sat chatting at the store.

Soon afterward, on a visit to Houston to see his uncle and cousins, Ali was inspired by the seemingly lucrative financial possibilities of starting his own business in Houston. His cousin already owned a mom-and-pop-style grocery store and video rental outlet in Houston. Ali hoped to build on his cousin's business. With a loan from his cousins, Ali signed a lease on a then-vacant store in a strip mall. Within a few months of the visit, Ali, Nadia, and their two young children had moved from Toronto to begin life anew in the United States.

The process of settling into life in Houston was difficult. On occasion, the responsibilities of managing the store while taking care of two young children would overwhelm Nadia, leaving her feeling helpless and in tears. The family lived in a small two-bedroom apartment in a gated community in a newer multiethnic neighborhood near Bissonnet Street, a ten-minute drive from Hillcroft Avenue. Ali and Nadia woke daily at about 8:00 a.m., prepared breakfast, got the children dressed, and left them with "Aunty," an elderly Pakistani woman. Aunty provided day-care services for the young children of South Asian families in the neighborhood. The store closed at 10:00 p.m., but Ali and Nadia often stayed well past midnight preparing for the next day. More often than not, the children would be asleep by the time Nadia and Ali picked them up from day care. It was usually two in the morning by the time they returned to their apartment, only to begin again in another six hours.

Confined to the store for most of their waking hours, Ali and Nadia forged friendships with customers. Their socializing was relegated primarily to phone calls and leisurely chats when the customers visited the store. Most customers came with their families. Several often stayed at the store for an hour or longer browsing movies, watching songs from Hindi films on the large flat-screen television in the store, and chatting with us and with other customers. Conversations ran the entire gamut of topics and included small talk about the weather, gossip about the private lives of Bollywood stars, nostalgic reminisces about Bollywood films from the 1970s and the 1980s, and often-intense discussions on topics such the military conflict between India and Pakistan and the U.S.-led war on terrorism.

It was through such conversations that Nadia had learned of Aunty. At that time, Nadia had been looking for a day care center. "It is not possible to get work done here with the kids running around. I also can't just leave the kids at a regular day care center," Nadia said, expressing her concerns about leaving her children with someone she did not know and who was not South Asian. When she mentioned this to a few of her customers who also had young children, they suggested Aunty who was from Pakistan. After a reassuring and positive meeting with Aunty, Nadia felt comfortable enough to leave the children in Aunty's care.

It was also through such interactions that Nadia met a middle-aged Pakistani Muslim woman who ran a Pakistani food catering business from her home as a way to supplement the family's income. Ali and Nadia ate only halal meat and would chide me for eating non-halal food. Ali and Nadia spent nearly all day at the store, leaving both of them with little time to prepare home-cooked meals daily. Nadia was thrilled to find affordable home-cooked halal Pakistani food. Soon afterward, Nadia began recommending the catering service to her customers, going as far as taking food orders from interested customers.

On occasion, Nadia and Ali would bring the children to the store. The children would spend the day at the store, running around, building towers and houses out of videocassettes and DVD covers. Nadia hated leaving them at day care and would often become sad and deeply concerned at not having them with her during the day. "You know, Aunty was telling me the other day that my daughter cries a lot after we leave her. I am so worried about her. . . . When we take our children to Aunty's place, she won't let go of me. She keeps crying as I try to pull away: 'Mommy, don't leave us here! Mommy, I want to come with you!!'

It breaks my heart to leave them there every day, but what can we do? It is even more difficult to have children running around the store with the customers present."

The struggle, Nadia and Ali often told me, was going to be worth it. "I want to expand this business—maybe even open a coffee shop in the store. No one has done that with a *desi* video store here. . . . I also want to open another video store," Ali would often say, dreaming aloud. Nadia also had dreams—a house in Sugar Land. Once, late into the night, we had gone to a twenty-four-hour Home Depot to pick up paint for shelves at the video store. "This is the only time I can come here. It is impossible to come here during the day when our store is open," Ali had said, apologetic about the late-night trip. As Ali and I surveyed the aisles for paints, I noticed Nadia looking wistfully at the glossy colored pictures of model rooms and houses. "I cannot wait to have my own house one day," she said as she saw me approaching her. "Our apartment is such a mess. I am so tired after working all day. I barely have any energy to set up the apartment . . . but when I have my own house, it will be different. It will be the most beautiful house!" At the end of the day, family-driven imperatives provided the ultimate payoff for Ali and Nadia: "I am doing this for my children," Ali said to me whenever things seemed to become unbearable.

Ali and Nadia, owners of a South Asian ethnic video and DVD store, Canadian citizens, and permanent residents in the U.S., had become embedded in the transnational Muslim heritage economy as they began life anew in Houston. Relying primarily on financial support from relatives in Houston, Ali and Nadia on a daily basis negotiated the pressures of family life while running a small business. Although Ali's cousin provided him with the financial resources to open the video and DVD store, Ali and Nadia missed the emotional support previously provided by Ali's brother and sister and extended family in Canada. Ali had completed his college education in Toronto but had not been successful in finding employment in the corporate sector. He was content with running his own business, in spite of the stresses of owning a small business catering to a niche clientele. The only silver lining to the struggle was, as Ali repeatedly told me: "We'll struggle now so my children can have a better life."

These fragments of Ali and Nadia's life reveal the significance of family labor in the everyday operations of ethnic business, and especially the importance of women's labor (Yanagisako 1995). There appears to be an expectation that immigrant wives will participate in the management of family businesses as an extension of their "spousal duties along with cooking, cleaning, and child rearing" (Das Gupta 2006: 79). In so doing, women like Nadia blur boundaries between work and home (Dhaliwal 1998) as well as point to structural difficulties that limit the possibilities for advancement for working-class and lower-middle-class South Asian female immigrants (Shankar 2008: 151–152). Indeed,

> Ethnic businesses—which capture the South Asian mainstream's endorsement for embodying the entrepreneurial immigrant spirit—are built on the back-breaking yet invisible labor of these women, who because of the overlap between home and work suffer extreme isolation. Rarely do they get the chance to retrain for another job or improve their language skills. Once again, gender subordination is harnessed to the story of immigrant success, which in turn forms the bedrock of the model minority myth. (Dhingra 2012: 79–80)

Ali and Nadia's life experiences in Houston not only illustrate the significance of women in family businesses but also speak to the ways in which transnational Islam is embodied in everyday life, and the practices of place making. Recall that Ali began each workday by playing audiotapes of Arabic recitations from the Qur'an, believing that it blessed his business and made "each day auspicious." Recall also the diversification of the business to include an array of Muslim commodities. Ali and Nadia observed the alcohol prohibition and only ate halal meat that had been cut and prepared according to Islamic precept. During the month of Ramadan, Ali and Nadia fasted every day for a month. Each evening at sundown, Ali would close the store to break the fast at the local neighborhood mosque. The privileging of a Muslim identity in Ali's reflections that he was "more Muslim" than he was Canadian or American is aligned with discourses such as "Muslim first" in the United States and "I am hundred percent Muslim" in Great Britain (Kibria 2011) and suggests a self-conscious positioning as a Muslim.

Shahid: "We Are Nothing without Our Community Here"

I had taken a few days off from volunteering at Nadia and Ali's video and DVD store to spend some time with Pakistani and Indian radio programmers/hosts for this research. I had just finished interviewing an Indian radio programmer at his medical clinic in southwest Houston. It was early November. The sun shone brightly, with no discernible sign of the impending winter. As I made my way to the bus stop nearby, I noticed a familiar face in a car gesturing to me. It was Shahid, a twenty-seven-year-old Pakistani journalist I had first met at the Pakistan Independence Day Festival, less than a week into my fieldwork in Houston in 2001. Shahid worked as an assistant editor for a Houston-based Urdu-language Pakistani newspaper and reported on news and events taking place within the Pakistani community locally. Shahid shared a one-bedroom apartment with a Pakistani man who worked as a salesperson at a Pakistani boutique in Hillcroft.

Shahid and I had attended the same private school in Pakistan, although at different times, and this shared experience had provided a starting point for our acquaintance. In fact, the affinity was immediate. When I first met Shahid, I was living at a Pakistani owned and managed motel and trying to find affordable housing in southwest Houston. Shahid would hear none of it. "How can you even think about staying at a motel? We are from the same school—you have to stay with me." Although I soon found an apartment in a building complex in southwest Houston and never took up Shahid on his offer, Shahid and I sometimes met for tea or dinner. As an editor for a local Pakistani newspaper, Shahid was well connected and became a valuable interlocutor. As I immersed myself in research, I briefly lost contact with Shahid and had not seen him for nearly two months until this November afternoon.

Shahid gestured to me to get into the car. We exchanged greetings. Shahid was silent and looked tired and preoccupied. Several empty coffee cups and worn-out and discolored pages from Pakistani Urdu- and English-language newspapers lay scattered on the front passenger seat and the back seats. The car ashtray overflowed with cigarette butts. Shahid looked embarrassed and flustered as I started to pick up an open oilcan, with oil spilling out, lying at the foot of the front passenger seat.

"I'm sorry—I haven't had much time to clean the car. You can just toss the can in the back," Shahid said to me, and started to drive toward Hillcroft Avenue.

I could sense that something was not right. On all prior occasions when I had met Shahid, I had found him to be smiling, confident, and self-assured. On this particular day, however, Shahid appeared particularly tense, anxious and nervous. After chatting a little about my various encounters with Pakistani interlocutors since we had last met, he asked if I had time for lunch at a Pakistani restaurant nearby. Hungry after a long morning, I was only too happy for an opportunity to get lunch and catch up with Shahid. "But I have to make a stop first," he said. As I surveyed the car, I asked him how he had been. "I quit working at the newspaper," he said dramatically. "The editor and I got into an argument and I just quit," Shahid explained. "Are you working?" I asked, concerned about how he was managing these days. "Yes, I am working at an American fast food restaurant. I have to get up so early in the morning now. My routine has changed completely. I am looking for a job. I don't want to be an assistant manager at the restaurant. It is not for me."

We reached an empty parking lot facing a multistory concrete building that served as the warehouse and storage facility for several of the retail outlets in southwest Houston. Shahid asked me to wait in the car while he went inside to speak with a Pakistani entrepreneur. I picked up a week-old edition of the *Pakistan Chronicle*, the oldest English- and Urdu-language weekly newspaper in Houston, and quietly flipped through the newspaper. It was a good twenty minutes before Shahid returned. Shahid appeared frustrated: "It's the same everywhere. You need to have connections and contacts to get a job even here . . . they don't care about your qualifications. It's no different from Pakistan."

I nodded in agreement about the limits of meritocracy and educational qualifications acquired in Pakistan, especially for those without technical training and education in the sciences that carried value in the energy-sector-dominated economy of Houston. I began suggesting jobs Shahid could explore, including relocating to another city that might have better job prospects for him. Before he had a chance to respond, we had reached one of the more popular Pakistani restaurants on Hillcroft Avenue. We ordered food and sat down at a table. "Perhaps this is an opportunity for you to explore something new," I suggested, picking up our conversation and trying to put a positive spin on his current predicament. Shahid looked at me, surprised and perhaps even a bit offended at my suggestion. "I like it here . . . I like Houston. I don't want to leave! Besides I want to start something of my own soon. Here people forget you very quickly. If you are not in the public eye for very long, everyone forgets you. The news that I am no longer working hasn't gotten around yet, but when it does, I know that people will lose interest in me. I don't want that to happen."

It was at that moment that I realized the extent to which Shahid's social identity, and, indeed, his claims of status in Houston were dependent on the local Pakistani networks and infrastructure that grounded his life in Houston. As a single male immigrant, Shahid lacked locally based kin relations and social networks or what sociologist Nazli Kibria has termed "family social capital" that is, "the status and resources available . . . through membership in a family network" (2011: 37). It became clear to me that without a public and productive role in the Pakistani community, Shahid feared becoming invisible, his presence erased from the memory of the only people he knew in the city. It was this fear of invisibility and erasure that had so terrified him. The fear was nowhere clearer than when Shahid said, nervously and tentatively: "I need the Pakistani community here."

We finished lunch and Shahid stopped on our way out to chat with a few people he recognized. Shahid did not say much as we got in the car and headed to my apartment complex, only a couple of blocks away. As Shahid dropped me off, he said: "Perhaps Nadia or Ali knows of someone who is looking to hire? Can you please ask them if they know someone who is hiring? Please pray that things get better for me."

Shahid, a journalist by training and profession, and also a part of the elite in his ancestral village in Punjab in Pakistan, found himself at a crossroads after resigning from his job at the Pakistani newspaper. When I first met Shahid, he had been in Houston for less than two years. His social life, and indeed all aspects of his public life, were centered in the Pakistani Muslim community and mediated the loss of status and kinship ties of his ancestral village in Pakistan. For Shahid, the Pakistani ethnoreligious community not only provided status, fellowship, and employment but also provided the capital to manage risk and marginality in Houston. Even though his current employment at an American fast food restaurant provided him with a job and financial security, it provided him with neither the cultural capital nor the access to the ethnoreligious and social networks that might endow status within the local Pakistani community.

Kaiser: "Where Does One Have the Time to Make Friends?"

After spending a long day at a Muslim community center on Bissonnet Street, I realized I had missed the last bus back to Hillcroft Avenue. Not finding a public pay phone nearby, I entered a Pakistani restaurant to see if I could use its phone to call for a cab. As I waited in the restaurant's nondescript and sparsely furnished lobby, I witnessed a curious exchange between two restaurant employees—a middle-aged Pakistani and a young Mexican man. The middle-aged Pakistani man, Kaiser, was speaking haltingly in broken English. Although only in his late fifties, his leathery face and the stark lines across his forehead gave the appearance of someone much older. The younger Mexican man, wearing an apron over loose pants and a shirt, answered in a mix of English and Spanish. The conversation was fractured yet apparently intelligible to both. From what I could understand of the conversation, Kaiser was trying to teach his Mexican colleague how to bake naan bread. After the young Mexican man returned to the kitchen, I turned to Kaiser, and asked him in Urdu whether I could use the phone to call a cab company. "Of course, you can," he replied in Urdu.

As I waited for the cab, Kaiser and I started chatting. I sensed that Kaiser was eager for company as he freely opened up about himself. Kaiser had been in Houston for only a year and a half. "I work almost fifteen hours daily, seven days a week," Kaiser said to me. "Do you have any family in Houston?" I asked a bit tentatively, not wishing to encroach on his privacy. "No, I share a room with another Pakistani man. Like me, he is also from Karachi."

"What brings you to Houston?" I asked him.

"I worked for the Pakistani Navy. I was on the staff of a ship that was bringing cargo from Karachi to the Port of Mexico. We remained on the ship as the cargo was unloaded. Then as we were about to return, I jumped ship . . . and ran. I have three daughters at home—all of them were at a marriageable age. . . . I had to stay here! Otherwise there was no way I could have earned enough money and gotten them married. Son, I cannot read or write—how can a man like me support a family in Pakistan? This was the only way."

In spite of the struggles and anxieties of his current life situation, Kaiser remained unfailingly proud that at the age of almost sixty he was in good health and able to work long hours. In my conversation with Kaiser, I tried to remain sensitive while approaching the issue of his family in Pakistan. "You know, I don't know when I'll see them again . . . but at least my daughters are settled. If I had stayed in Pakistan, there was no way I could have gotten them all married," he repeated for the umpteenth time. Looking back, perhaps Kaiser's repeated assertions were meant as a reassurance to himself: the uncertainty and loss of family networks and kin that had accompanied his journey to Houston had been well worth the risk now that his daughters were married.

Did he have any friends here? I had asked him. "Where does one have the time to make friends?" Kaiser had laughed. After a workday that began early in the morning and ended only after the restaurant has closed late into the night, Kaiser walked to an apartment nearby that he shared with one other man, exhausted and too tired to do anything but sleep. In addition to his demanding work schedule, Kaiser tried to make time to go to the neighborhood mosque for prayers. Beyond working at the restaurant and sporadic visits to the neighborhood mosque, Kaiser had neither the time nor the money to socialize. Indeed, Kaiser tried but failed when I asked him to recall the last time he had gone beyond five miles from the immediate area.

Kaiser's "family social capital," including social and kinship-based networks that endow status and provide capital for constructing social identity and negotiating rights as a citizen, was based in Karachi. As an undocumented worker employed in a Pakistani restaurant, Kaiser remained isolated, a "dispensable" body (Agamben 2005) in the neoliberal economy, one for whom success was conceptualized in relation to the fulfillment of obligations to his family in Pakistan. The sole provider for his family, Kaiser had literally jumped ship—lacking locally based kinship relations and networks, finances, or language skills—and embraced a bitter and lonely struggle only because it seemed the most assured way of accumulating wealth for his daughters' dowries and marriage expenses in Pakistan, even if it meant a life of confinement in the recognizable space of a South Asian business.

Kaiser's experience highlights the contradictions of embeddedness within the transnational Muslim heritage economy, which can be experienced as security as well as confinement within ethnic spaces (Kwong 1997). On the one hand, employment at a Pakistani restaurant provided Kaiser with a livelihood and enabled him to meet his financial obligations to his family in Pakistan. At the same time, however, the cultural familiarity of his workplace also exacerbated his marginality and abjection as an undocumented working-class immigrant.[8]

Rashid: "It's Allah's Will"

Rashid, a thirty-nine-year-old single Pakistani man, worked at a Pakistani supermarket only a couple of blocks away from Nadia and Ali's store. On occasion, Nadia and I would visit the store for groceries. I would often catch a glimpse of Rashid cleaning and stocking the shelves, attending to the customers, or managing the cash register. Rashid dressed in the traditional Pakistani clothing of a loose kameez and shalwar, with a white Muslim netted cap covering his head. Rashid's only breaks during his fourteen-hour-workdays were quick visits to the nearby mosque for prayers. During the month of Ramadan when Muslims fast for thirty days from sunrise to sundown, Rashid volunteered at the mosque to serve hot Pakistani meals for the congregation of men and women who had gathered to pray and break the fast at sundown each evening.

It was at the mosque that we first became acquainted. Ali and I happened to be seated next to Rashid to break the fast when we struck up a conversation. After meeting a couple of times, I asked Rashid if he would be willing to let me record his life story. Rashid, soft spoken and unfailingly polite, was reluctant at first. "*Bhai* (brother), what do you want to know? I am just a simple man trying to make a living here. All my waking hours are spent at the store. *That* is my story," Rashid said in Urdu. Eager to help me with the research, however, Rashid proceeded to mention the names of several Pakistani community leaders and successful entrepreneurs whom I could interview instead. "They are the ones who have 'made it' here. You should interview them," he had insisted. I remained insistent that I wanted to interview him and even agreed to spread out the interview over several meetings whenever he had the time. Rashid finally relented. "All right, come to the supermarket in the afternoon. It is our least busy time," Rashid said. The next day I arrived at the supermarket at the appointed time. With only a couple of customers present, Rashid took a break to speak with me. We did not get too far along before Rashid would have to leave to attend to a customer, run chores, or sign invoices for the new stock of goods that arrived several times a week. It was through these often-interrupted conversations that I learned of Rashid's life in the U.S. and Pakistan.

* * *

Rashid was born in Karachi, the eldest of five siblings—two brothers and two sisters. Rashid's father, a contract construction worker, never had a steady income and it was often difficult for the family to make ends meet. The family lived in a low-income neighborhood where most inhabitants were Mohajirs, that is, Muslims who had migrated from regions in India to Pakistan in the years following the country's formation in 1947. Like many Indian Muslims during the time of Partition, Rashid's parents had also left behind their ancestral home in Delhi, with dreams of a better future in Pakistan. Yet material success remained elusive as Rashid's grandfather and later his father struggled but failed to find professional success. It seemed Rashid was destined for the same fate. Rashid's mother passed away when he was still a teenager, leaving Rashid and his father with the responsibility of providing for the entire family. Rashid left school after completing the eighth grade and remembers his teenage years as being rather uneventful. His younger brothers and sisters continued to attend school while Rashid helped his father maintain the household.

In the 1980s, as Rashid reached adulthood, his neighborhood became engulfed in ethnic violence among Mohajir, Pathan, Sindhi, and Punjabi ethnolinguistic communities. The violence centered on competing claims for entitlements, rights, and privileges in the city.[9] The city quickly divided itself spatially along ethnolinguistic affiliations. "Violence was everywhere," Rashid told me, as he recalled the names of several of his childhood friends who had lost their lives during those years. As violence accelerated, Rashid's family gathered their meager belongings and left to join distant relatives in the city of Lahore. In spite of the move, the financial situation of Rashid's family remained dire. A distant relative who had immigrated to Canada several years earlier returned to Pakistan on a visit a few months after Rashid's family had arrived in Lahore.

With limited financial resources and even fewer career opportunities in an unfamiliar city, Rashid approached his uncle and asked if he would sponsor his visit to Canada. "People like me can't even dream about coming to Canada or America. It had just never occurred to me. Where would we get the money for me to travel there and what would I do even if I got there? I had not even completed high school and I did not even know any English," Rashid said matter-of-factly. "It was Allah's will that my uncle returned to Pakistan when he did. It is Allah's will that I am here. There is no other explanation, is there?" Rashid's visiting relative, owner of a small business in Toronto, agreed to sponsor his visit. Pooling family finances, Rashid traveled to Canada almost a year later, desperate for a new start and the financial security that had eluded him in Pakistan.

Rashid never truly felt settled in Toronto. He was helping his uncle with the business yet never found his own footing or independence. Most of the money Rashid earned during this period went to support his family in Pakistan and to pay back the loans he had taken from relatives. By 1998, Rashid had been in Toronto for a few years and had learned to speak conversational English. Rashid decided to travel to Houston, armed with the knowledge that Houston was home to a large Pakistani population, and a belief that the United States might offer more financially lucrative opportunities. Soon after he had arrived, Rashid began working at a Pakistani supermarket, sharing a one-bedroom apartment with two male coworkers. Rashid smiled as he repeated: "It is Allah's will that I am here. From the money I earn here, I will be able to settle my family in Pakistan. . . . You know, I feel blessed that I have been able to finance my sister's wedding. . . . I cannot ask for anything more."

I appreciated Rashid's candor in speaking with me and I wanted to learn more about his life in Houston. However, we lost touch for a few months primarily because of Rashid's busy work schedule. I returned to the supermarket in early spring 2002, expecting to continue from where we had left off. To my surprise, Rashid was nowhere to be found. Perhaps it was his day off, I thought. I approached Sohail, one of his coworkers and roommates, and asked about Rashid. "You haven't heard?" he said somewhat nervously.

According to Sohail, about a month previously, Rashid had shown up to work early in the morning and was just about to raise the metal shutters of the supermarket and begin the workday when two men who had been waiting in the parking lot of the strip mall approached him. The two men turned out to be federal agents who took Rashid into custody. Sohail had not been able to visit Rashid and did not know why Rashid had been incarcerated or what had made him the target of federal surveillance. "Someone who did not like him must have given his name to the police," Sohail speculated. "We don't know what to make of it. He didn't do anything," Sohail concluded. A few weeks later news circulated that Rashid had been deported to Pakistan because he had overstayed his visa in the United States.

Although I had not known Rashid for long and my interactions with him had been limited to our conversations at the mosque and the supermarket, his alleged deportation was disturbing, bringing to the forefront the precariousness, dispensability, and vulnerability of Muslim male immigrants like Rashid following 9/11. In the absence of any verifiable information regarding Rashid's situation or even whereabouts, his detention and deportation were explained primarily through speculation. In a period of heightened surveillance and covert government operations and erosion of civil liberties and freedoms, and one in which details of surveillance, incarceration, and deportation remain outside purview of public information, gossip and speculation are a rational response and resource for a community that perceives itself under threat. Sohail's speculation that Rashid's disappearance could be explained by his incarceration and then deportation is premised on the circulation of countless stories of the U.S. government's surveillance of Muslim immigrants and especially single Muslim men. Speculation as a resource is based on a dominant framing of male Muslim as terrorists and as the legitimate objects of arbitrary and excessive state intervention and disciplinary practices.[10] Ironically, it is this extraordinary surveillance, the experience of abjection, and the curtailment of civil liberties that allows noncitizens like Rashid, otherwise invisible to mainstream

U.S. society, to become visible in narratives of U.S. imperialism (Puar 2007).

In Pakistani ethnic media such as radio programs and at cultural events like the Pakistan Independence Day Festival, the achievements of Pakistani professionals and entrepreneurs are routinely celebrated, positioning such accomplishments as the normative and exemplary immigrant experience. The celebration of accomplished professionals and entrepreneurs illustrates the classed hierarchies of privilege within Muslim immigrant communities that render inequalities and exploitation invisible. It is telling that as I attempted to build contacts with Pakistanis from different ethnolinguistic, religious, professional, and class backgrounds in Houston, no one directed me to the unemployed, the struggling, or the undocumented. Indeed, even in the case of the highly skilled Pakistani labor force experiencing unemployment, serendipitous encounters led to me to Amjad and his friends. When I asked community leaders for leads for individuals whom I could contact for this research, I was always pointed to success stories as if documentation and research on South Asian Muslim immigrants was inherently about stories of definitive success, material prosperity, and the achievement of the American dream. Recall, for example, Rashid's belief that I interview community leaders since they were the ones who had "made it here," and that confined all day in a supermarket, he did not have a story worth telling.

This emphasis on financially secure and upwardly mobile members of the community contributes to making the working poor like Rashid, Kaiser, and Shahid barely present in most representations and discussions of the Pakistani or the Muslim immigrant experience. This emphasis also glosses over how privileges, rights, and entitlements available to all citizens and resident noncitizens are in fact unevenly distributed across society. Moreover, Rashid's self-effacement emerges as a strategy to mediate such exclusions. It obscures his success in providing financial capital for his sister's wedding in Pakistan and remaining grateful and optimistic in the face of a life characterized by trauma, hardship, and struggle. It begs the questions: Why is it that Rashid's struggles and resilience in beginning life anew first in Canada and subsequently in the United States are not perceived as successes worthy of acknowledgment? How are ethnic spaces of commerce such as the

South Asian ethnic economy refashioned as a transnational Muslim heritage economy complicit in such exclusions?

The immigrant experience of individuals like Rashid reveals an unsettling truth about the ways state policy and surveillance make certain citizens and noncitizens more dispensable than others. Consider Rashid's dilemma. Becoming "out of status," that is, overstaying the legally permissible length of stay in the United States, Rashid was allegedly first detained in police custody and subsequently deported to Pakistan along with hundreds of other men, without legal recourse and without any consideration of his life situation. In 2002, reports of airplane flights full of Pakistani Muslim men who had become "out of status" and were forcibly deported to the home country had appeared on U.S. television and in the mainstream press. The sight of airplanes leaving American soil made a public spectacle of the expulsion of Muslim citizens and noncitizens who were deemed undesirable in U.S. society at best and a threat to the United States at worst. Indeed, Rashid's situation reveals what Hansen and Stepputat (2005) have termed "a form of life that is beyond the reach of dignity and full humanity and thus not even subject of a benevolent power" (17).

Being a Muslim provided Rashid with a sense of community and belonging, as well as spiritual respite from the struggles and pressures of his life. In Rashid's narrative, invocations of Allah's blessings are central to his explanation of his difficult life situations. Rashid had insisted to me that it was indeed Allah's blessing that a man of his limited means and skills had been able to come to Canada and subsequently the United States. Rather than point to structural barriers and the difficulties he had faced in Canada or the United States, Rashid interpreted his life as "Allah's will" and believed it was due to Allah's blessings that he had been able to finance his sister's wedding in Pakistan. Such invocations of Allah might be read as an attempt to find a higher meaning in a society in which he was marginal and invisible—and ultimately dispensable.

Conclusion

In this chapter, I have attempted to critically analyze the transformations and development of the South Asian ethnic economy in Houston and relate these transformations to the everyday life of individuals embedded in these spaces of commerce. The critical mass of Pakistani Muslim immigrant population, the growth of Pakistani ethnic businesses, variegated engagements between Pakistani Muslim immigrants and coreligionists with ancestral affiliations in other countries, and geopolitical contexts such as the tensions between Hindu and Muslim communities in Houston have had the effect of radicalizing consumption and economy. By the late 1990s, these developments fractured the South Asian economy along the lines of religion and resulted in the formation of a transnational Muslim heritage economy that is connected through financial networks to production and consumption nodes in North America, Europe, Asia, Africa, and the Middle East and the Gulf States. The mass circulation of Islamic religious commodities, the increasing centrality of Islam in mediating patterns of consumption, and a realignment of Pakistani Muslims within the Muslim ummah characterize the transnational Muslim heritage economy.

Transformations in consumption patterns and the ethnic economy in Houston provide an important context for examining lived experience within the transnational Muslim heritage economy, notably the experiences of entrepreneurs who provide the capital for starting and managing ethnic businesses and the working class and working poor who provide the labor for these businesses. Like Ismaili Muslim professionals, Pakistani ethnic entrepreneurs, and the working class and the working poor employed in Houston's South Asian ethnic economy are perceived to embody the American dream and positioned in public discourse as "self-employed, self-sufficient, boot-strapping immigrants who have become successful without government intervention" (Dhingra 2012: 1). The individual life histories and biographies of Pakistani ethnic entrepreneurs, the working class, and the working poor reveal a unique set of challenges that include the experience of poverty, marginality, racism, and various forms of violence and abjection and belie homogenizing discourses that flatten the heterogeneity of experiences within the Pakistani Muslim communities in Houston. The individual life experiences discussed in this chapter also make visible the recourse to religion to mediate multiple marginalities, exclusions, and forms of oppression under the U.S. regimes of surveillance as well as within ethnic spaces of commerce. Indeed, in spite of difficult life situations, Nadia and Ali, Kaiser, and Rashid shared in a strong belief in the value and the ultimate payoff of hard work for family success. Indeed, as gleaned from these biographies and narratives, racial inequalities and advancement are not mutually exclusive (Dhingra 2012). Rather, the pursuit of the American dream, reworked as individual effort and success in the service of family rather than the self, reveals agency and resilience that coexist with experiences of racism, marginality, discrimination, and abjection.

4

"I Have a Very Good Relationship with Allah"

Pakistani Gay Men and Transnational Belonging

The Pakistani Muslim American gay male represents a multiply hyphen-ated[1] and complex figure, confounding easy categorizations in classifi-catory schemes of subjectification. Stigmatized in diasporic nationalist projects,[2] Pakistani Muslim American gay men draw on South Asian histories and epistemologies of same-sex sexual eroticism and relation-ships in constructions of diasporic identities.[3] Criminalized for a devi-ant sexuality in transnational revivalist Islamic movements that espouse literalist interpretations of Islam, Pakistani Muslim American gay men nonetheless mobilize Islam in fashioning a religiously conceived trans-nationality. Marginalized and racialized in Anglo-centric queer move-ments and organizations (Das Gupta 2006), Pakistani Muslim Ameri-can gay men draw on Western epistemologies of sexuality to construct a gay identity. Homogenized as the Muslim "other" in post-9/11 U.S. policies supporting the war against terrorism, policed by the state, and marked outside emergent forms of nationalism and patriotism in the United States (Puar 2007), Pakistani Muslim American gay men build alternative communities and counterpublics (Munoz 1999) to claim rights, entitlements, and privileges as Americans.[4]

Though stigmatized, criminalized, marginalized, racialized, and ho-mogenized, Pakistani Muslim American gay men narrate their lived experience in terms of invocations of South Asian epistemologies of same-sex sexual eroticism and relationships and narrative tradi-tions, a religiously conceived transnationality, and appropriations of Western epistemologies of gay identity. The complex intersections of race, religion, sexuality, and transnationalism in what I call "transna-tional Muslim American sexual cultures" advance the exploration of heterogeneity of the Pakistani immigrant experience and guide the inquiry in this chapter. The narratives examined in this chapter are a corrective to the heterosexual transnational Muslim population movements and community formations typically represented in scholarship on Muslim Americans. Moreover, Pakistani Muslim American gay men problematize classed and gendered classifications, given that these groupings include highly skilled labor as well as middle-class and the working-class men. Indeed, in this grouping, differences of class, professional affiliations, educational attainment, sectarian affiliations, and citizenship status are subordinated to a shared identity as Muslim American gay men.

In this chapter, I employ a cultural analysis to explore the everyday life and constructions of transnational identities among Pakistani Muslim American gay men in Houston. The analysis disavows liberalist notions of a transparent and monolithic queer sexuality that have guided Western human rights activism in the non-West[5] and instead employs cultural analysis to explore everyday negotiations of religion, race, sexuality, and transnationalism in Muslim American communities during the current period of globalization.[6] In particular, I draw attention to culturally constructed male sexualities that are informed by South Asian narrative traditions, and epistemologies, language, and cultural idioms of homosociality and same-sex eroticism and relationships; the increasing centrality of belonging to a transnational Muslim ummah; and the appropriation of Western terminologies and categories of sexuality in constructing a gay identity.

I argue that the transnational Muslim American sexual cultures described in this chapter invoke South Asian scripts in ways that complicate dominant understandings of homosexuality in the West and in contemporary revivalist Islamic movements. Pakistani gay men refer to notions such as *yaar* (friend) and narrative traditions to fashion a nonheteronormative diasporic identity. A due consideration of such transnational registers makes visible South Asian Americans who typically "are written out of national memory entirely" (Gopinath 1997: 469–470) and rendered invisible in diasporic projects that conceptualize diaspora in terms of heterosexuality.[7] Hegemonic constructions of the diaspora take recourse to an imagined cultural authenticity that perceives queer identities "as a threat to the cultural integrity of South

Asian immigrants" (Shah 1993: 119). Indeed, as historian Nayan Shah argues, this "rhetoric is lethal and well understood by immigrants and their children, who are unceasingly chastised for shedding their "culture" and acquiring the degenerate and destructive values of white societies. The notion of culture here is a fossil—solid and petrified" (ibid.).

I also argue that Pakistani Muslim American gay men experience multiple marginalities—exclusion not only from diasporic nationalist projects but also discourses and projects of nationalism, patriotism, and nationhood in the United States. Significantly, the recent expansion of U.S. nationalism to incorporate homosexual subjects illustrates a conundrum for gay Pakistani Americans. Terming such expansion of U.S. nationalism as "homonationalism," Jasbir Puar argues that such expansion "sanctions some homosexualities, often through gendered, racial, and class sanitizing, in order to produce 'monster-terrorist-fags'; homosexuals embrace the us-versus-them rhetoric of U.S. patriotism and thus align themselves with this racist and homophobic production" (2007: 46). U.S. national homosexuality then, accommodates certain racialized and classed categories of homonormative U.S. citizens and subjects in post-9/11 projects of U.S. patriotism and nationalism while omitting "others," as I will demonstrate further in this chapter. This mutuality between the state and U.S. homosexual nationalism presents a challenge for the nonheteronormative Pakistani Muslim American subject—a site for inclusion if pacified through its appropriation of homonormativity (Duggan 2003) and the promise of freedom and sexual diversity on the one hand (Reddy 2011) and a racialized Muslim-as-terrorist (Rana 2011) who is outside inclusionary state projects of nationalism on the other.

Even as Pakistani Muslim American gay men negotiate marginality if not exclusion from nationalist projects, such negotiations are further complicated by a professed belonging to Islam in constructing identity and community. For the interlocutors discussed in this chapter, belonging to Islam is increasingly central in mediating such exclusions. Moreover, much as is the case with the working class and the working poor discussed in chapter 3, in the face of state-sanctioned violence and racism in the United States, religious beliefs provide, as anthropologist Junaid Rana suggests, a "source of refuge when confronting racism . . . [and] allow[s] them to cope with the seemingly vexing assumptions about the religious and social comportment that [Pakistanis] embody" (2011: 172).

Three caveats are in order before continuing further. One, the data presented in this chapter reflect transnational sexual cultural formations through the lens of a very specific group of gay Muslim Americans, that is, Muslim men of Pakistani descent who reside in Houston and with whom I interacted during the period of my ethnographic research. My intention in this chapter is to ground the analysis of transnational Muslim American sexual cultures within the specificities of the individual experiences of my interlocutors. I follow anthropologist Richard Parker (1999), and similarly approach the documentation of Pakistani Muslim American gay narratives and lives as "a collection of fragments, slices of life, bits and pieces" (Parker 1999: 23) rather than a totalizing or definitive account of transnational Muslim American sexual cultural formations. Relatedly, the omission of the experience of transnationality of lesbian and bisexual Muslim American women in this chapter is primarily due to my lack of interaction with lesbian interlocutors. Scholarly study of nonheteronormative women is an important and essential project and a necessary direction for future research on Muslim Americans.

Two, this research documents the formation of transnational Muslim American sexual cultures during a specific time period, that is, the first decade of the twenty-first century. The data and analysis do not reflect developments and changes, or the cultural politics of Muslim American sexual cultural formations since the time I completed the research. Indeed, the transnational Muslim sexual cultural formations that I attempt to document in this chapter are always in the making, shaped by shifting emphases on varied transnational registers of invocation and affiliations, as well as changes in individual dispositions in constructions of sexuality.

Finally, in referring to South Asian cultural epistemologies as well as accommodations of same-sex sexual eroticism in Islamic traditions and communities historically, my aim is not to project transnational sexuality into the past, or erase the specificity of how accommodations of same-sex sexual eroticism emerged in South Asia and in Muslim communities historically. Rather, I refer to South Asian and Islamic histories to illustrate the sources of cultural capital in negotiating multiple exclusions and marginalities, and forms of oppression and subordination given geopolitical and cultural specificities of the Pakistani Muslim American experience in the early twenty-first century. Here I follow Nayan Shah (1993), who has argued:

> Recovering histories both of the ancient and recent past challenge us all to understand the possibilities of alternative sexualities and social arrangements. Through mobilizing histories, reappropriating languages, and other cultural strategies, we may be able to gain affirmation and support within South Asian immigrant communities for queer desires and relationships. Simultaneously, these cultural strategies may unexpectedly destabilize the self-definitions of South Asian lesbian and gay communities. (123)

A consideration of the transnational circulation of South Asian epistemologies and histories of same-sex sexual eroticism and relationships then "enables a simultaneous critique of heterosexuality and the nation form while exploding the binary oppositions between nation and diaspora, heterosexuality and homosexuality, original and copy" (Gopinath 2005: 11). In approaching emergent transnational Muslim American sexual cultures this way, this chapter attempts to reinscribe Muslim American gay men into nationalist, religious, and racial narratives and histories, question the very terms of such engagements, and suggest new ways of accounting for gay Muslim lives in the early twenty-first century.

South Asian Epistemologies and Histories of Same-Sex Sexual Love and Relationships

I had been out to dinner with a couple of friends when we decided to stop at a popular gay bar in the Montrose District of Houston. In recent decades, Montrose has emerged as one of the primary centers for gay business establishments as well as residence that are located inside the Loop.[8] Montrose is located near several universities as well as the Museum District, home to numerous institutions dedicated to the arts, notably the internationally renowned Rothko Chapel, the Menil Collection, and the Contemporary Arts Museum. Montrose is also one of the few pedestrian-friendly areas in a city renowned for privileging highways and cars.

After a leisurely late evening at the bar, we took a stroll down the street, and I saw a young man approach me. I did not recognize him at first. "I am Aamir. I think we met at the mosque a couple of weeks back . . . you were there with a friend of mine," he said as we stood in the brightly lit parking lot next to JR's, a prominent gay bar. Aamir continued, "I saw you come into the bar, but I wasn't sure if I should come over and say hello. I had actually left to go home but drove back because I thought I would take my chances and say hello!" Perhaps noticing my confusion, Aamir said rather emphatically, "I don't think too many Pakistanis come here. I am not out [of the closet], but there are few gay Pakistani friends with whom I come to JR's. It has now become a part of my life."

Aamir was born in Karachi, Pakistan. His family had emigrated from India to Pakistan at the time of the formation of Pakistan in 1947. One of Aamir's maternal aunts had immigrated to the United States and had resided in Houston since 1981. Aamir's parents divorced when he was seven years old, and Aamir's maternal aunt sponsored Aamir's mother's immigration to the United States. In 1995, Aamir, his eldest brother, and his mother moved to Houston, primarily because of the availability of better educational opportunities for Aamir and his brother. Aamir's brother had completed his education in business management in New England and had stayed there, eventually marrying a Pakistani American colleague. While living with his mother in a two-bedroom apartment in a gated community in southwest Houston, Aamir was a full-time undergraduate student at the University of Houston and worked part-time as a teller at a bank. His mother worked as an office administrator at a private company.

Over the course of the next several months, Aamir and I became good friends and I socialized often with Aamir and his Pakistani gay friends. In this group of Pakistani gay men, differences in age, class, educational background, Muslim sectarian affiliations, and profession were subordinated to a shared self-identification as gay Muslim men. Aamir's friendship circle consisted of second-generation Pakistani Americans, twice-migrant Pakistanis, and recent immigrants from Pakistan. Shahrukh, a recently naturalized American citizen, worked as a waiter at an upscale American restaurant. Salman was a second-generation Pakistani American who had recently completed his graduate education in social work. Salman was in the process of moving back to Houston, where he was born and had lived until his pursuit of educational opportunities took him to Canada. Saif, a recent Pakistani immigrant who was born and raised in Karachi, worked as a salesperson at a local health food store. Saif's boyfriend, Imran, worked at a hair and beauty salon in the evenings and attended community college part-time. Imran, who had grown up in South Africa, had come to the United States for college and had met Saif through Aamir.

In spite of their differences, these men embodied culturally constructed male sexualities that were informed, in part, by South Asian scripts of homosociality and same-sex sexual eroticism and relationships and South Asian narrative traditions. My ethnographic research with this group of men revealed two salient South Asian cultural scripts that appeared in everyday conversations. The notion of *yaar*, usually translated as "friend" in Urdu and Hindi, exemplifies one such script that recurred in my conversations with my interlocutors to describe the ideal romantic partner. As used by my interlocutors, yaar refers to culturally constructed romantic friendships that are not fully translatable or legible in the English language and epistemologies of Western sexuality. A second cultural script pertains to a narrative tradition, specifically the genre of "personal experience tales," that has been documented in studies of Pathan women in northern Pakistan (Grima 1991). This narrative tradition also framed the retelling of traumatizing and difficult life experiences among my interlocutors. Analytic consideration of these scripts illuminates two transnational registers and sources of cultural capital in emergent transnational Muslim American sexual cultures.[9]

Yaar

In seeking relationships, my Pakistani gay male interlocutors search for men who share their religious and ethnic background. Although these Pakistani men venture regularly into predominantly gay spaces—for example, the bars, clubs and other gay-owned business establishments in the Montrose District (and beyond) in Houston—they often experience these places with other Muslim gay men. In conversations over

dinner, at a bar, or sitting in a cafe, these men readily espouse their preference for a Pakistani Muslim boyfriend. While we were having coffee
at a café in Montrose, Aamir said to me:

> I definitely want to be in a relationship with another Pakistani guy
> [pause]. We would be able to understand each other more [pause]. We
> would have the same religion and culture [pause]. I think our relation-
> ship would be more successful because of this.

Aamir had paused before continuing:

> Basically, I want a yaar, you know? [I want] someone who can be a spe-
> cial friend with whom I can share everything."

On another occasion, Shahrukh similarly invoked the notion of
yaar to describe what was missing in his relationship with Mario, a gay
Mexican American man in his twenties, whom he had been dating for
a couple of years. Even though he cared deeply for Mario, Shahrukh
was unsure if the relationship had a future. When I asked Shahrukh
why, he had paused, searching for the right word to describe his concerns. "I don't know what it is [pause]. Mario and I have a great sexual
relationship, and I know that he loves me but [pause] I don't know how
to describe it [long pause]. I want to be with someone who is a friend,
[pause] a *dost* [friend]."

These brief fragments from everyday conversations converge on the
invocation of the notion of yaar to describe the ideal relationship or
"special friendship" as Aamir termed it. There are several interchangeably used words for "friend" in Urdu and Hindi, among them *dost*,
humsafar, saathi, and *yaar*. The appropriation of these words among my
interlocutors shows the subversive potential of these words to encapsu-
late same-sex sexual friendships. Shahrukh, for example, had used the
term dost and Aamir had used the term yaar. The pauses in the conversation in both instances, as both Aamir and Shahrukh searched for the
right word in English, and code switching between Urdu and English
illustrate the difficulties in translating the notions of yaar or dost. For
diasporic subjects like Aamir and Shahrukh who appropriate Western
classifications and categories of sexuality in constructing a gay identity,

such pauses are suggestive of "disidentification" (Munoz 1999; Medina 2012), a strategy of resistance that "works within and outside the dominant public sphere simultaneously" (Munoz 1999: 5), and indexes "a multiplicity of interlocking identity components" (ibid.: 8). Aamir and Shahrukh, for example, resisted using English and words like "friend" and "boyfriend," persisting instead in situating romantic friendships within South Asian cultural linguistic specificities.

The language use among diasporic gay Pakistanis demonstrates the transnational circulation of scripts for making meaning of South Asian same-sex sexual eroticism and friendships between men, and between women as well. For example, in an autobiographical essay in one of the first anthologies of gay and lesbian South Asians in the diaspora (Ratti 1993), the writer using the pseudonym Ayyar, eloquently describes his quest for the ideal relationship in a manner that resonates with the usage of term yaar by my interlocutors, Aamir and Shahrukh. According to Ayyar:

> Over the past few years I have come to realize that my meandering path through romance, sexual liaisons, and friendship has been, and still is, but a search for a singular relationship that can encompass all three of these elements. Such a bond is embodied in the concept of yaari. A yaar is an individual with whom one feels a deep, almost intangible connection. . . . For me a yaar embodies elements of both a friend and a lover, and I yearn for just such a connection with a man in my life. . . . There is really no English equivalent for this concept, no word that approaches its breadth and depth. *Friend* is not enough. *Buddy* is superficial, reeks of Budweiser beers and backslapping in bars. . . . A world of romantic images revolves around yaari. There are tales of yaars dying for one another. Even a wife must many a time take a backseat to a man's yaar. (1993: 167)

Despite the contemporary political and cultural climate in South Asia that criminalizes and attempts to efface homosexuality from national and cultural histories and experiences (Dave 2012), there is ample evidence and an extensive history of same-sex sexual relationships. These histories suggest that sexual identities across the spectrum are enacted and solidified in South Asia. Recent anthologies that traverse a variety of literary genres—autobiography, fiction, poems, plays, and prose extracts—from Bangladesh, India, Nepal, Pakistan, and Sri Lanka document the rich repertoire of literary representations of same-sex sexual eroticism and relationships between men, and between women in South Asia over time and space. One such anthology is tellingly titled *Yaraana*, which is translated as "friendship" in Urdu, (Merchant 2011); it represents myriad traditions and contexts in historicizing same-sex relationships. Another anthology, *Same-Sex Love in India: Readings from Literature and History* (Vanita 2001), similarly includes excerpts from religious books, legal and erotic treatises, story cycles, medieval histories and biographies, modern novels, short stories, letters, memoirs, plays, and poems translated from different South Asian regional languages into English. The anthology counters "homophobic myths existing in India and elsewhere that homosexuality was imported to . . . India, from elsewhere, like the West. This history of homoeroticism is to assure homoerotically inclined Indians of a long Indian tradition which did not view same-sex love as inferior" (George 2002: 93).

Just as these anthologies illuminate transnational contexts for understanding same-sex sexual eroticism and relationships in South Asia historically, ethnographies of contemporary South Asia also document variegated constructions of same-sex sexual relationships between men and between women in South Asia today. These studies make visible the embodied experience of same-sex sexual intimacies in contemporary South Asia.[10] The excerpt that follows provides one exemplary narrative from a study of Bangladeshi men:

> We were friends for a long time and then started flirting and making jokes about how attractive we found each other. . . . One evening we were at his house and were lying on his bed and talking. The next thing I knew we were hugging each other madly. We took off each other's clothes and made out for hours. Our affair continued for a year. . . . Emotionally and physically we were close as any lovers. (S. Khan 1997: 12)

The complexities of same-sex relationships are represented in South Asian media and popular culture and suggest the discursive production of nonheteronormativity in public culture. Writing about the exchange of sexually explicit homoerotic *Holi* (Indian festival of color that marks the beginning of spring) greeting cards between male friends in the city of Banaras in India, anthropologist Lawrence Cohen conceptualizes these exchanges as expressions of love, passion, and friendship (Cohen 1995). Cohen notes that the graphic drawings of erect phallus, a primary visual motif in the cards, referred to a worldview of non-heteronormative male desire. In his discussion of same-sex relationships among men in contemporary Pakistan, Badruddin Khan suggests the same: "Love between men is, in fact, exalted, and tenderness, affection, and deep friendships are not uncommon. Unlike the macho backslap that passes for camaraderie in the West, men frequently hold hands while walking, and it is not uncommon to see men embracing" (B. Khan 1992: 99). Elaborating further, Khan states that homosociality among Pakistani men "is generally perceived as requiring tenderness, passion, good humor, and gracious permissiveness rather than harsh dominance" (ibid.: 97–98).

Male friendships in South Asia demonstrate the potential for encapsulating sexual desire and love, in part because of the cultural permissibility of the intense male bonding that is expressed in single-sex institutions, notably schools, or through the socialization that brings together young men and creates gendered public cultures of leisure activities, entertainment, sociality and living, such as eating, working, and sleeping in shared quarters (Derne 2000). Moreover, the permissibility of sexually intimate friendships in South Asia may also be a result of "the close emotional bonding and physical affection between male friends while discouraging premarital heterosexual social life, and the prevalence of boarding schools and arranged marriage" (Dynes and Donaldson 1992: xii).

Homosociality recurs as a major theme in South Asian popular culture, notably Hindi language Indian cinema.[11] Such cinema is one of the primary sources of entertainment and leisure activities in India and elsewhere in South Asia.[12] The supremacy of the bond of friendship between men and the subordination of heterosexual love to such bonds finds expression in Bollywood cinema, most overtly in films produced in the 1970s and the 1980s. The theme of several popular films centers on the almost-sacred quality of male friendships, in which men willingly sacrifice the love of their beloved (a woman) for the love of their friend (a man). In depictions of a love triangle involving two male friends in love with the same woman, a subgenre in romantic films in Bollywood cinema, for example, the woman typically "remains out of the picture, while the two males decide between themselves who will have her" (Prasad 1998: 83–84). Indeed, the idealization of dosti that makes "images of male bonding readily available for a queer male viewership" (Gopinath 2005: 102) is complicated by a "simultaneous investment in misogyny and patriarchal kinship arrangements" (ibid.).

Homosociality is also notable in popular songs in Bollywood cinema that "talk of undying friendship between men [and] are part of the repertoire of popular verse" (B. Khan 1992: 99) and represent one of the sites of queer desire and identification, from which queer diasporic South Asians negotiate heteronormativity (Waugh 2001).[13] In the often-cited example of a song from a classic Indian western, *Sholay* [Flames], directed by Ramesh Sippy in 1975, legendary superstars Amitabh Bachchan and Dharmendra sing a song that celebrates male friendship. The capacity of such songs for queer appropriation is apparent in the subversive readings of the song as "a diasporic gay male anthem of sorts, sung at gay pride parades from New York to London to San Francisco" (Gopinath 2005: 101).[14]

The script of yaar invoked by my Pakistani Muslim American gay interlocutors demonstrates the transnational circulation of South Asian language of same-sex eroticism and its appropriation as a communicative practice in everyday conversations about love and relationships. Intense homosociality, male bonding, and friendships emerge from within dominant patriarchal kinship patterns and socialities. Moreover, the consideration of discursive and historically contingent sites for constructing nonheteronormative male sexualities throughout South Asia is important in the analysis of Pakistani Muslim American gay men because of the convergences in colonial, postcolonial, and transnational South Asian histories that transcend the boundaries of the nation-state in South Asia.

Transnational Circulation of Ideologies of Filial and Kinship Obligations

Pakistani Muslim American gay men also invoke culturally specific South Asian scripts that reference narrative traditions, notably the genre of "personal experience tales" (Grima 1991), as shown in the narrative of Shahrukh. Shahrukh sometimes came over for dinner when he was not busy working as a waiter at an upscale restaurant. He would stay for hours as we indulged in a marathon viewing of a week's worth of the episodes of daytime soap operas that we both liked to watch while we ate takeout from a nearby Pakistani restaurant. Having arrived in the United States on a student visa, Shahrukh began working part-time at a jewelry stand in a mall in California while attending college in the mid-1990s. After a few years of working at the jewelry stand, Shahrukh convinced the stand owner to file his employment-based immigration application. "I put up with the low pay and the long working hours seven days a week. I was so unhappy. I had no life. But what other choice did I have?"

Shahrukh's immigration- and employment-related difficulties were exacerbated by a traumatizing and difficult route coming to terms with his sexuality. One evening, Shahrukh became especially emotional as the conversation turned to our difficult individual experiences navigating U.S. immigration bureaucracy. Shahrukh said to me:

> Being gay has been a curse for me. You know, when I lived in California, I was not out of the closet. My life was so simple then. And now, my life is just upside down. Can you believe how unlucky I am? I was waiting for my immigration to come through and I couldn't leave the U.S. for several years. My mother would call me regularly from Karachi, and ask me to return. She would always ask: "When will you return? When will you return? I am not well. I miss you. Please come soon." A few years ago, when she passed away, I could not even attend her funeral. Is there anything worse than not being able to see your mother's face for the last time, and to be with her in her time of illness?

Shahrukh's deeply affecting narrative, one of personal misfortune, equated his absence from his mother's life, her funeral, and his inability to travel to Pakistan, with failure as a son to fulfill his filial obligations toward his mother. Shahrukh was in tears as he continued: "I believe that it is because of my homosexuality that I couldn't see her. . . . Anyway, I can't do anything about it now except live with this curse for the rest of my life. I cannot imagine that I will ever be completely happy."

Shahrukh's path to acquiring a green card had required a sacrifice of family and fractured family and kinship relations based in Pakistan. Shahrukh's retelling of his experience invokes, what anthropologist Benedicte Grima has termed "personal experience tale," that is, individual narratives that typically relate to illness, catastrophe and misfortune (1999). According to Grima, her Pathan female interlocutors in Peshawar, Pakistan retold stories of personal misfortune by emphasizing sacrifice, honor, suffering, and courage in personal narrative (ibid.). In Grima's analysis, this narrative construction is a counterpart to the gendered notions of honor and status that have been documented as central markers for conferring social respectability for Pathan men.[15] For Pathan women, Grima argues, honor implies "tears and endurance of hardship" (ibid.: 79).[16]

In the case of Shahrukh, one finds a regendering and diasporic refashioning of such narrative traditions, situating narratives of misfortune, loss, and sacrifice in the context of the specificities of Pakistani Muslim American life and as a response to individual experiences navigating racialized immigration policies that restrict mobility and travel outside of the United States. Shahrukh's tale reflects his personal experience with U.S. immigration bureaucracies in the post-9/11 period, demanding personal sacrifice and entailing loss and hardships in the form of a subordination of family and kin relations to immigration practices and procedures, even as state practices around immigration ironically attempt to profess and promise freedom and access to opportunities in the global neoliberal capitalist economy (Reddy 2011). Moreover, the assumption of linearity in gay population movements from the East to the West and the elusive promise of sexual freedom in the United States undergird U.S. immigration policies and apparatus, undermining not only the prevalence of same-sex sexual cultures in the non-West but also circularity of population movements.

In an ironic twist, the same U.S. government apparatus that regulates family immigration and gives rise to dislocations such as those Shahrukh experienced penalizes single working-class male Pakistani immigrants in practices of surveillance, control, and discipline of Muslim immigrants. As Rana aptly argues: "The impermanence of work and family life that transnational migration brings . . . has produced affective registers that disrupt normal conceptions of respectable domesticity enabled by middle-class heterosexual marriage" (2011: 119). In this configuration, queerness transcends identity politics centered on nonheteronormative sexualities and instead references homosociality and homosexuality "as a referent of visible racial and classed abjection" (ibid.).

Even as Shahrukh attempted to build a life as an openly gay man in the United States, his sense of his failure in fulfilling his filial responsibility toward his mother appears to have tarnished his quest for fulfillment, contentment, and happiness: "I can't do anything about it now except live with this curse for the rest of my life. I cannot imagine that I will ever be completely happy." Ironically, it is this personal angst that allowed Shahrukh to accept his homosexuality as a core aspect of his identity. This rationalization allowed him to build community and a life as gay male, even as the remembrance of his mother's death, expressed through a personal experience tale, emphasized loss, hardship, and sacrifice.

Heteronormativity and Pakistani Diasporic Nationhood

For my interlocutors, hegemonic ideologies of diasporic nationhood privileging heterosexuality and premised on the exclusion of nonheteronormative diasporic subjects exemplify another register for negogitations of transnational belonging.[17] Women and gender studies scholar Gayatri Gopinath (2005) aptly terms such exclusions the "symbolic effacement of queer subjects from a 'home' space nostalgically reimagined from the vantage point of the diaspora" (17). The constructions of the diasporic nation in terms of heterosexuality marginalize Pakistani Muslim American gay men in public performances of diasporic nationhood, for example, the Pakistan Independence Day celebrations in Houston. Foreshadowing the discussion of the Pakistan Day Festival in the next chapter, here I refer to the understandings of the Festival from the perspective of the interlocutors discussed in this chapter. When I asked Aamir whether a gay Muslim group or organization could participate as a group at the annual Pakistan Day Festival in Houston, he was emphatic: "There is no way would they be allowed because the community would not accept it at all. That is for sure. . . . There would be some sort of an incident . . . some sort of a violent incident. Someone would have just gone and physically hit someone at the stall."[18]

The exclusion of South Asian LGBTQIA (lesbian, gay, bisexual, transgender, queer, intersex and asexual) organizations from the India Day and the Pakistan Day Parades in New York City coincides with the rise of Hindu extremism in India, the exclusion of Indian Muslims and "deviant sexualities" from the Indian nation, and Islamic revivalism in Pakistan (Prashad 2000). Discussing the tensions that erupted over the participation in the India Day parade in New York of the South Asian Lesbian and Gay Association (SALGA) as well as a progressive women's organization, Sakhi, anthropologist Johanna Lessinger (1995) states: "India Day Parade organizers felt that homosexuals were a disgrace to 'the Indian community.' Some also invoked family values, arguing that official acceptance of SALGA's presence [at the India Day Parade] might send the wrong message to the young people watching the parade" (64–65).[19]

As I was making plans to attend the Pakistan Independence Day Festival in Houston in 2002, I invited Aamir to accompany me. Aamir was emphatic in his refusal: "My mother will be going with some of her friends. I have no interest in going." He continued, "Why should I go someplace where I am not wanted? I'll just end up feeling awful. . . . Besides, none of my other gay friends will be there. They know what the Festival is like and they would never attend it either." Aamir's belief that as a gay man he did not belong at an event dedicated to celebrating Pakistani heritage points to the profound sense of exclusion experienced by men who are marked outside of the diasporic imagined community.

The conception of the diasporic Pakistani nation in terms of heterosexuality, and increasingly through religion (as I discuss in the next chapter), stigmatizes homosexuality by alienating gay subjects in diasporic communities. On several occasions, Aamir reiterated his tremendous fear of being ostracized by his heterosexual Pakistani peers if he were to come out to them. Aamir underscored this heightened alienation from his peers during the course of a formal interview late one evening at my apartment:

I know the type of people they are, I would never share this with them. Ever! I have realized that they do not really respect gay people at all.

Whenever they talk about gays or lesbians they start to make fun of them. If a guy appears to be effeminate, they start to make fun of him. . . . They are not my friends. . . . [If they ever found out, they] . . . I would have been totally left out and ignored. Everyone would start making fun of me.

The oppressive and exclusionary heteronormative ideologies have contributed to the formation of alternative organizations that are inclusive of LGBTQIA individuals (Das Gupta 2006) in major cities across the United States. These include SALGA in New York City, Khush Desi in Washington, DC, Sangeet in Chicago, Trikone in San Francisco, Satrang in Los Angeles, Trikone Tejas in Austin, and the Massachusetts Area South Asian Lambda Association (MASALA) in Boston. It is important to note, and pertinent for this discussion, that similar organizations were conspicuously absent in Houston, in spite of its large South Asian population. LGBTQIA South Asians in Houston have thus far avoided forming social and civic organizations centered on intersectional issues of religion, ethnicity, and sexuality. Rather, Pakistani Muslim American gay men have forged religiously conceived informal social networks as safe spaces that compensate for the experience of marginality in diasporic public cultures and community formations.

Negotiations of Belonging in the Global Muslim Ummah

The marginality in, if not exclusion of, Pakistani American gay men from the broader ethnic community on the basis of sexuality coexists with appropriations of South Asian epistemologies of same-sex sexual eroticism and relationships and narrative traditions and professed belonging to Islam. Religious appropriations, and the centrality of Islam in fashioning transnational identities as gay men, intersect with ongoing revivalism in Islam globally.[20] Revivalist movements in Islam, especially those associated with Wahabi Islam emanating from Saudi Arabia, sustain literalist interpretations of homosexuality in Islamic scripture.[21] This literalist perspective characterizes homosexuality as "an aberration and violation of nature" (Duran 1993). It positively affirms and rewards heterosexuality and denounces, criminalizes, and punishes any public expressions of homosexuality. Moreover, these readings of the Qur'an represent homosexuality as a Western import (Rahman 2010). In so doing, these interpretations ignore the rich and varied repertoire of same-sex eroticism and relationships in South Asia discussed earlier in this chapter.

Most Islamic scholarship on homosexuality takes as its starting point literalist interpretations as the irrevocable and absolute truth without due consideration of geopolitical, economic and social contexts. Notably, these interpretations "mistake or transpose state repression for sexual repression, essentially denying any productive effects of juridical structures" (Puar 2007: 13–14). Moreover, this scholarship scarcely, if at all, examines the historical contingency of scriptural knowledge, especially in relation to the rise of revivalist movements in Islam in the late twentieth century and the early twenty-first century. This scholarship barely examines the production of scriptural knowledge through its interaction with the lived experience, or the "variance in how homosexual conduct existed or exists and was or is understood in Islamic societies" (Rahman 2010: 950).[22] Providing insight into the global circulation of Islamic ideologies that espouse the impossibility of accommodating same-sex desire in Islam and in Muslim countries, and its intersection with production of the Muslim-as-terrorist concept following 9/11, Puar (2007) states: "Queer secularity most virulently surfaces in relation to Islam because Islam, the whole monolith of it, is often described as unyielding and less amenable to homosexuality than Christianity and Judaism, despite exhortations by some queer Muslims" asserting sameness with Christian and Jewish counterparts (Puar 2007: 13–14).

The work of Islamic scholars such as Scott al-Haqq Kugle (2003; 2014) provides compelling insight into accommodations of same-sex sexual eroticism and relationships in Islam historically. Going against the grain of dominant interpretive understandings of nonheteronormative sexualities and Islam, Kugle argues: "In comparison with many other religious traditions . . . Islam is a religion that has evaluated sexual life positively. Articulating the integral relationship between spirituality and sexuality is one way that the Prophet Mohammad challenged his society. It remains for us, today, to continually struggle with that challenge. The system of norms, rules, and laws created by Muslims in the past does not absolve us of this challenge. . . . Muslims in pre-modern times certainly were not shy about discussing matters of sex" (2003: 190–191).

Given the denigration of homosexuality in literalist interpretations of Islam, what then are the strategies through which Pakistani gay men position themselves as Muslim members in a global Muslim ummah? For Pakistani Muslim American gay men in Houston, literalist interpretations of Islam have not led to a rejection of religion or even a distancing from religious life and sources of authority.[23] Rather, Islam is central to their lives as gay men, rupturing scholarly interpretations of Islam and Muslim communities as monolithic and incapable of non-heteronormative accommodation. Indeed, although literalist interpretations dominate scholarship,[24] critiques of this view show how literalist interpretations of homosexuality in the Qur'an and the hadith have increasingly co-opted alternative representations and understandings of homosexuality in Islam.

In the case of my interlocutors, belonging to Islam finds expression in constructions of an individual relationship with Allah and a reinterpretation of select parables in the Qur'an, deference to Muslim forms of authority, and construction of religiously informed sexual practices. Thus, religious identity and sexual identity are simultaneously collapsed in certain instances and then made incompatible in the case of the Pakistani Day Festival where the nation structures the space between religion and sexuality. Moreover, belonging to Islam has been critical in the formation of inclusive transnational Muslim counterpublics such as the informal friendship circles within which my interlocutors like Aamir are embedded, as well as the Internet-based transnational Muslim LGBTQIA networks such as Al-Fatiha.

Clearly the literalist interpretations of homosexuality and Islam have deeply affected Aamir, who has given considerable thought to his Muslim identity:

AHMED AFZAL (AA): Would you say you are a religious person?
AAMIR: I won't say that I pray five times a day. I fast during Ramadan, and pray whenever I can. But I know that I have a good relationship with

Allah. I know that I am very spiritual. . . . I really feel that whatever
I asked for from Allah, he has given me. . . . I do not feel guilty that
I am gay or believe that Allah does not like me because I am gay. I
think he likes me more now.

AA: What do you mean?

AAMIR: I have accepted that I am gay . . . whenever I have prayed, Allah
has always given me whatever I have asked for. So that makes me
think that Allah loves me more now because maybe, now I am being
honest with myself or maybe . . . I don't know . . . I just know that I
have a very good relationship with Allah.

As if to reinforce self-positioning as a Muslim, Aamir repeated:

I wouldn't say that my relationship with Allah has been harmed by my
homosexuality. I would say that my relationship with Allah has become
even stronger and Allah really loves me. So it makes me think that I am
being really loved by Allah, so how can this be possible that Allah hates
me or that I cannot be a Muslim?

Aamir sought to reinterpret Islam through an individual relationship
with Allah in ways that attempted to reconcile sexuality with religion
and to position himself within the Muslim ummah. This point was also
made by Muslim gay men in a recent study that shows how individual
relationships to Allah provided comfort while developing a stronger
religious identity (Kugle 2014). In my interpretation, the construction of an individual relationship between Aamir and Allah allows an
ongoing and lifelong dialogue that incorporates new concerns, situations, and issues, instead of a relationship that is premised on finality
and resolution.

Aamir's ongoing process for understanding his relationship with
Allah also focused on rethinking mainstream Muslim interpretations
of the Qur'an. In analyzing the position of homosexuality within Islam,
the meaning of the parable of Prophet Lut in the Qur'an is a key reference that has been the subject of much debate among Muslims. The
story of Lut is interpreted in literalist readings of the Qur'an as a con-
demnation of, and punishment for the pervasiveness of homosexuality

in the people of Lut, and its reiteration in hadith.[25] Aamir contested literalist and hegemonic interpretations of the parable of the Kingdom of Lut. On one occasion when this topic came up, Aamir shared his interpretation:

> In the Qur'an, there are several things that we are not supposed to do, but we do them anyway. I would say that it depends a lot on the interpretation. I think, whatever the Qur'an says about homosexuality, like the Kingdom of Lut, I think they were not destroyed because of their homosexuality but because they were corrupt. They were raping people . . . I think it is a matter of interpretation.

Aamir's characterization of the destruction of the Kingdom of Lut as a consequence of corruption and rape rather than a particular sin indicates the availability of alternative readings of the parable. Indeed, some scholars attribute the destruction of the Kingdom of Lut to transgressions such as the absence of appropriate hospitality accorded to strangers and the engagement of the people of Lut in several types of sin, and do not see the destruction of the Kingdom of Lut as representing a particular sin.[26] That a hegemonic interpretation of the parable of the Kingdom of Lut circulates globally speaks to the globalization of Wahabi revivalist movements in Islam rather than a parable that is in fact open to multiple interpretations. Moreover, these interpretive possibilities are significant in that they enable a critique of violence and corruption that is upended from the perspective of same-sex sexual eroticism and relationships.

Religious Leaders and the Mediations of Sexuality

Deference to religious forms of authority provides another example of the practices through which my interlocutors expressed their religiosity. Glimpses of Salman's religiosity, for example, can be discerned in his solicitation of counsel from the Imam at a local mosque and community center in Houston. Salman, an openly gay second-generation Pakistani American Muslim, had recently completed his graduate education in social psychology in Canada and was in the process of moving back to Houston, where he was born. I had met Salman through Aamir during one of Salman's visits from Canada. We were sitting at a cafe in Montrose when Salman shared me with me:

> You won't believe this, but I was married. I got married to a Pakistani woman in Houston. We knew each other before we got married. She was a student here. I didn't know that I was gay, although I had always felt attracted to men. I always felt different and anxious. I just did not know what to do, so I went to see the Imam at one of the mosques here for advice. I went to the Imam and told him that I was starting to feel very depressed and that I did not know what to do. I was just beginning to realize that I wanted to be with other men, and not women. The Imam advised me to get married. He said, "everything will be alright when you get married." So I followed his advice and got married to my friend from college. But things didn't get better. I just got more and more confused. I mean my wife and I had sex and everything but something just did not feel right. We eventually divorced.

This experience however, had not negatively impacted Salman's deference to a religious leader in personal matters. Indeed, when I asked if he still had faith in the counsel of religious leaders like Imams, he replied without any hesitation: "Anyone can be wrong. It wasn't the Imam's fault that things didn't work out with my wife." As Salman elaborated on his plans to return to Houston in order to work with a local community health organization, he said, "I can't wait to return. I would love to be in a relationship when I return." Even though Salman embraced his homosexuality after his marriage ended, he maintained a sense of faith in Muslim religious forms of authority, indicating that for my Pakistani Muslim gay interlocutors, Muslim identification is premised on individual negotiations of religious belonging that defy generalities.

My conversations with Aamir, Shahrukh, Salman, and Imran compel a rethinking of dominant and hegemonic understandings of Islam that represent Islam as irrefutably intolerant of homosexuality. Instead the data presented in this chapter suggests the capacity for accommodation in the global Muslim ummah. Indeed, it is this possibility of accommodation in Islam and within the Muslim community that allows my interlocutors to draw on religion as a source of capital in fashioning transnational identities and subjectivities.

Appropriations of Western Categories of Sexuality

My interlocutors self-identified as gay men in part by drawing on Western categories of sexuality and sexual orientation to construct a gay social identity. My interlocutors, who were either born in the United States or came to the United States with their families as teenagers, had appropriated a gay male identity, evidenced through narrative as well as fragments of everyday life and sociality. Significantly, this self-identification coexists with the conception of an ideal romantic friendship in terms of South Asian cultural scripts. The coexistence of "gay" to define "self" and "yaar" to characterize the idealized sexual partner demonstrates a complexly constructed sexuality in which a range of vocabularies and epistemologies intersect each other. These intersections index the hybridity of the Pakistani Muslim American gay men who navigate multiple cultural and epistemological spaces.

Access to media technologies such as the Internet and familiarity with gay businesses and neighborhoods in Houston allow young Pakistani gay men to construct gay identities and forge transnational communities centered on specificities of social locations as Muslim American gay men of Pakistani descent. Indeed, it is in the mass-mediated, deterritorialized gay chat rooms and LISTSERVs on the Internet, in gay bars, clubs, and cafes in Houston, and through serendipitous encounters with each other that connections are made, friendships are forged, and a religiously conceived gay community formed. Aamir's narrative illustrates this.

It was only a couple of months after Aamir had immigrated to the United States that he first began to explore "the gay scene" in Houston through the Internet. Although he hesitated to visit a gay bar or a club, he joined an online Yahoo group for gay Muslims and soon began correspondence with Imran, an eighteen-year-old Pakistani Muslim gay man. Imran's family had resided in the United Arab Emirates since he was a toddler. After completing his high school education in Saudi Arabia, Imran moved to Houston to attend the University of Houston. Aamir attended the same university and met Imran soon after he arrived in Houston. Imran, who was out to his immediate family and living with his married sister and her family in Houston, began exploring the gay bars and clubs in the Montrose District on his own.

Soon after they had met and become friends, Imran asked Aamir to accompany him to a gay bar. Aamir laughed as he recalled:

> I used to be very rigid and thought that I would never go to a gay club or bar. . . . I don't drink and . . . I was not looking to hook up with another guy. . . . I did not want to play around [sexually] with other guys.

In the summer of 2001, during the annual Gay Pride weekend in Houston, Imran insisted that Aamir accompany him to the gay bars in the Montrose District. Aamir was present when Imran recounted that weekend to me. Imran laughed as he remembered: "Aamir was so nervous. He kept looking around to see if someone he knew was there. He kept telling me: 'Let's go home.'" Aamir interjected: "But he took me to JR's . . . it was packed so I felt a little more comfortable. . . . Anyway, we went there and I saw another *desi* [South Asian] guy there so I turned to my friend and said, 'hey there is another *desi* guy here.' We were just standing there watching him and he came up and approached us. It was Shahrukh. We started talking and the three of us became friends after that."

Even as my interlocutors perform and construct a gay identity, they also challenge "gay" as a global category of self-identification that presumes a homogeneous, monolithic identity for all homosexual men (Manalansan 2003). Indeed, much like Filipino gay men in New York City, these men do not see the transnational registers discussed in this essay as a premodern and "prior condition before assimilating into a gay identity" (ibid.: 186). Similar to the bakla in anthropologist Martin Manalansan's ethnographic study, my interlocutors also mobilize culturally specific South Asian scripts, language and cultural idioms, and belonging to Islam "as a way to survive . . . within the racial, ethnic, class and gendered spaces of America" (ibid.).

Indeed, the appropriation of Western terminologies and categorizations of sexuality and sexual orientation by Muslim American gay men is not an affirmation of the "Gay International," that is, the globalization of Western categories of sexual identification and the production of modernity among nonheteronormative communities in the non-West (Altman 2001). Political scientist Joseph Massad (2008), for example, critiques the international human rights regimes in protesting gay rights violations in the Arab world in the name of liberation and freedom as Western imperialism that has had the effect of "destroying social and sexual configurations of desire in the interest of reproducing a world in [their] own image" (14). Although Massad provides valuable insights regarding the problematic modalities for Western gay rights activism in the non-West and especially in Muslim countries, he relegates culturally constructed sexuality among Muslim gay men primarily to acts of sexual penetration and misses the lived experience and the depth, variety, and mythologies around constructions and accommodations of same-sex eroticism and relationships in the non-West.

In spite of the appropriation of Western categories of sexual identification, and participation in the larger LGBTQIA spaces, the experience of racism has undermined the incorporation of communities of color, and contributed to the emergence of South Asian LGBTQIA organizations (Das Gupta 2006).[27] In an anthology of the South Asian gay and lesbian experience in the diaspora, Rakesh Ratti (1993) laments the centrality of whiteness and the marginality of queers of color in mainstream LGBTQIA public cultures and spaces: "There is a patronizing, sometimes indulgent attitude. Cliques of gay white men in the Castro area of San Francisco, for instance, think that they are the center of the universe. They often regard non-white gays as poor, wide-eyed Third Worlders who come to the Castro to sip coffee and pay homage. . . . The acceptance is but surface" (172). Nayan Shah similarly notes the salience of such exclusions in the formation of alternative organizational structures: "In a society where South Asians are rendered either invisible or alien, South Asian queer organizations have developed to create safe spaces. These spaces are defined by race and often displace class difference" (1993: 127).

The appropriation of Western categories of sexuality may be characterized as a political project that emerged to acquire visibility but does not indicate inclusion in the larger American gay communities. Indeed, this political project is undermined through its intersection with post-9/11 racialized categorizations of Muslim Americans as militants, jihadists, and anti-American Islamists and as legitimate objects of state-sanctioned regimes of surveillance and violence. The emergence of homonationalism "corresponds with the coming out of the exceptionalism of American empire. . . . This brand of homosexuality operates as a regulatory script not only of normative gayness, queerness, or homosexuality, but also of the racial and national norms that reinforce these sexual subjects" (Puar 2007: 2). The rise of U.S. homonationalism serves to build support for U.S. regimes of imperialism, including the global war on terrorism, and alienates LGBTQIA Muslims, unless they conform to and perform a state-sanctioned pacified homonormativity.

Given these racialized exclusions, Muslim American gay men and women have formed counterpublics.[28] I had remained in touch with Aamir after I returned from Houston in the autumn of 2002. In the summer of 2003, Aamir called me and was clearly excited and eager to share the "good news" that he recounted to me:

> The founder of Al-Fatiha from Washington, DC, was in Houston recently, and [he] met with me and some of my friends. He wants us to start the Houston Chapter of the Al-Fatiha Organization.

Al-Fatiha takes its name from the title of the first chapter in the Qur'an and means "the opening." Al-Fatiha is a progressive Islamic movement as well as an Internet-based international organization (Minwalla et al. 2005). Al-Fatiha does not have regional offices; rather, it has local chapters in major cities in the United States, Canada, the United Kingdom, and South Africa. Al-Fatiha organizes international conferences that provide safe spaces for men and women to come together and discuss issues relating to spirituality, emotional and mental wellness, "social justice, peace, and tolerance" (ibid.: 116).

The incorporation of Pakistani Muslim American gay men in Houston into a transnational LGBTQIA Muslim organization represents emergent transnational Muslim counterpublics that are intertwined with the politics of queer organizing in the United States. Specifically, as a counterpublic, Al-Fatiha appropriates a Western language of sexual identity centered on LGBTQIA identifications to construct a minority sexual community, and "validates and produces minoritarian public spheres while at the same time offering a potent challenge to the white heteronormativity of majoritarian public spheres" (Halberstam 2005: 128). These counterpublics are mass-mediated via the Internet and exemplify important sites for creating transnational communities, alliances, and networks across national, cultural, and linguistic borders and boundaries. Al-Fatiha is grounded within geographically bound histories and specificities, however. For example, Al-Fatiha emerged in 1997 through the initiative of a Pakistani Muslim American gay male activist (Kugle 2014) and is registered in the United States as a U.S.-based nonprofit nongovernmental organization, exemplifying its intersection with the cultural politics of LGBTQIA visibility, organizing, and activism in the United States.

For my interlocutors discussed in this chapter, Western terminologies and categories of sexuality are only one of the constitutive registers in constructing transnational identity, not a totalizing discourse of selfhood. Muslim American gay men appropriate Western terminologies in constructions of public selfhoods and identity as gay men, and they visit bars, clubs, and cafes in predominantly gay neighborhoods and localities to forge alliances and build friendships with other gay Muslim men. However, these intersections are mediated by the experience of racism, and geopolitical developments such as the post-9/11 U.S.-led war on terrorism and the rise of homonationalism that have had the effect of alienating LGBTQIA Muslim Americans.

Conclusion

In this chapter, a cultural analysis of emergent transnational Muslim American same-sex sexual cultural formations has focused on South Asian scripts of homosociality and same-sex eroticism and relationships, and narrative traditions; the increasing centrality of belonging to a transnational Muslim ummah; and the appropriation of Western terminologies and categories of sexuality in constructing a gay identity. These registers foreground a cultural analysis of everyday negotiations of religion, race, sexuality, and transnationalism among gay Muslim American, and problematize the exclusively heterosexual focus of research on transnational Muslim population movements and community formations in the United States in the early twenty-first century.

Intertwined with such negotiations of religion, race, and transnationality, a nonheteronormative Muslim sexuality acquires visibility and finds expression in South Asian scripts, language, and cultural idioms of homosociality and friendship. The transgressive fluidity of boundaries of friendships illuminates a register of selfhood that situates emergent gay Muslim American sexual cultural and community formations in transnational contexts. The evocation of the genre of personal narrative tale associated with women in Northern Pakistan (Grima 1991) and in narratives of Muslim American gay men included in this research points to a second South Asian cultural script that is mobilized to externalize hopes, fears, and sacrifices associated with sexualized, gendered, and racialized lives as gay diasporic Pakistanis.

Decentering notions of Islam as a militantly heteronormative religious tradition that criminalizes same-sex sexual eroticism and relationships, the lived experience of gay Muslims discussed in this chapter emphasize spaces of accommodation and negotiations of belonging within a global Muslim ummah. Accommodations of same-sex sexuality in premodern Islamic cultures further create possibilities for an inclusive positioning of LGBTQIA Muslims within the ummah. As Islamic scholar, Scott Siraj al-Haqq Kugle (2003) notes: "With the Qur'an's vivid portrayal of diversity at so many levels of the natural and human world, it would be logical to assume that this diversity of creation plays out on the level of sexuality as well. It is also plausible to assert that, if some Muslims find it necessary to deny that sexual diversity is part of the natural created world, then the burden of proof rests on their shoulders to illustrate their denial from the Qur'anic discourse itself" (196).

Even though my interlocutors appropriate and mobilize Western notions of sexuality in constructions of identity, these notions do not represent a totalizing discourse of selfhood and subjectification. Indeed, Muslim American gay men also challenge Western categorizations of sexuality that are premised on a modernist impulse to homogenize complex cultural realities of same-sex eroticism and relationships. These appropriations take place within a larger geopolitical context marked by the rise of U.S. nationalism and nationhood that realigns queer Americans with projects of U.S. imperialism and engagements in the Muslim world. These realignments present a conundrum for Pakistani Muslim gay men like my interlocutors, who draw on Islam in fashioning transnational identity, and illustrate the complexities of emergent transnational Muslim American same-sex sexual cultural formations in the early twenty-first century.

5

The Pakistan Independence Day Festival

The Making of a "Houston Tradition"

The Pakistan Independence Day Festival is a high-profile annual event organized by the Pakistani American Organization[1] in Houston, Texas. According to official estimates released by the organization, on August 11, 2001, between 5,000 and 7,000 men, women, and children in Houston attended the annual Festival, which celebrates the founding of Pakistan as a sovereign nation-state on August 14, 1947. Financed by membership dues, private donations, and corporate sponsorships, the Festival is a major source of revenue for the organization. Advertised as a "family event," the Festival begins early in the evening and continues late into the night.

Independence Day is celebrated on August 14 in Pakistan. In Houston, the Festival takes place on the Saturday closest to August 14 to ensure the widest participation by Pakistani Americans. This flexibility is important because of the Festival's emphasis on catering to its target audience, middle-class families, professionals, and students who might be at work or in school during the workweek. The Festival's Muslim heritage is indexed through the flexible timing of the event with respect not only to Pakistan's independence but also to the Islamic calendar. In 2010 and 2011, for example, the celebrations were deferred for several weeks because of Ramadan, the ninth month of the Islamic calendar, which is marked by fasting, prayer, and worship. Unlike the solar calendar, the dates of the Islamic calendar change each year, moving backward by about eleven days each year depending on the sighting of the new moon. During the years when August 14 falls during Ramadan, the Festival is combined with the three-day-long post-Ramadan Eid celebrations.

From the late 1970s until the mid-1990s, when the small population of a few hundred Pakistani immigrants in Houston first celebrated the founding of their homeland, the Festival took place either at a university auditorium or at a large multipurpose hall in southwest Houston. During the 1970s and 1980s, the Festival was a largely informal and modest cultural event. It provided Pakistani students and families an occasion to socialize around a major commemorative festival selected from the repertoire of celebrations in the homeland. Faisal, a Pakistani male entrepreneur who had been a student in Houston during the 1970s, provided insights into the social life of Pakistanis in Houston during this period. Faisal had arrived in Houston in 1971 to pursue his undergraduate education at the University of Houston. According to Faisal:

> We started going out to clubs . . . if there were an India or a Pakistan Independence Day program, we would attend the program. Hindi movies were initially shown at the University of Houston on a 16mm projector. . . . I don't know how we got them . . . I remember we got *Mughal-e-Azam* (a critically acclaimed and immensely popular Indian film on Muslim Mughal ruler, Akbar) that I saw at least a few times. A few of us were quite involved in putting together private film screenings at the University. We enjoyed the songs and the dialogues in these films. We would also occasionally get together and organize live musical nights - some of us who played a musical instrument would perform. We would also sometimes invite people from the outside [to perform].

Faisal returned to Karachi, Pakistan, in 1988 after completing his degree and building a career in hotel management in Houston. He remained in Pakistan, finding employment at a five-star luxury hotel in Karachi, eventually marrying and raising a family. Still, friendships and associations forged over twenty years routinely brought Faisal back to Houston. It was during one of his trips, in the spring of 2002, that we were introduced to each other through mutual friends and began correspondence. Faisal's memories and experiences of Pakistani solidarity in Houston, notably through participation in Independence Day programs as well as other cultural events, played an important role in his continued relationship with the city.

By the 1990s, in large part as a result of the rapid growth of the Pakistani immigrant population and the thriving South Asian ethnic economy, the Festival became more elaborate and ritualized. The Festival's increased formality and scale is intertwined with a set of seemingly unchanging routines and rituals, which I first observed in August 2001, a month before 9/11. At that time, the celebration took place at the Reliant Astrodome Complex, otherwise known as the Astrodome, a Houston landmark built in 1965. As is customary at most Pakistani public ceremonies and events, the Festival begins with a recitation of several verses from the Qur'an. The recital is followed by an official ceremony that is presided over by the mayor of Houston and the elected officials of the Pakistani American Organization. The ceremony, a linguistic mix of Urdu, English and Arabic, continues. Certain Arabic words such as the *Bis'millah* ("in the name of Allah"), *Al-hamdu'llah* ("praise to Allah"), *Insha'llah* ("if Allah wills it") reveal the widespread use of sacred words as a way for Muslims to recognize other Muslims (Metcalf 1996) and endow the ceremony and social interactions at the Festival with religious meanings.

During the ceremony, certificates of acknowledgment are awarded to preselected members of the local Pakistani community and to Pakistani students who have graduated from private and public primary, middle, and high schools. Pakistani children and youth who have memorized the Qur'an in its entirety are also acknowledged during the ceremony, again indexing the embeddedness of religion at the Festival. The children and youth who finish memorizing the Qur'an earn the title *hafiz*. Becoming a hafiz is an exalted accomplishment and a universal Islamic belief that transcends Muslim sectarian differences. Becoming a hafiz is presumed to bring rewards in the "hereafter," guaranteeing the person entrance to heaven. A hafiz also plays an important role during the month of Ramadan, when the entire Qur'an is recited over thirty days. In the context of the Pakistani community in Houston, being a young hafiz has added significance, symbolizing the relevance of religious education and accomplishments among youth and second-generation Muslim Americans. Honorees make their way to the stage to receive commemorative silver plates inscribed with their names and pose for photographs with the mayor and the officials of the Pakistani American Organization.

Live performances begin almost immediately after the ceremony has concluded. Pakistani children dressed in ethnic attire, representing the ethnolinguistic regions of Pakistan, perform folk and patriotic songs on the makeshift stage in front of hundreds of people sitting in rows of chairs. A concert featuring a musical group from Pakistan invited especially for the occasion sustains the celebratory mood. Next, a local Pakistani theater group performs a play written specifically for the occasion. Rising to moments of high melodrama, the play typically focuses on intergenerational conflict and tensions centered on Pakistani cultural authenticity. For example, during the Festival in 2001, the play focused on a conflict between an older man dressed in traditional Pakistani clothing and a younger man, dressed in western attire—jeans, T-shirt, and a leather jacket. The conflict centered on pervasive concerns that appear in discourses within Pakistani immigrant communities: Is the second generation more American than they are Pakistani? Have they lost their cultural values and become American? Are American and Pakistani identities mutually exclusive? The play ended with an affirmative resolution as the actor representing the second-generation asserted his Pakistani-ness and Muslim identification, and the actor representing the first generation opened his mind to Westernized presentations of self.

A Pakistani food court, an entertainment enclave for children, and almost a hundred stalls of Pakistani businesses, Muslim schools, and Islamic community centers line either side of the Exhibit Hall, providing vibrant and bustling backdrops for the staged performances. Although the exact number and types of Pakistani businesses vary from year to year, it is the high number of local Pakistani businesses that makes the Festival recognizable and familiar to the attendees. The food court offering Pakistani cuisine similarly fulfills an expectation attendees have from the Festival. The mix of individuals present—cohorts of men and women, and families dressed in colorful formal Pakistani attire, or western casual wear—remains unchanged in the visual topography of the Festival.

* * *

The Pakistan Independence Day Festival is a celebratory event that represents long-distance nationalism and diasporic place making. At the

Festival in August 2001, a marching band composed of Shia Ismaili Muslim men performed the Pakistani national anthem. The marching band members were dressed in identical dark blue jackets and trousers, knee-length white boots, and a red, blue and gold lapel crisscrossing the shoulders. I walked toward the entrance of the hall to join the hundreds of people with camcorders and cameras in their hands who had gathered, eager to capture the formal commencement. The mayor of Houston entered the hall, accompanied by the members of his staff and the president of the Pakistani American Organization. The band stopped marching midway through its performance but continued to play the anthem. The mayor and the organization's president walked toward the stage. Once on stage, the ceremony began with a recitation from the Qur'an, followed by a speech by the mayor. In his speech, Mayor Lee Brown congratulated the Pakistani community on Pakistan's Independence Day and emphasized the contribution of Pakistanis to Houston's diversity and economy. At the end of the speech, Mayor Brown presented a certificate to the organization's president and declared August 11, 2001, as Pakistan Day. The mayor shook hands with the board members of the organization and made his way out of the stadium. The president of the organization then proceeded with the ceremony.

The formal commencement of the Pakistan Independence Day Festival in Houston that I describe above invoked in me memories of the Independence Day ceremony and parade in Pakistan and played out strikingly similarly to the festivities in Pakistan. I have vivid memories of watching the ceremony and the parade broadcast live on state-controlled television while growing up in Pakistan. It was a family occasion. The entire family would wake up early. Blurry eyed, my brother and I would make our way to the roof of our house to hoist the flag of Pakistan on a makeshift flagpole. Soon afterward, we would congregate in the living room for a leisurely, traditional holiday brunch of oil-drenched fried bread, sweet halwa, and chickpea curry, and watch the live broadcast of the parade, and subsequent special programming on television. The president of Pakistan, dressed in formal Pakistani attire, led the parade, which included a marching procession of men representing the different branches of the armed forces. Elaborately designed and vibrantly colored floats, each representing an ethnolinguistic region

of Pakistan, combined with the solemnity of the proceedings to com-
memorate the lives of the members of the armed forces and nationalist
leaders who had died during the violent formation of Pakistan in 1947
and during the subsequent wars between India and Pakistan in 1965
and 1971.

In the United States, ethnic celebratory events like the Pakistan Independence Day Festival are ritualized cultural performances that are
important occasions to reflexively and creatively stage a Turner-esque
"social drama" through which specific groups and communities negotiate relationships with multiple regimes of power and authority.[2] Most
studies of South Asian cultural festivals in major cities in the United
States represent such festivals as secular.[3] I argue that the Pakistan Independence Day Festival in Houston is an important occasion for the
production of Islam. As I discuss in this chapter, Islam is integral in
ideologies of Pakistani nationhood and therefore embedded in performances of long-distance nationalism such as the Festival. It is this centrality of Islam that has enabled a reframing of the Festival as a transnational Muslim celebration that is inclusive of Muslim communities
from throughout South Asia. The transnational Muslim heritage economy discussed in chapter 3 has been central to such transformations.
Local Pakistani businesses and private donations finance the Festival
and point to the intertwining of ethnic businesses with festive cultures.

This complexly authored performance is not only bound to diasporic
nationhood, histories, and religion but also intertwined with geopolitical contexts of subjectification. Following 9/11, although Islam continued to shape the Festival's organization and form, the Festival had
also repositioned itself as a Houston tradition authenticating the local
Pakistani communities as Houstonians. The Festival was reframed as
a practice of cultural citizenship through which Pakistani Americans
in Houston made claims to space, rights, entitlements, and privileges
in the United States. As a practice of cultural citizenship, the Festival
became implicated in "racial rearticulations" (Omi and Winant 1986) as
it attempted to mediate fears and vulnerabilities associated with the surveillance of Muslim Americans.[4] Given the post-9/11 hostility toward
Muslims and especially South Asian nationality groups in the United
States, the organizers projected the Festival as a "Houston tradition,"

as I will demonstrate in this chapter, situating the Festival within discourses and practices of multiculturalism in contemporary U.S. society.

The dominant ideology of Pakistani nationhood that is performed at the Festival is built on an imagination of Pakistan as a sovereign nation-state for South Asian Muslims. Pakistan came into existence on August 14, 1947. Its creation came about in large part because of the failure of the volatile decades-long negotiations over power sharing between Muslims and Hindus following the end of British colonial rule, and structural inequalities such as those between Hindu landowners and Muslim laborers in parts of colonial India, that became mapped onto religious oppression.[5] As British rule ended, colonial India was divided into two sovereign nation-states, predominantly Hindu India and predominantly Muslim Pakistan. As examined in much nuance by South Asian historians, the moment of independence from British colonial rule and its aftermath were marked by unprecedented scales of forced migrations of Hindus, Sikhs, and Muslims.[6] Fearing persecution and marginality in Hindu-majority India, Muslims fled with the barest of essentials to territories in Pakistan. Hindu and Sikh communities, who had resided for generations in regions that became a part of Pakistan, similarly feared loss of economic opportunity, social status, and political power under Muslim rule and fled to India. This two-way mass migration was less than an orderly, systematic, and peaceful process. These mass migrations resulted in widespread Hindu-Muslim-Sikh violence, mass rapes, arson attacks, mass abductions, and forced religious conversions.[7]

In spite of such violent histories surrounding Pakistan's formation, the partition of British colonial India is represented in official Pakistani historiographies as a celebratory moment of freedom from Hindu majoritarian rule, the inevitable creation of a safe haven for Muslims of colonial India, a victory of Islam in the Indian subcontinent, and the unification of all Muslims of the subcontinent (Bose and Jalal 1996). Scars and silences around the atrocities and violence persist to this day, as evidenced in the celebratory narratives of freedom and postcolonial sovereignty that are performed on occasions such as the Independence Day Festival in Pakistan and among Pakistani communities in cities like Houston. The embeddedness of a religious imperative in constructions of Pakistani nationhood indexes the Islamization of the Festival.

Islamicizing the Festival

The embeddedness of Islam in the Festival and within institutional structures such as the Pakistan American Organization of Houston became apparent during the course of my interview in November 2001 with Mohammad Omar, the president of the organization and the organizer of the annual Pakistan Independence Day Festival:

MOHAMMAD OMAR (MO): We do not have programs where liquor is consumed or served.

AHMED AFZAL (AA): Is that because of religious reasons?

MO: Yes, people are not allowed to bring their own liquor [to the events].

AA: This has been the case since the inception of the organization?

MO: Well . . . let's say since 1986.

AA: Why, did something happen in 1986 to make this the official policy?

MO: It was something that was always understood. But at one time it was violated and when that happened . . . we made a clear policy . . . that we would not allow the consumption of alcohol [at our events]. We would not provide it and no one [would be allowed to] bring it to the events.

    The second thing that I did once I got elected [as the Pakistan Organization's President] was to change [the Organization's] bank accounts into non-interest based accounts. . . . We did this because many of our members are Muslims. They felt that the organization's accounts should be interest free [in accordance with Islamic precepts that prohibit the accumulation of interest on monies invested].

    The third thing is that there is no mixed [gender] dancing at any of our events. There really isn't even any dancing by women on the stage at formal events because that is not really looked up to. Because see, all of our events are family based events. We do not have events that cater to singles, for example. We have events in which young people participate in large numbers but all of our events are family oriented programs. So all of our programs reflect that—the family values—to make sure that there is no [display of] revealing dresses on the stage, or any loose [sexually inappropriate] song being played . . . or mixed dancing on the stage. *This is a part of our Pakistani culture that we want to preserve* [my emphasis].

The observance of the alcohol prohibition, the restrictions on mixed-gender dancing on stage, and the definition of permissible attire for men and women at the Festival construct Pakistani normative social behavior and public life as irrefutably Islamic. At the Festival, a cordoned-off section for holding communal evening prayers further emphasizes the portability of Islamic rituals in place-making practices. In the construction and performance of a transnational Pakistani nationhood, the Festival fetishizes ancestral affiliations in terms of Islam, the faith of most but not all Pakistani immigrants in Houston. Although the majority of attendees at the Festival are Sunni Muslims, the religious community constructed at the Festival transcends national, cultural, sectarian, and ideological divisions within Islam.

The fetishizing of the homeland (Naficy 1993) as Muslim is a partial representation of Pakistani history and heritage that renders invisible the country's religious diversity. Nonetheless, the fetishizing has had the effect of allowing for the inclusion of non-Pakistani Muslim groups, notably Muslims from India and Bangladesh, within a religiously conceived Pakistani nation. This became evident in my conversation with Omar. As we spoke about the profile of the majority of members of the organization, Omar's response pointed to this reconfiguration of the Pakistan Independence Day Festival as a transnational South Asian Muslim festive culture:

> MO: The membership of the Pakistani-American Organization has always
> been open to all people of Pakistani origin, which we interpret as all
> the people from the sub-continent. So we have Muslims from India
> who are a part of the organization [and] have served on the Board of
> the Pakistan Organization also [my emphasis].
>
> AA: Really?
>
> MO: Yes, we felt that [in terms of] culture and religion we have a lot of
> commonalities, and we also share a lot of common social activities,
> so why not bring them to the platform. And I think this is the right
> approach. We should be more inclusive. But as you know, lately the
> [South Asian] community has grown so much . . . it is so big, that it
> is mostly Pakistanis who are members, but yes, we have some Indian
> Muslims and Bangladeshis who are members . . . we don't discriminate on this basis.

The inclusive positioning of Muslim immigrants from India and Bangladesh by the Festival organizers illustrates a complex strategy for constructing transnational belonging in terms of religion. The strategy to include Muslims from India and Bangladesh within a religiously conceived Pakistani nationhood affirms the official ideology that imagines Pakistan as the homeland for all South Asian Muslims.

The inclusion of Muslims from India and Bangladesh in constructions of a transnational Pakistani nationhood finds interlocutors within Pakistani immigrants in Houston because of the global transformation in religious belonging and revivalism in the early twenty-first century that has had the effect of subordinating affiliations with an ancestral homeland to religion.[8] In the case of the Indian diaspora in the United States, for example, Hindu and Muslim Indian immigrants are implicated in political struggles over the definition of "Indian-ness." Since the 1990s, right-wing Hindu religious groups have acquired increasing visibility and influence in establishing the terms of Indian identity and nationhood.[9] These religious organizations are not only influential sources of power and authority in India but also assert a strong presence among Indian communities in the United States (Prashad 2000). The development of Muslim religious infrastructure, such as mosques, community centers, and Islamic schools, similarly connects Pakistani Muslims to Muslim communities from elsewhere in South Asia and beyond, and plays increasingly central roles in defining Pakistani-ness in relation to Islam. The refashioning of a Pakistani cultural festival must also be attributed to the shared Muslim experiences of objectification, persecution, and surveillance by American statecraft, and in projects of governmentality. The Festival then provides a celebratory space for the affirmation of emergent religious alliances, networks, and affiliations in post-9/11 U.S.

Representations of a Muslim Festival in the Local Pakistani Media

In Houston, dominant ideologies of Pakistani nationhood that are premised on belonging to Islam are also discursively produced in Pakistani media, notably the weekly English-language Pakistani newspaper, *The Pakistan Chronicle,* as well as on Pakistani radio programs.[10] *The*

Pakistan Chronicle prints a pre-Festival multipage special supplement that carries advertisements paid for by Houston-based Pakistani businesses and professionals. Messages take up an entire page or half a page and include personalized greetings on Pakistan's Independence.

A consideration of a few of the celebratory messages that appeared in the special edition supplement during the week prior to the Festival in 2001 provides insight into the ways in which ideologies of Pakistani nationhood circulate globally through locally produced Pakistani media in Houston and intersect with the transnational Muslim heritage economy. These mass-mediated representations resemble messages and nationalist rhetoric that dominate the state-controlled media, notably television and radio in Pakistan, during the weeks leading up to the Independence Day celebrations in Pakistan. A photograph of Mohammad Ali Jinnah, a Muslim nationalist leader and the first president of Pakistan, frames the front page of the special edition. A black-and-white photograph of Jinnah is juxtaposed with a flowing Pakistani national flag. Beneath the newspaper's name, large green lettering announces "We Are Here!" Below this assertive pronouncement of arrival and presence in Houston are photographs of six different Pakistanis who will be recognized in the awards ceremony at the festival. The text carries a statement attributed to Jinnah that reads:

> At this supreme moment [of Pakistan's Independence], my thoughts are with those valiant fighters in our cause who readily sacrificed all they had, including their lives, to make Pakistan possible. . . . Those of our brethren who are minorities in Hindustan may rest assured that we shall never neglect or forget them. . . . I recognize that it is the Muslim minority provinces in this subcontinent who were pioneers and carried the banner aloft for the achievement of our cherished goal of Pakistan.

In these celebratory messages, visual images are integral to the message conveyed. In several advertisements, in addition to the photographs of eminent Muslim nationalist leaders, photographs of local public officials are placed prominently. As a system of representation (Hall 1997), these visual images are codes that intend to produce and represent legitimacy through invocation of a relationship or affiliation with a higher and recognizable public authority. Meaning, as cultural

THE PAKISTAN INDEPENDENCE DAY FESTIVAL >> 163

- We as proud Pakistanis celebrate our country's Independence Day: Long Live Pakistan.
- All Car Bare Center and Body Shop would like to take this opportunity to remind all our country's people that Pakistan, the land of the pure, was created for the Muslims of Indian sub-continent. Let us not forget millions of men, women and children freedom fighters that made the ultimate sacrifice. We are a proud Pakistani American community. Pray for a stronger Pakistan.
- Attorney and Counselor at Law would like to congratulate the entire Pakistani community [on] a very happy 54th birthday of Pakistan, and would like to salute all the freedom fighters — especially the founding father, Quaid-e-Azam Mohammad Ali Jinnah, and the poet of the East, Dr. Allama Iqbal.
- We hope and pray that this anniversary lays a foundation for further uniting and organizing Pakistanis [from] coast to coast and from Mehran to Khyber Pass.
- Congratulations to the Government of Pakistan and the Pakistani community for being the atomic power!
- Mohammad Ali Jinnah: A leader who stood to carve out an independent homeland for Muslims. His vision of Pakistani progress, prosperity, and self-reliance is becoming a reality. Be Proud Pakistani Americans.
- American First National Bank would like to congratulate all the Pakistani community on their 54th Independence Day.
- We should take a moment here, and reflect on what we can do to enhance the prestige and status of the great people of Pakistan.

Fig. 5.1. Advertisements, *Pakistan Chronicle*, August 2001

theorist Stuart Hall has argued, depends "not on the material quality of the sign, but on its symbolic function" (ibid.: 26). Further, "it is social actors who use the conceptual systems of their culture and the linguistic and other representational systems to construct meaning, to make the world meaningful and to communicate about that world meaningfully to others" (ibid.: 25). Photographs of Mohammad Ali Jinnah serve to create a representational affiliation between individual middle-class Pakistani immigrants and Pakistani nationalist leaders. Just as the photographs of Muslim nationalist leaders invoke long-distance nationalism, the photographs of the mayor of Houston posing with a Pakistani entrepreneur fulfill a similar function by implying a personal relationship and affiliation with local forms of power and authority.

In Houston, it is through these concrete mass-mediated representational practices that Pakistani entrepreneurs and middle class professionals attempt to authenticate and perform a long-distance Pakistani nationalism. In these messages, themes of nationalism, freedom, struggle and sacrifice, unity, and nuclear strength (see figure 5.1) serve as symbolic codes through which to fetishize Pakistani history, heritage, and past primarily through the lens of the dominant ideology of Pakistani nationhood. Moreover, invoking discourses centered on Pakistan as the nation for all South Asian Muslims, these advertisements also include Indian Muslims. Note for example, Jinnah's statement in the advertisement: "Those of our brethren who are minorities in Hindustan may rest assured that we shall never neglect or forget them." I return to this particular issue later in the chapter when discussing ongoing transformations of the Festival in Houston.

At moments such as the Pakistan Independence Day anniversary celebrations, the geographical distance that separates Pakistan from Pakistanis in Houston is dissolved. A reterritorialized Pakistani nationhood, community, and identity are produced and performed at the Festival and represented through visual and textual messages in Pakistani mass media. It is, for example, the Pakistani owner of the All Car Bare Center and Body Shop, or the American First National Bank based in Houston, who invokes themes of sacrifice and pride. It is not a territorially ambiguous professional, but a locally identifiable attorney in Houston, who celebrates Pakistan's independence.

Festive Cultures and the Transnational Muslim Heritage Economy

In the early twenty-first century, local nodes in the transnational Muslim heritage economy provide the requisite financial capital to organize ethnic festivals in the United States.[11] In turn, festival organizers commodify ethnicity, religion, nationhood, and heritage, presenting them as goods to be purchased.[12] At the Festival, the stalls of Pakistani businesses are evidence of a locally thriving Pakistani ethnic economy. These businesses purchase stalls and participate in the Festival with a market-driven imperative. For Pakistani businesses and professionals, the Festival provides a unique and high-profile opportunity to display and advertise a range of consumer products and services targeting a niche Muslim consumer. Businesses include insurance companies, real estate and travel agents, fashion boutiques, video and audio retail outlets for Pakistani and Indian music and films, and Pakistani clothing and accessories for women. Other stalls advertise the services of immigration lawyers, Disc Jockeys and video recording services for private social gatherings.

The presence of distinctively Pakistani material goods and services is far more than a display of merchandise, however. It is a feast for all the senses, where one can see, hear, and taste Pakistani-ness.[13] Sensory perceptions are vital conduits of cultural memory and cultural otherness for ethnic groups in multicultural societies in the West.[14] In the case of the Cultural Festival of India in New Jersey, for example, "food accrues considerable significance . . . because of the sheer number of social practices (weddings, deaths and religious ceremonies and rituals) that occur around the preparation and consumption of food in Indian culture" (Shukla 1997: 229).[15] Similarly, at the Festival in Houston, Pakistani cuisine is a significant site in the commodification of Pakistani cultural heritage.[16]

Pakistani cuisine assumes an important function as a site for endowing authenticity and a register for invoking nostalgia for the homeland during the Festival. In spite of the wide array of Pakistani businesses present at the Festival, the Pakistani restaurants are easily the most popular venues for attendees. The aesthetics of Pakistani cuisine—the colors, aroma, and flavors of Pakistani spices and foods—create a sensory perception of Pakistani authenticity at the Festival. The stall of Sheikh Chili's Restaurant, one of the oldest and most successful Pakistani restaurants in southwest Houston, is among the more popular businesses present. The bustle of people at the restaurant's stall adds to the air of festivities.

Excitement built in the weeks leading up to the August 2001 Festival, when Pakistani businesses, which prominently displayed the Pakistani national flag, offered special sales and discounts as a part of a mix of festivities and conspicuous consumption. For example, on the night before the Festival, Funplex Family Complex hosted a live concert featuring popular Pakistani musical artists specially invited from Pakistan. Funplex, a Pakistani-owned and -managed multipurpose entertainment facility, features an air-conditioned amusement park, two cinema theaters that screen first-run Hindi-language Indian films several times daily, a bowling alley, restaurants, and a video game arcade.

Pakistani radio programs, broadcast on three AM frequencies throughout Greater Houston, aired a series of eclectic programs and business promotions before and during the Festival. Several radio programs invited local community and religious leaders for live on-air chats to discuss key events in Pakistan's history as well as the life of Pakistani Muslim nationalist leaders. Prerecorded Pakistani patriotic songs were played repeatedly throughout the broadcasts. Several radio programs invited school children—second-generation Pakistanis—to the studios to participate in quizzes on Islam and Pakistan's history and culture. Prizes given to children who answer a question correctly included Muslim prayer mats, copies of the Qur'an, and free dinners at local restaurants. Other radio programs engaged with the listeners in similarly creative ways, inviting listeners to call in and sing patriotic songs, recite verses from the Qur'an, and answer questions relating to Pakistan's history.

While the Festival is deeply embedded in the transnational Muslim heritage economy, following 9/11, the Festival was repositioned as a Houston celebration in large part to mediate the racialized othering of Muslim communities. This repositioning illustrates the active engagements between festive cultural formations and exigencies of geopolitical contexts of subjectification. Moreover, such repositioning brings to the fore the role of the organizers as architects of the Festival who reshape symbolic meanings associated with the Festival.

9/11 and the Making of a "Houston Tradition"

> The Pakistan Independence Day Festival is the biggest public event organized by a Pakistani community organization not just in Houston but also anywhere in the United States. Over 7,000 people attended it last year. . . . It has become a Houston tradition.
> —President, the Pakistani American Organization of Greater Houston[17]

The post-9/11 civic engagements and oral life history narrative of Mohammad Omar, referenced earlier in the chapter, illustrate active decision making on the part of the organizers to characterize the Festival as a Houston tradition. This characterization frames the Festival as a practice of cultural citizenship that is central in claiming rights, privileges, and entitlements as U.S. citizens.

In November 2001, two months after the Festival, I spoke at length with Mohammad Omar, an important Pakistani community leader activist in Houston and one of the primary organizers of the Pakistan

Independence Day Festival. Much had changed since I attended the Festival in August 2001. September 11 had had a devastating effect on Muslim Americans in the United States. In the weeks and months following September 11, several hundred Muslim men with ancestral affiliations in the Gulf States, the Middle East, and South Asia were interrogated, deported, or detained in police custody. At this moment of increased hostility toward Muslims and scrutiny of Muslim infrastructure and institutions, Pakistani American community leaders and activists like Omar found it politically expedient to become involved with mainstream politics, influence public policy and opinion, and defuse popular perceptions of Muslim Americans as militants, terrorists, and foreigners.

In the months following the attacks, it seemed that Omar was everywhere. Less than a week after the terrorist attacks of 9/11, a Pakistani-owned and -managed auto mechanic shop was torched and vandalized by unidentified motorists near Bissonnet Street in southwest Houston. The arson attack contributed to heightened fears and vulnerabilities within the Muslim American community in Houston. The attack was the subject of news reports and feature stories in mainstream and Pakistani ethnic media. In most of the media coverage of the arson attack, Omar was just as prominent, if not more so, than the actual victims of the attack. Indeed, the arson attack appeared to be visually and textually mediated through Omar's figure and words. Omar appeared on several Pakistani radio programs to discuss the arson attack and reiterate his support for anyone experiencing such violent reprisals. In the *Pakistan Chronicle*, the report of the arson attack included a prominent photograph of Omar with his arms around the son of the business owner, offering support and counsel. Another article on the attack published in the *Houston Chronicle*, the oldest and largest circulating English-language newspaper locally, also quoted Omar at length:

> I condemn this act of cowardice, this chaos in the world. Why do innocent people have to be victims? Why do we have to go through this? It is sad that anyone is questioning our patriotism. We should remain calm even in the face of people's bigotry. People should live their normal lives . . . don't argue with anyone. . . . I appeal to the community to please stay calm. (Pugh 2001)

Emphasizing the severity and seriousness of the arson attack, Omar stated that his office had received calls from Pakistani business owners fearful of reprisals after the terrorist attacks. "All this is very sad for us," Omar said concluding his plea.

A few days later, in a large hall in a nondescript strip mall on Bissonnet Street, nearly a hundred individuals had gathered in a demonstration of interfaith solidarity with the local Muslim communities. Omar as well as representatives from all major Muslim, Jewish, and Christian religious organizations and communities constituted the panel of speakers. The meeting provided an important public forum to discuss the reported harassment of and violence toward Muslims locally and nationally. The atmosphere was somber as representatives discussed the radically transformed political climate in the country. All representatives proposed specific initiatives to promote a more modern and assimilative vision of Islam. "I took the lead to organize this meeting," Omar tells me. "Through the programs at the Pakistani American Organization of Greater Houston, we hope to promote a greater understanding and knowledge of Islam."

Less than a month following the terrorist attacks, a national television network featured a panel discussion with prominent Muslim leaders in Houston to discuss the relationship between Muslim immigrants, Islam, and global terrorism. The panelists included representatives from locally based Muslim religious organizations. Again, Omar was featured as one of the panelists. On this occasion however, Omar was identified as the spokesperson for the Islamic Society of Greater Houston, the local chapter of the international Islamic Society of North America. Speaking on the occasion, Omar emphasized the need for increased interfaith outreach, including "opening the doors of mosques to non-Muslims so that they can learn about Islam. We should encourage Muslims to visit their neighbors [and] approach people in their neighborhoods and educate Americans about Islam. . . . Terrorism has nothing to do with Islam. In fact, it contradicts completely the teachings of Islam."

Omar's active mediation between mainstream and Muslim Houston is critical for understanding his characterization of the Festival as a Houston tradition and part of a broader civic engagement. Such civic engagements are similarly intended to diffuse the perception of

Pakistani Muslim Americans as terrorists, and to emphasize their position as Houstonians embedded in the local community. This self-presentation as Houstonian appears as a salient theme in Omar's oral life history narrative.

Mohammad Omar: "Houston Is Very Much Like the City I Am From"

Mohammad Omar was born in Pakistan in 1950. Most of his extended family had migrated from colonial India to Pakistan and settled in cities in the Punjab in the years following the creation of Pakistan in 1947. Omar's father, a bureaucrat in the newly established Pakistani government, was assigned to the city of Hyderabad in the province of Sindh. In 1974, Omar completed his engineering degree and began his professional career at an engineering firm in the city of Karachi. Subsequently, Omar entered the public service commission's exam and, at twenty-four years of age, was assigned to the Pakistan Power and Water Department in the Government of Pakistan.

I interviewed Omar at his multistory mansion in a posh multiethnic suburb in southwest Houston. He began by describing his early life in Pakistan. He beamed with discernible pride as he talked about the value of the education he received in Pakistan, and the opportunities afforded to him:

> There really was no other way that I could have received the education that I did receive, had it not been for the system of Pakistani education. Then to be able to go to engineering school—I could afford it and I had the opportunity to learn English. I could come here because of my education in Pakistan. So I owe everything—whatever I have achieved—to Pakistan. I think the Pakistani nation has made tremendous sacrifices for people like me to get here and we tend to forget that sometimes.

In spite of bright prospects for career growth in Pakistan, Omar aspired to come to the United States to pursue higher education. He had recently married a doctor when he received a letter from the University of Illinois accepting him into the graduate program in civil engineering. Family discussions followed regarding the desirability of moving to the United States only six weeks after his marriage. Omar left his wife in Karachi, where she was pursuing her residency, and traveled to the Midwest in spring of 1976 to begin his graduate education. His wife joined him soon after. When Omar completed his education, the couple relocated to New York City, where they lived for a few years and started to raise a family. In 1980, Omar and his family moved to Houston where they had lived since. As a highly skilled professional, Omar traveled first to the Midwest, then to New York City, and finally planted roots in Houston. "We love Houston" Omar said with undisguised pride and affection for his home as he continued:

> Houston is very much like the city I am from—not on the same scale— but Houston is also the kind of city where everyone knows everyone else. It is not like New York where no one knows anybody. In Houston, you tend to see the same faces and you kind of know who everyone is, and that is what [my hometown of] Hyderabad was all about. Hyderabad was a small town, where everyone knew everyone. And the weather is more to our liking as well. We never liked the snow in New York. Houston is also an inexpensive place. Since we moved, it has been the best thing for us.

When I mention his presence at public forums and interfaith activities following 9/11, Omar smiles:

> No one outside our community knew of the Pakistani American Organization before 9/11. It was just a community-based organization. We are not a [numerically] strong community like say, the Mexican or the Chinese communities, but after 9/11, people in Houston know about the organization. In fact, the organizers of interfaith activities turned to us to learn more about Pakistani immigrants in Houston. I take pride in that . . . that I now have a public forum and can use it to dispel misconceptions about Muslims.

Omar thoughtfully shared his concerns regarding the vulnerable situation of Muslim immigrants in the United States following 9/11:

> The events of 9/11 have been a huge setback for Muslims in the United States . . . there is no question about it. There is a tremendous amount of . . . anxiety to the point of hatred among Americans against individuals

who they believe are responsible for September 11. A lot of the people here cannot differentiate between terrorists and Muslims. They blame entire nationality groups and religious communities. This perception is certainly a cause of concern for us. In the last two decades, we had made so much effort to become involved in public life and inter-faith activities, and network with other religious groups in the city. . . . Just recently, the Pakistani American Organization provided money and volunteers to aid local communities during the floods in Houston. Most of the families who were affected were not Pakistanis but we felt it was our responsibility and obligation as citizens of this country and as Houstonians to help in any way that we could. 9/11 completely undermined these efforts. It is almost as if we have to start all over again. It is just very sad.

Omar's remarks demonstrate his keen awareness of the gulf between Muslim Americans and other Americans in spite of his personal and civic engagements in Houston. His discussion of local crises during which local Pakistani communities initiated outreach activities, for instance, illustrates efforts to situate Pakistani Muslims within the local milieu as Houstonians.

Given the vulnerability and the emerging visibility of Pakistani immigrants in the public sphere in the United States, it was not surprising that during our conversation Omar repeatedly referred to the Festival as "a Houston tradition" and characterized Pakistani immigrants as Houstonians. Omar's characterization of a Pakistani cultural celebration that invokes long-distance Pakistani nationalism and belonging to Islam as "a Houston tradition" may well have been shaped by the fear of persecution, intense government scrutiny, and the police detention of Muslim immigrants.

Aligned with such rearticulation of the Festival, Omar and the other Festival organizers attempted to rearticulate Pakistani ethnoreligious identity. A few months after the September 11 attacks, for example, the Pakistan Organization changed its name from the Pakistan Organization of Greater Houston to the Pakistani *American* Organization of Greater Houston. This renaming was a politically expedient act through which the organization attempted to position itself, and the Pakistani immigrant population, within the fabric of U.S. society and emphasize its "Americanness."

Omar's depiction of the Festival as "a Houston tradition" is also significant because it points to a strategic reframing of the festival as a vitally important practice of cultural citizenship.[18] As Sunaina Maira astutely notes, "Cultural citizenship is an important notion for South Asian Americans because legal citizenship is not enough to guarantee protection under the law with the state's War on Terror, as is clear from the profiling, surveillance, and even detention of Muslim Americans who are U.S. citizens" (2009: 82). Cultural citizenship allows minorities to establish themselves as communities with distinct social claims while also placing themselves in the broader context of mainstream U.S. society.

At the same time, Omar perceived 9/11 as having "completely undermined these efforts." As he said to me: "It is almost as if we have to start all over again." The active civic engagements in interfaith dialogue and outreach, a strategic repositioning of the Festival as a Houston tradition, and the change in the organization's name emerge as strategies for starting over. These rearticulations find expression in Omar's hope for greater engagement of the second-generation in mainstream political society. Elaborating on this, Omar said to me:

> We have to [use this] as an opportunity to create good will for ourselves. No matter how many times I, as a representative of the Pakistani community here, speak on the radio or to the press, it will not have the same impact as each member of our community taking this responsibility seriously and talking to his or her neighbors, customers, coworkers, and friends about Islam and Muslims. Opportunities are all around us. We need to use every opportunity to create a positive image of our community and religion.

Omar paused before continuing:

> I think now more than ever, we need the younger generation in our community to take an active leadership role in our communities and become more involved in the political process in the country. I see young Pakistani Americans serving as interns at city hall . . . and it is really encouraging to me. I really do believe that the younger generation is the bridge

between Muslim Americans and American society and we have to look at them to defuse the hatred toward Muslims.

Omar's optimism points him toward a more hopeful future. His sense of opportunity prevails despite an oppressive context. Indeed, his hope "to defuse the hatred" lies in the civic mindedness and participation in American institutions by the younger generation, as he repeatedly emphasized to me.

From an Indoor Festival to an Outdoor Parade

By the year 2001, the Independence Day celebrations, which had originated in the 1970s on a much more modest scale, had transformed into an elaborate event and a complex practice of long-distance nationalism, transnational belonging, and cultural citizenship that was attended by thousands of South Asian Muslims. It is a testament to the dynamic nature of cultural celebrations that the Festival had taken a new form by the year 2009, as shown in the Parade organizers' message (figure 5.2).[19]

Aslaam O Alaikum—Maire Humwatano [translation: May Allah's greetings be with you, my fellow countrymen]

The great nations rise to occasion when given a challenge. It will be the first time ever we are going to celebrate Pakistan Day Independence Celebrations by parading the streets of our great city of Houston, TX.

This celebration is to share our great heritage of Pakistan with U.S.A. And let this great society be made aware that Pakistan has stood shoulder to shoulder against terrorism and has made tremendous sacrifices.

In a recent military action within Pakistan four million people were displaced in order to crush the terrorists. When we join hands on August 16, parading the downtown Houston streets we will show our solidarity here and abroad.

This parade is a moment of pride and celebration shared by each one of us. Each one of us has a role to play to make this parade one for the memories.

Pakistan Day Parade will feed homeless people working with Star of Hope and have a blood center on the day of the Parade to bring our great society together.

Your enthusiasm and support has left us spellbound and invigorating. We look forward to march with our young generation leading our parade as leaders of tomorrow.

Thank you and God Bless Us All.

Pakistan Zindabad! America Zindabad! [Translation: Long Live Pakistan! Long Live America!]

Fig. 5.2. Organizer Message, Pakistan Day Parade, Houston 2009

The venue for the Festival shifted from the Reliant Stadium complex, home of the Astrodome, to an open-air parade through five city blocks that concluded at Tranquility Park in downtown Houston. Parades claim public space differently from Festivals in that the use of city streets rather than an enclosed space significantly increases engagement with the wider city. Indeed, Omar's emphasis on educating Americans about Islam and Pakistani heritage came to fruition in some ways through this change of venue, which obligates public interaction. Children and families parading in festive clothing, smiling and singing, through a cultural celebration that includes outsiders also has the effect of humanizing people.

Furthermore, Tranquility Park was a symbolic site for ending the Parade. The Pakistan Day Parade website provided the following historical background and description for Tranquility Park:

> Tranquility Park, named for the Sea of Tranquility, is filled with grassy embankments and serene pools while situated right next to City Hall in downtown Houston. The cool oasis of fountains and walkways was built to commemorate the first landing on the moon by the Apollo 11 Mission. Opening to visitors in 1979, the park was dedicated on the tenth anniversary for the first lunar landing. Neil Armstrong's words from the moon "Houston, Tranquility base here; The Eagle has Landed" are written in many languages on plaques placed at the entrance of the park. The mounds and depressions on the park's surface represent the cratered lunar surface.[20]

This description situates the Pakistan Day celebrations much more overtly within the local milieu by emphasizing Tranquility Park's uniquely American roots. In so doing, the Parade organizers reaffirm the Festival as a "Houston" event that is intertwined with American memories and imaginaries associated with the Park. The first moon landing was an extraordinary story of human ingenuity and American achievement. Tranquility Park is also the venue for ethnic and community-centered events such as the Children's Festival and the Houston International Festival, further situating the Pakistan Day Parade within local genealogies of festive celebrations. Moreover, as the organizers said in their message, "it will be the first time ever we are going to celebrate Pakistan Day Independence celebrations by parading the streets of our great city of Houston, Texas."

Such self-reflexive realignments of the Pakistani community within a multiethnic and multireligious local milieu point to a metaphoric coming out of the Pakistani community into mainstream American society. That coming out is punctuated by bringing the Pakistani community to the mayor, by finishing the parade at the park near city hall, by standing "shoulder to shoulder against terrorism," and by caring for Houston's poor. It represents an active engagement with sources of power and authority to diffuse perceptions of the foreignness of the Festival and to rearticulate transnational Pakistani Muslim festive cultures as part of diverse cityscape. The respatializing makes the Festival into a more self-conscious performance of cultural citizenship mediated through long-distance nationalism to Pakistan and transnational belonging to Islam in a post-9/11 U.S. society. Recall the organizer's message: "When we join hands on August 16, parading the downtown Houston streets, we will show our solidarity."

Houston-based South Asian radio programs (the subject of next chapter) and Internet-based social media and networking websites had also acquired greater significance as the Pakistan Day celebrations become more public, and available for consumption by outsiders. The 2009 parade was sponsored by ten South Asian radio programs and newspapers. The parade organizers also maintained Facebook and Twitter pages with regular updates and news about the parade and uploaded video clips of the event on YouTube and other public media streaming websites, indicating by all measures that the Festival had entered the twenty-first-century world of social media. These media practices also point to how the Festival was poised to transform further, evolving into a more democratized and mass-mediated practice of cultural citizenship and transnational belonging.

Conclusion

The Pakistan Independence Day Festival, a celebratory event that marks Pakistan's formation as a nation-state in 1947, was first organized in Houston in the 1970s at rented public halls or university auditoriums as intimate and informal affairs, occasions for the nascent Pakistani population made up primarily of students to socialize and build community. With the rapid increase in the Pakistani population and the growth and development of South Asian ethnic and religious infrastructure and enterprises since the late 1980s, the Festival turned into an elaborate celebration that took place at the Reliant Astrodome complex. The Festival began to include live musical performances, staged dramatic skits on the theme of diasporic Pakistani nationalism, stalls of local South Asian businesses and services, Muslim organizations and community centers, and a food court featuring cuisine from several Pakistani restaurants in Houston.

Islam is embedded in ideologies of Pakistani nationhood that are performed at the Festival and circulate within the larger Pakistani ethnoreligious environment in Houston. Given the intersection of nationhood and religion in official Pakistani nationalism, Islam has been central in the structure and proceedings at the Festival. The late 1990s, however, marked a critical transformation of the Festival as a transnational Muslim festive culture rather than simply a Pakistani cultural festive tradition that was inclusive of Muslims with ancestral affiliations to postcolonial nations in South Asia. These transformations occurred in concert with the emergence of the transnational Muslim heritage economy in Houston that provides much of the financing for the Festival.

The Festival reveals a tremendous capacity for adapting to local developments as well as geopolitical contexts of subjectification that enable its characterization as a practice of cultural citizenship. Conceptualized through the lens of cultural citizenship, the Pakistan Day Festival is an affirmation of the empowered role of Pakistanis in defining their interests as a racially marked ethnoreligious minority group. These adaptations are guided by the organizers, such as Omar. Following 9/11, the change in the name of the organization that plans the Festival from the Pakistan Organization of Greater Houston to the Pakistani American Organization of Greater Houston, and the characterization of the Festival as a "Houston tradition," indicate the deployment of festive cultures to lay claim to rights, privileges, entitlements, and space in a diverse metropolis. Moreover, these changes in the Festival provide a context for Pakistani Americans to position themselves as Houstonians and as U.S. citizens, engage issues of socioeconomic and political inequalities, invisibility, and marginality, and mediate the vulnerabilities and the threat of persecution, surveillance, and objectification by government agencies. The Pakistan Day Festival is produced out of "negotiating the often ambivalent and contested relations with the state and its hegemonic forms that establish the criteria of belonging within a national population and territory" (Ong 1996: 738). The transformation of the Festival from an indoor event into an open-air parade that ends at a venue associated with multicultural events and city government further reframes the Festival as a Houston tradition and as a practice of cultural citizenship, situating Houston's Pakistani communities within specificities of the local milieu.

6

"Pakistanis Have Always Been Radio People"

Transnational Media, Business Imperatives, and Homeland Politics

Radio is a ubiquitous presence in Pakistani public life in Houston. For the Pakistani community that is dispersed throughout the greater Houston metropolitan area, radio is a site of connectivity and convergence that transcends boundaries of class, gender, generation, and geography. In 2001, there were fifteen Pakistani radio programs on the air (see tables 6.1–6.3), a high number even for a city with one of the largest Pakistani populations in the United States. A decade later, in 2011, the number had increased to more than twenty programs. As an assemblage of "expertise, material circuitry, listening practices, and sound" (Bessire and Fisher 2012: 20), radio exceeds "any singular heuristic and entails putting multiple interpretative frameworks to work" (ibid.). Pakistani radio in Houston, for example, may be conceptualized as a community-based initiative, a business venture intertwined with the transnational Muslim heritage economy, a mass-mediated practice of diasporic nationhood and transnational religious belonging, or a practice of cultural citizenship.

The Houston-based Pakistani radio programs provide a number of benefits: news reports focusing on culture and politics in South Asia, the Muslim world, and beyond; culturally specific entertainment such as airplays of Indian and Pakistani songs and music; information about local South Asian businesses and services and a calendar of local South Asian cultural and religious events; and a venue for advertising South Asian ethnic businesses based in Houston.[1] Mohammad Omar, whose narrative appears in the preceding chapter, routinely appeared on these radio programs as an invited panelist or as a promoter for an upcoming event of the Pakistani American Organization of Houston.

On one occasion, Mohammad Omar said to me: "You must include radio programs in your research. The programmers really help us promote our cultural events, and provide such a good service to our community." Indeed, Pakistani radio is an important facet of postcolonial and diasporic South Asian histories, experiences, and community life. Moreover, given the paucity of research on radio engagements in new immigrant communities in the United States, it begs greater analysis and consideration.

The uses of radio following 9/11 provide a testament to the intertwining of radio with diasporic histories and experiences. In the weeks after 9/11, Pakistani radio in Houston emerged as an important forum to discuss issues such as hate crimes directed at Muslims; Muslim self-presentations in the mainstream public sphere; and the U.S.-led war on terrorism. For example, community leaders appeared on radio to offer support to victims of hate crimes and to address concerns over government surveillance in localities in southwest Houston such as Hillcroft Avenue and Bissonnet Street. Listeners called in with a broad range of questions, transforming radio into a vital resource during this period of crisis. They asked some version of the following questions: Do Pakistanis on student visas have to report to immigration agencies? Would the government deport Pakistanis who had overstayed their tourist or work visa? Can people be fired from their jobs because they are from Pakistan? Will federal agents be visiting businesses? What should one do if approached by federal agents? These and similar questions indexed the fears, anxieties, and vulnerabilities within the Pakistani American communities in Houston and also pointed to an absence of transparency and clarity in government intentions and programs following 9/11.

Radio programs also engaged with issues of public self-presentation of Muslims, and the tense negotiations between assertions of a Muslim identity and the effacement of difference. As reports of the harassment of Muslim women wearing the hijab (head scarf) circulated among Muslim communities in Houston, some community leaders encouraged women who wore the hijab to go out in groups rather than alone. The suggestion provoked heated debate and controversy on one of the Pakistani radio programs in Houston. During an on-air panel discussion, one community leader suggested that women consider not wearing the hijab until things had calmed down. "Should we stop practicing our

religion and abandon our religious practices just to be safe?" another
Pakistani American man involved in a community-based organization,
exasperated and angry, reacted to the suggestion.

Radio also provided an outlet and a voice to express a critique of the
U.S.-led war on terrorism and subsequent occupation of Iraq, military
engagements in Afghanistan, and drone strikes in Pakistan. The drone
strikes, for example, raised questions about U.S. imperialism and the
continuing war on terrorism on the one hand and the sovereignty of the
Pakistani nation-state on the other. These engagements blurred distinctions between radio production and reception, as discourses became
shaped by the on-air interactions among listeners, radio hosts, and
invited panelists. The perceived U.S. governmental involvement in the
Palestine-Israel conflict, U.S. economic engagements in Saudi Arabia,
the Gulf States, and the Middle East, and the U.S.-Pakistan relationship
were also the subject of discussion on Pakistani radio, indicating critical
mass-mediated engagements with a broad range of geopolitical situations that transcended both locality and the war on terrorism. Community leaders appeared on radio and voiced support for the United States
but also offered a critique, referring to the failure of U.S. support for
Pakistan following the end of the Soviet occupation of Afghanistan in
the 1980s. Such concerns draw attention to the complicity of the United
States and the CIA with the "buildup of Pakistan's terrorist industrial
complex: military dictators, opium markets, terrorist training centers
set up to fight the Soviets" (Puar 2007: 72). For example, during an on-
air discussion, a community leader and activist grew increasingly pas-
sionate as he stated:

> After the Afghanistan and Soviet Union war, Pakistan ended up with 2.5
> million Afghan refugees. We never had a Kalashnikov culture in Paki-
> stan. We never had a drug problem in Pakistan. We never had a high
> crime rate in Pakistan. We never had such a high rate of terrorism in our
> country. Why did we end up having all? Because after the Afghanistan–
> Soviet Union war, nobody thought about Pakistan. The U.S. packed its
> bags and went home and started imposing sanctions. So the American-
> Pakistani relationship is a classic story of a one-sided friendship in
> which Pakistan has always stood up for its friends but nobody has ever
> stood up for Pakistan.

Pakistani radio in Houston is demonstrably a valuable communicative practice that is vitally important during periods of crisis. As evidenced from the preceding examples of on-air discussions of issues impacting Muslim Americans following 9/11, and as I argue in this chapter, the entanglement of Pakistani radio with the politics of the homeland and South Asian histories, transnational Islam, and racialized life experiences in the United States creates a contentious and dynamic auditory public space in Houston. In this chapter, I draw attention to the complexity of these entanglements to reveal the broadening of public spaces that engage with Islam and homeland politics. Conceptualizing Pakistani radio as a mass mediated practice of cultural citizenship, diasporic nationhood, and transnational religious belonging, I argue that Islam represents a discursive phenomenon that emerges through on-air discussions of Muslim lives following 9/11 and through radio texts and broadcasts on "Pakistani culture" and politics and current affairs in South Asia.[2]

A survey of the first Houston-based Pakistani radio program and the narrative of its hosts provides an important starting point for examining the ways in which radio mediated religious difference among the Houston-based Indian and Pakistani diasporic communities in the 1970s and the 1980s. Although contemporary radio programs draw on South Asian popular culture and media industries, notably airplays of songs from Indian film soundtracks and Pakistani classical, folk, and contemporary music, they have become recast as business enterprises. Several of these radio programs are hosted by Pakistani entrepreneurs who also own businesses in Houston. Radio hosts use these programs to advertise their businesses, market their products and services, and solicit sponsorship from other businesses in Houston's transnational Muslim heritage economy.

The repositioning of Pakistani radio programs as business enterprises has contributed to intense competition for sponsorship money from local businesses. On occasion, radio hosts have gone on the air and used their radio programs to externalize grievances and personal conflicts with other Pakistani radio hosts. As a technology that is deeply personal in nature (Douglas 2004) and centered on the "voice,"[3] Pakistani radio programs create a space for "agency and therapeutic self-expression" (Bessire and Fisher 2012: 22). Conflicts between radio hosts then recast radio as a site for mediating the anxieties and stresses around the loss of masculinity and heterosexual male privilege during a time when Muslim masculinity is rendered queer and nonheteronormative (Rana 2011). These on-air articulations of conflict are a response to the silencing of Muslim male voices and agency in constructions of Muslim masculinities as "monster-terrorist-fag" (Puar and Rai 2002) in heteronormative projects of U.S. imperialism and post-9/11 U.S. patriotism and nationalism (Ahmed 2002) as much as they are a product of market-driven exigencies and the competition for sponsorship money. Radio also provides Pakistani community with a voice to externalize opinions regarding politics in the homeland. On-air discussions regarding nuclear armament in South Asia and heightened political tension between India and Pakistan during the 1990s and the 2000s provide exemplary case studies illustrating the salience of religion in mass-mediated practices of diasporic nationhood, transnational belonging, and cultural citizenship.

The Beginning of Pakistani Radio Programming in Houston

The first Pakistani radio program, *Khekashan Ke Sitare* (A Galaxy of Stars), began broadcasting in Houston in 1978, cohosted by Mr. S. M. Saleem and his wife, Suriya. After an extremely popular twelve-year run, the program went off the air when Saleem passed away. The program was discontinued for a year before Saleem's friend, also a regular volunteer on *Khekashan Ke Sitare*, convinced Suriya to resume broadcasts. A dramatically revamped program began broadcasting in 1990 and has been on the air since.

I first met Suriya and Azhar, the current cohosts of *Khekashan Ke Sitare*, at the radio station just off of Hillcroft Avenue from which the program is broadcast. The managerial offices and the recording studios for the private radio station are located in a high-rise that also houses the offices of law and accounting firms, insurance companies, and travel agencies, among other service sector companies. The ambiance may at first underwhelm a visitor. The recording studio is devoid of any personal or cultural artifacts or larger-than-life celebrity photographs. In the seemingly nondescript space of the radio studio, it is the soundscapes that transform space into a transnational Pakistani place. The voice-centered mediation endows the space of the radio studio with cultural meanings, interpellates "listeners as members of audiences, collectives, and publics," and shapes affective experiences (Bessire and Fisher 2012: 21). The voice of the cohosts speaking in Urdu, the informality of conversations between listeners and the radio hosts during call-in segments, and the replay of Pakistani and Indian film songs transform aurality into "a sign of emotional directness, authenticity and immediacy" (Kunreuther 2006: 324).

It is difficult to describe the camaraderie between the two cohosts as they engage in effortless banter on issues both extraordinary and banal, with each finishing the other's sentence and moving from one topic to the next, and back to the first, all within a few minutes. It is equally difficult to define the genre of the radio program. The program is unscripted and invokes nostalgia and "deeply personal and vivid memories" (Douglas 2004: 3) of living room conversations between two old friends in Pakistan. The conversations have an air of indeterminacy, taking form through spontaneous interactions with listeners (Hutchby 1999). Often known to either or both of the cohosts, the listeners may call in to request a specific Pakistani song, contribute to the conversation between the hosts, or request information about a Pakistani event, business, or service that has been advertised during the broadcast. The airplay of an occasional song, often a classical or well-known contemporary Urdu song by famed Pakistani singers such as Noor Jehan and Mehdi Hasan, combines with the informality, immediacy, and intimacy of the program to create nostalgia for the homeland and invoke culturally specific modes of listening, conversation, and sociality.

Suriya and S. M. Saleem: Pakistani Radio Pioneers in Houston

On a late fall evening, I sat down with Suriya at Azhar's Pakistani restaurant on Hillcroft Avenue in southwest Houston. The sparsely decorated restaurant is more than just an affordable place to eat home-style Pakistani food. It is a site for Pakistani sociality, interaction, and place making that disrupts geographical boundaries between private and public spaces. Although well past 10 p.m., a steady flow of mostly South Asian men and women continue to arrive for dinner. People move from table to table, making small talk with friends and acquaintances.

The laughter and chatter reverberate throughout the entire restaurant. Amidst the constant flurry of sociality and gastronomic indulgence, I find a relatively quiet corner to speak with Suriya about the radio program. Dressed in a traditional *shalwar* (a loose trouser) and *kameez* (shirt), with a *dupatta* (head scarf) covering her head, Suriya is dignified, eloquent, and cordial.

Suriya recounts that S. M. Saleem, her late husband, an engineer by profession, is counted among the pioneers in radio broadcasting in Pakistan. He was a well-known artist and producer in the Drama Department at Radio Pakistan from the 1950s until the 1970s. At the time of Pakistan's formation in 1947, there were nine radio stations in British colonial India. Of these, Pakistan inherited only two: Lahore (5 KW) and Peshawar (10K). A new radio station was hurriedly set up in Karachi, then the federal capital of Pakistan. In 1951, the studios of Pakistan Broadcasting, a government agency, shifted to a Broadcasting House dedicated to radio production and programming. During this period, radio offered broadcast service for two hours in the morning, one and one-half hours during the afternoon, and five hours during the evening.[4]

Historically, radio has been embedded in state projects of nation building in South Asia.[5] Specifically, radio was central to the process of modernization "via the delivery and insertion of technologies, and/or inculcating values, attitudes and behaviors in the population" (Melkote and Steeves 2001: 38). In subsequent years, as battery-operated radio transistors became affordable and commonplace, radio began to reach the majority of the populace in rural areas, particularly villages without electricity. English and Urdu were the primary languages of the programming. As radio began to reach all corners of Pakistan, radio programming was extended to regional languages spoken in the different provinces and regions in Pakistan (Ahmad 2005).

From 1955 until 1970, socioeconomic development, advancements in media technology, and the availability of skilled technicians and artists were critical in giving shape and identity to Radio Pakistan (Page and Crawley 2001). Radio programming such as the dramatization of Urdu novels was forged during this period. It was also during this time that Saleem and his wife, Suriya Saleem, joined Radio Pakistan. Saleem produced dramas, and Suriya read news broadcasts in English.

In 1978, Suriya and her husband left thriving careers in radio broadcasting and immigrated to the United States. Suriya's brother, who had been based in Houston since 1958, sponsored Suriya's family for immigration. "We came here because of the better educational opportunities for our children. . . . Had my brother not been here [in Houston], perhaps we would have gone to another city. I only came here because of my brother," Suriya tells me when I ask her why they settled in Houston.

However, life was not entirely easy when they first arrived in Houston. In spite of their combined professional experience, Suriya and Saleem found it difficult to break into mainstream English-language radio industries that had historically marginalized nonwhite communities in radio production (Douglas 2004). Suriya does not dwell on the limited professional opportunities that were available for a person of color, particularly a nonnative speaker of English, in mainstream American radio. In focusing on Saleem's professionalism, entrepreneurialism, and commitment to Urdu-language broadcasting, Suriya's recollection reveals how advancement and racialized exclusions are not mutually exclusive:

> SURIYA SALEEM: [In] Karachi, Saleem *Saab* was already established in radio [in Pakistan]. When we came here, professionally he could not find a job in radio broadcasting. Everything was in English. There was nothing in Urdu. But since he had already been involved in radio in Pakistan, he started an Urdu-language program. There was an Indian radio program in Hindi but none in Urdu.
>
> The radio program had an established format with different segments—there was *Geeton Bhari Kahani* [musical dramas], theatrical plays, poetry recitals, and news broadcasts. He would spend weeks preparing for the program. He would get audiocassettes from Radio Pakistan. His guests from Pakistan—mostly artists and poets—would bring with them audio cassettes for my husband. He would invite them to speak and share their art on the air. It was all done very professionally. . . . It was not a commercial program but a community-based program that was funded entirely through private donations.

KEKASHAN KE SITARE (A GALAXY OF STARS): NOSTALGIA AND A
CULTURALLY CONCEIVED SOUTH ASIAN DIASPORIC COMMUNITY
Kekashan Ke Sitare represents an important diasporic space that mediated differences of religion and national origin among South Asian
communities in Houston. Invoking nostalgia through the airplay of
Indian and Pakistani music and songs and the production of dramatic
traditions associated with radio programming in India and Pakistan,
the program attempted to represent a culturally conceived diasporic
community that was inclusive of all South Asian nationality groups
who either spoke or understood Urdu. In an interview published on
23 October 1983 in the oldest South Asian newspaper in Houston,
the *Indo-American News*, Saleem explained the goal of the program,
emphasizing that the audience for his program included both Pakistanis and Indians in Houston. According to Saleem:

> The radio program is for people who want to remember their culture
> and language. There is not much of a difference in the Indian and Paki-
> stani culture. People on both sides listen to the same music and songs. It
> is for people who want to keep in touch with their roots and understand
> their origin better.

The program's production and reception were intertwined, making Pakistani radio programming into a site for diasporic community
building. Pakistani and Indian middle-class professionals, the majority
of whom were employed in the hospitals, aerospace industry, oil and
gas industries, and construction, constituted the primary audience for
the popular radio program. These professionals were not just listeners
but in fact assumed ownership of the program through financial contributions, volunteer work, and acting in the dramatic segments. Suriya
reminisced fondly about these collaborations:

> There were very few [South Asians] at the time but they all enjoyed help-
> ing out with the program. They would cooperate fully with us. . . . If they
> were visiting Pakistan or India, they would bring back audiocassettes of
> songs and Urdu plays. We had contacts at Radio Pakistan in Pakistan so
> we would get scripts of plays from them, and then dramatize them on

our radio program here. We also had a *Kekashan* Drama Unit made up of volunteers who were professionals in their fields.

Suriya's emphasis on community-based programming was responded to in kind by full participation of the South Asian community and demonstrates the program as a community-based initiative. The importation of source material from Pakistan during the 1970s and the 1980s further demonstrates the centrality of consumers in shaping the production process. The use of Urdu, however, complicates such democratizing practices and ideologies of inclusivity in media production.

Urdu Language and Negotiations of Religion in Building a Diasporic Community

Kekashan Ke Sitare was broadcast in Urdu, a language associated with the Muslim princely courts during the Mughal and the British colonial periods. It is also the primary language for the majority of the Pakistani immigrant population in Houston. Historically, Urdu has been central in discourses on nationhood and religious belonging in South Asia. In the early twentieth century, during the height of anticolonial nationalist movements in South Asia, the All India Muslim League, a major political party for Muslims, lobbied for the creation of Pakistan as a separate homeland for Muslims in South Asia. The All India Muslim League mobilized Urdu as a symbol of Muslim solidarity that was intended to unite Muslims divided by linguistic, ethnic, and regional differences.[6] Given the linguistic diversity of Muslim communities in South Asia, Urdu, with its past in the Muslim Mughal courts of Delhi and Lucknow and its prominence in anticolonial Muslim nationalism, appeared to be a viable candidate as the national language of South Asian Muslims. Indeed, "because [Urdu] was the only language common among Muslims of pre-1947 India—whose mother tongues were as widely apart as Tamil and Punjabi, or Gujarati and Pushto—Urdu served as a vehicle for the expression of larger-than-regional concerns" (Memon 1983: 106).

Despite its potential for uniting Muslims in anticolonial nationalist projects, Urdu proved untenable as a symbol of Muslim unity. If anything, in the postcolonial epoch in Pakistan, Urdu is a highly divisive and contentious symbol that represents the failure of accommodation of regional and minority linguistic interests in Pakistan. For example, at the time of Pakistan's creation, the Bangla-language speaking population had constituted the majority of the Pakistani population and was concentrated in East Pakistan. However, Bengali nationalists associated Urdu with the exclusion of Bengali Muslims in Pakistani statecraft and governance and its use as a systematic attempt to marginalize Bengali traditions, culture, and language in projects of Pakistani nationalism and nationhood (Kibria 2011). Student protests, mass resistance, and the growing alienation of Bengalis from the center culminated in the formation of an independent nation-state, Bangladesh, in 1971. The formation of Bangladesh out of postcolonial Pakistan fractured the narrative and illusion of Pakistan as the homeland and Urdu as a unifying symbol for South Asian Muslims.

Given Urdu's centrality in Muslim nationalism in British colonial India and its contentious position in the politics of cultural and national belonging in postcolonial Pakistan, it is particularly significant that Suriya and Saleem chose to use Urdu as the language of communication in their program and as an instrument for constructing a culturally conceived South Asian diasporic community. The paucity of archival material makes it difficult to gauge the discussions or the extent of resistance, if any, within Houston's South Asian population in the 1970s and the 1980s regarding the use of Urdu. However, my conversations with Suriya suggest that the use of Urdu was motivated by Suriya and Saleem's fluency in the language. Moreover, their language choice indicates efforts to replicate Urdu-language radio programming with which they were most familiar. Regardless, given the complex colonial and postcolonial contexts that implicate language, Saleem and Suriya nurtured their relationship with their listeners by excluding on-air discussions of contemporary South Asian politics and religion.[7] As Suriya emphasized to me:

> We wouldn't do anything that would upset someone's religious sentiments. . . . See, one of the things that we have tried to ensure over the years is to stay clear of politics, particularly the politics of the India-Pakistan or the Bangladesh-Pakistan relationships. We have several

Hindu, Sikh and Muslim listeners from India and Bangladesh and we would never hurt their religious or political sentiments.

Pakistani Radio in Houston since the 1990s

Kekashan Ke Sitare, in its twenty-third year of broadcast when I carried out my field research in Houston during 2001–2002, had become part of a widely diversified Pakistani media landscape that included more than fifteen regularly scheduled Pakistani radio programs, several newspapers in English and Urdu, Indian radio programs, South Asian DVD and video stores, and multiplex cinemas that screened first-run Hindi language feature films several times daily. Additionally, since the mid-1990s, the Internet had emerged as an increasingly important mediated space for the almost instantaneous global distribution of Indian and Pakistani films, television soap operas, and music. The broadcast of Pakistan- and India-based satellite and cable television networks in Houston provides one more piece of a media assemblage (Rai 2009) through which Indian and Pakistani music and popular culture circulate globally and reach diasporic audiences.

Given the paucity of listener-based reception studies of contemporary non-English language programming and among new immigrant communities in the United States (Douglas 2004), it is difficult to generalize Pakistani radio listening patterns in Houston. My ethnographic research on radio audiences complicates conventional understandings that indicate listenership primarily among newly arrived immigrants and the first generation and decreasing levels among the second and the third generations.[8] Indeed, several Pakistani radio programs are hosted by second-generation students, professionals, and entrepreneurs. Other programs are hosted by first-generation Pakistanis and include men as well as women. It is also reasonable to assume that Pakistani radio programs reach a considerable percentage of the Pakistani community in Houston. In the vast majority of the structured oral life histories that I collected as well as conversations with hundreds of interlocutors throughout the period of my research, radio reoccurred as a topic of discussion, reflecting the significance of Pakistani radio within the larger Pakistani community in Houston. Certainly, not all Pakistani Muslims in Houston listen to these radio programs. In fact, some listeners try to distance themselves from these broadcasts because of the eruption of on-air conflicts between radio hosts that are perceived to reflect negatively on the Pakistani community. Shahzad, a host of a Pakistani radio program, described a love-hate relationship that most Pakistani listeners have with radio as of 2001:

> People *do* listen to the radio. . . . Although it is kind of funny because the average Pakistani in Houston does not want to ever admit that he listens to the Pakistani radio programs. When you talk to most people, they always say: "We don't listen to the radio." Then five minutes later they will tell you, "Oh, this host said this on the radio and that fellow said that . . ." So, I never accuse them of not listening because I know that even if they are not listening to my radio program they are listening to some other program. We all do. Yes, some people in North Houston do not have as much exposure because some of the stations do not reach that far.

Shahzad's description of a vexed audience demonstrates a significantly different relationship with listeners than that described by Suriya in terms of a close-knit, well-known, and supportive audience. The difference is, in large part, a function of the increase in the number of radio programs. Digital technologies and new web-based social media sites such as YouTube, Twitter, and Facebook are further transforming Pakistani radio, deterritorializing the reach of radio and its availability in multiple geographical contexts that extend far beyond Houston. These ongoing transformations in the reception of radio indicate "a dialectical relationship between oligopoly control of radio programming and technology on the one hand and technological insurgencies defying this control on the other" (Douglas 2004: 16).

Contemporary Pakistani radio programming also complicates the pervasive conception of non-English-language radio programming solely through the lens of community-based radio stations centered on cultural activism and production (Hinkson 2012).[9] For example, Pakistani radio in Houston represents a wide range of professional, class, and Pakistani ethnolinguistic and Islamic sectarian backgrounds and affiliations. These differences, often subsumed within the homogenizing category of Pakistani American radio programming, demonstrate multiple communities within Houston's Pakistani population, as I illustrate through the range of case studies discussed in this book. One program, for example, hosted by a retired Pakistani American and his wife airs mostly Punjabi music and songs and caters to the Punjabi-speaking Pakistani and Indian communities.[10] Another program, Radio *Naya Andaz* (New Style), promotes itself as "pollution-free" radio, a reference to the politics of Pakistani programs. This program is hosted by three second-generation Pakistani Americans as well as a Pakistani immigrant who arrived in Houston in the late 1990s. Another program, *Sangeet* Radio ("Pleasant Melody"), casts itself as a family radio program and "the total family choice in entertainment" for South Asians. Yet another, *Pehli Dhadkan* (First Beat), which is cohosted by a team of first-generation Pakistani and Indian entrepreneurs, focuses on Indian and Pakistani film music and songs and also airs interviews with visiting actors and musicians from India and Pakistan. *Radio Baseerat, Iqra Radio*, and *Ahmadiya Islam* feature religious programming and cover current affairs from a religious perspective. The circulation of Islamic discourses on these three programs has implications for the democratization of religious interpretations through the presence of programming by Ahmadiya community.

Several programs are hosted by married couples and demonstrate continuities between Houston's first Pakistani radio program, which was also hosted by a Pakistani couple, and the radio programs on the air today. Beyond such continuities, the inclusion of women as radio hosts in Houston (as well as in Pakistan) may be explained in two ways. One, radio programs reflect a privatization of public space given the generic conventions of Pakistani radio that are premised on an intimacy and informality of experience that is reminiscent of living room conversations. Conceptualized this way, radio programs then create the possibility of female engagements in mediated practices of place making that blur boundaries between work and home. Two, in recent years, Pakistani radio has repositioned itself as a business enterprise. The participation of women as hosts is well aligned with the inclusion of women in South Asian family businesses (Dhingra 2012). However, complicating the logic of structural limitations that are seen to inhibit the possibility for advancement for women in the economic sphere (Shankar 2008), several of the female cohosts are community activists and entrepreneurs who manage and run their own businesses, such as hair and beauty salons and fashion boutiques. As such, women hosts and cohosts of these radio programs are equally invested in the repositioning of radio as business enterprise.

Repositioning Pakistani Radio as Business Enterprise

Through specificities in content, radio programs claim distinction and compete for a dedicated listener base as well as finances and sponsorship from businesses in the transnational Muslim heritage economy.[11] Programming on commercial radio in Houston is characterized by a relative ease of entry and a low cost of operation for each program, which at least partially explains the expansion of Pakistani radio programming in Houston in the 2000s. Each host, also the producer of the program, pays a monthly fee to the radio station in exchange for on-air time and use of the studio facilities for recordings and broadcasts. Almost all of the hosts/programmers of the Pakistani radio programs are professionals or entrepreneurs who advertise their businesses on their programs. In order to make a profit, a radio host/programmer will also advertise other businesses.

Perhaps because of the relative ease of entry into the radio market, Suriya, the cohost of *Kekashan Ke Sitare,* is highly skeptical of the quality of programming on Houston's Pakistani radio in the 2000s.

> SURIYA SALEEM (SS): Now there are just so many radio programs. . . . Nowadays, whoever feels like it just starts a radio program. Earlier, you couldn't just purchase a time slot from the radio station to go on air. Ours was a community-based program on KPFT [the nonprofit National Pacifica Radio]. KPFT did not charge us anything but received funds through donations. We worked like this for 12 years— from 1978 until 1989. . . . We try, as much as possible, to keep our sponsorship low—we just don't have time in a two-hour time slot to advertise very many businesses.
>
> AHMED AFZAL (AA): I wonder if you have any thoughts on the Pakistani radio programs here?
>
> SS: See, the majority of radio hosts would never have been able to have their own radio program in Pakistan. You need to have the right

professional background and voice, and knowledge of broadcast [radio] production. Now, whoever has money can just pay for a time slot and begin a radio program. Radio programs are being approached from a business point of view. It is a quick way of making money . . . everyone wants more and more sponsors.

Shahzad, a middle-aged Punjabi Pakistani Muslim American entrepreneur who hosts a politics-based radio talk show, similarly referred to financial imperatives in order to explain the relatively high number of Pakistani radio programs in Houston in the 2000s.

SHAHZAD: I began the radio program [because] it is a good source of advertisement for my business. Earlier, I would just go to other people's shows and advertise with them. . . . When I got into the real estate business, I initially advertised with some of the other radio programs. But the cost became prohibitive. When I was advertising on 5 different programs, it became too much money for me to spend. So I figured, why not start my own radio program? I had an opportunity to get an hour on this station, so my wife and I decided to do our own show.
AA: Did you have any prior experience in radio broadcasting?
S: As you know, S. M. Saleem was a very famous radio personality, and he started the first Pakistani radio program in Houston—a very professional radio program. . . . We used to organize fund-raising drives for the radio every three months. . . . This was in 1983 and 1984. I started going to the radio station and volunteering at *Kekashan Ke Sitare.* . . . We bring these [listening] habits from Pakistan. Pakistanis have always been radio people and newspaper people—that is where we have typically gotten our information.

Although Saleem and Suriya had drawn on their vast experience at Radio Pakistan to create *Kekashan Ke Sitare,* a professional background in media broadcasting and/or academic education and training in media studies or communication is not a pre-requisite for entry into the commercial Pakistani radio market in Houston today. The ease of entry, combined with the low labor and resource cost for running a radio program and a rich available repertoire of South Asian songs and music, make it a highly attractive avenue for entrepreneurs and professionals who are looking to market their businesses or services to a targeted South Asian Muslim consumer base. At a bare minimum, a good supply of CDs of Indian and Pakistani songs alone, interspersed with commercials read aloud by the radio host/programmer to advertise businesses, will suffice to defray the cost of broadcasts.

Despite low entry costs, there is intense competition for sponsorship from South Asian businesses in Houston. This competition has sometimes contributed to rather volatile airings of personal conflicts and grievances between radio programmers, examples of which I will discuss in the next section. The public airing of grievances has played a major role in the denigration of radio by some segments in the South Asian communities in Houston.[12] Several of my interlocutors, also listeners of the Pakistani radio programs, narrated accounts of personal conflicts and in-fighting between Pakistani radio hosts/programmers. A few interlocutors distanced themselves entirely from Pakistani radio, and some even tried to steer me away from researching radio based on their perception that these on-air broadcasts of personal fights represented the Pakistani community in a negative light. An upper-middle-class Pakistani female interlocutor, for example, whom I had met several months into my research on Pakistani radio, expressed embarrassment and dismay. "Oh, I wish I had met you earlier. I would have pointed you to another direction—we are doing so many *good* things in Houston," she stated.

On-Air Conflicts and Grievances, Sponsorship Imperatives, and the Recuperations of Muslim Masculinity

In the 2000s, Pakistani radio emerged as a volatile site for airing personal conflicts and grievances between radio hosts, much at odds at first with the elevated, formal, and respectable position of radio in practices of nation building in Pakistan discussed earlier in the chapter. In one instance, a Pakistani radio host used his radio show to make allegedly inflammatory statements about specific religious leaders and minority Muslim sectarian communities in Houston. Nabeel, a cohost of a Pakistani music and variety radio show, had worked as the liaison between the radio hosts and the radio station management when the conflict erupted. In this case, a Shia Muslim radio host caused conflict by insulting a Sunni Muslim cleric. Nabeel recounted the aftermath of the episode in detail.

> NABEEL: The [management] never used to monitor the programs on air. But with these types of conflicts on the air, it has created a lot of disturbance within the community. . . . The mullahs showed up at our office the next day . . . we were getting phone calls and emails from listeners expressing their disappointment and even anger. It was a serious issue. . . . There was a protest outside of the radio station. It had apparently gotten to the point where the radio station manager had exclaimed, half jokingly that there would be no more Pakistani radio programs on the air because they caused so much problems. I remember my boss at the station asked me: "Why do the Pakistanis always have to fight?" He didn't understand what was going on, or what was being said, except of course, that it was potentially libelous and inflammatory.
>
> AHMED AFZAL (AA): What is the main reason for these conflicts?
>
> NABEEL: It is ego problems mainly. Everyone thinks that they are the leader of the community. They think that because they are doing radio that they are leaders. They think that they are celebrities.

Personal conflicts and "ego problems" as Nabeel aptly put it, are intertwined with the desire to make money through private sponsorship by primarily Muslim and South Asian businesses, organizations and services. In a formal interview, Shahzad discussed in animated detail, the infighting that has characterized some of the programming in Houston:

> SS: I think a lot of it has to do with the advertising money. Most of the squabbles that I have seen have to do with the competition over the advertising dollar. It is still going on . . . the infighting . . . slander . . . personal attacks . . . name-calling . . . yes, there has been a lot of that. . . . The community is much divided and whoever likes, can verbally attack another. That is why no one respects Pakistani radio programs today. It is very much seen negatively in the community.
>
> AA: But it just seems a little difficult to believe that it would be so easy to do this on-air?

ss: The radio station management has taken a stand against those who
slander and have even taken certain Pakistani programs off the
air. What we Pakistanis have exploited the most in the United
States is free speech. These radio host/programmers term slander
as free speech and use it as a license to hurl abuses at people . . .
or settle personal scores . . . say even the worst things without any
consideration. . . . Pakistani radio programmers in Houston have
taken full advantage of, and misused, freedom of speech.

It is in large part because of such perceived misuse of freedom of
speech that Nabeel added a tag line to his radio program—*Radio Naya
Andaz: Pollution-Free Radio*. When I asked Nabeel to say more about
this, he explained at length:

People are more cautious about what they say on the air. But still some
radio hosts will bring up religious issues or controversial issues so that
their ratings go up. They thrive on the word of mouth publicity through
controversies. . . . Radio programs are meant to strictly provide information and entertainment, and unite the community and not divide it. We
have been doing our show for the past six years and never once had a
problem. We support charitable events, and speak about charitable and
civic causes, but we do not bring up religious or political issues on the
air. That's why we added "Pollution Free Radio" as our tag line—to differentiate ourselves from other radio programs.

Competition for advertising dollars and listenership provides viable
explanations for the eruptions of personal controversy on Pakistani
radio. This also illustrates the discursive deployment of radio for articulating Islamic sectarian differences, notably between Shia and Sunni
Muslim communities in Houston. Conflicts between Pakistani and
Indian radio programmers further complicate the scenario and suggest
a mapping of historically situated colonial and postcolonial differences
between Indians and Pakistanis onto the space of radio in Houston. For
example, as Nabeel recalled to me:

A couple of years ago, a radio program supported a live show with
[Indian film superstar] Aamir Khan and then a [local Pakistani] news-

paper reported that the shows contributions were going toward supporting the Indian army in Kashmir. . . . It became a big issue. It caused conflict between the Indian and Pakistani communities here. The conflict
was not just about radio. It was about telling people not to shop in Indian
grocery stores, and restaurants.

I suggest that the competition for sponsorship and listeners provides
only a partial explanation of on-air conflicts between radio programmers, however. Rather, the abjection, marginality, and racism experienced by Muslim men in mainstream U.S. society also find expression
in the uncensored and volatile grievances that are aired on radio. The
airing of personal grievances represents an extension of the spirited and
emotional discussions of the situation of Muslims following 9/11 that
I discuss at the beginning of this chapter. Racialized Muslim subjectification is produced not only in race regimes and labor flows but also
in Islamophobia in the late twentieth century. As Junaid Rana (2011)
has astutely argued, in the 1980s through the 2000s, U.S. foreign policy
constructed terrorism as an enemy of the state and a legitimate site of
state violence and biopolitics. It marked and produced certain nationality groups, such as Pakistani immigrants, as a terror threat. Using
notions such as moral panic and Islamic peril and terror, Rana (2011)
shows how global racial systems incorporate the "dangerous Muslim" as
a racial category that is policed by the state. Moreover, this category is
central in anti-immigrant ideologies, practices, and narratives that construct illegality and criminality.

Examined through the lens of this racialized construction of the
Muslim, the on-air mediations of personal grievances and conflicts,
and participation in radio in general, reveal a desire to claim a voice
denied in the mainstream and a "yearning for some form of public discourse, [and] for a place where less slick and less mainstream opinions
could be articulated" (Douglas 2004: 19). During the more than three
decades of Pakistani radio in Houston, mainstream American airwaves
continue to feature English-speaking, accentless voices from dominant
sociopolitical perspectives while Pakistani radio has blossomed into
multiple niche markets. In the process of creating these alternative public spheres, "the profoundly embodied nature of listening and sounding
makes radio deeply entangled with the inner lives and political agency

of its users" (Bessire and Fisher 2012: 4). Personal grievances and conflicts then provide a context to both assure and recuperate a Muslim masculinity that is rendered deviant and a terror threat, and an agency that is constrained in the United States.

Radio, Homeland Politics, and Negotiations of Transnational Religious Belonging

The use of the airwaves to mediate grievances as well as to negotiate marginality within the specificities of life in the United States extends to discussions of volatile and potentially divisive issues such as politics and religion in South Asia. Several of the programs rebroadcast news segments that are produced by the state-controlled Pakistan Radio. These broadcasts are available on the Pakistan Radio website. Ease of access has enabled Pakistani radio programmers/host in Houston to include the rebroadcasts as a regular segment in their program. Through such programmatic investments today, Pakistani radio emerges as a mass-mediated practice of diasporic nationhood and transnational religious belonging that includes coverage of homeland politics. This investment is a departure from the ideology of *Kekashan Ke Sitare*, which was premised on an explicit exclusion of potentially divisive and exclusionary discussions of homeland politics.

In this section, I explore Pakistani radio in relation to homeland politics and the embeddedness of transnational religious belonging in such practices through a consideration of the on-air discussions during the 1990s and the 2000s around the militaristic tensions and armed conflict between India and Pakistan. In 1998, India and Pakistan both detonated nuclear weapons in rapid succession, leading to global concern and criticism, including threats of sanctions from several donor countries, including the United States. Complicating this scenario were demonstrable feelings of national pride among several Indian and Pakistani communities in the homeland and in the diaspora. As Vijay Prashad characterizes the reaction: "These folks took the explosions as a transnational dose of Viagra, as jingoism became a substitute for the traditions of anti-imperialism and anti-racism fostered by previous regimes" (2000: 136). Religion was implicated in such assertions and performances of pride, with some Pakistanis conceptualizing the nation's nuclear arsenal as the "Islamic atom bomb" and as the "the beginning of the resurgence of Islamic power."[13] Theorizing such performances of religious pride, Prashad states:

> The virulence of this kind of pride may make it easier to live as a subordinate population in the United States, but it certainly does not transform the fact of subordination (as a minority in the United States). These events severely compromised the moral capacity of desi peoples to fight for social justice. In turn, the cleavages created between peoples from the different subcontinental states has widened on religious lines as Indians are pressured to be aggressively Hindu and Pakistanis are asked, in turn, to be publically Muslim. (Ibid.: 137)

Such assertions reflect a sense of disempowerment and racialized abjections of Muslims within U.S. imperialism as well as the rise of right-wing Hindu politics in the 1990s in India and Islamic revivalist movements in Pakistan and its diaspora. As primordial expressions of religious nationalism (Ludden 1996), these assertions reiterate antagonistic Muslim and Hindu collective identities that are intertwined with the colonial and postcolonial histories and experiences referenced earlier in the chapter and discussed in the context of the formation of Pakistan in chapter 5. Defining India as Hindu and Pakistan as Muslim obscures the multicultural and multireligious heritage of both nations, which have historically drawn on a variety of cultural, religious, regional, and ethnolinguistic influences. Moreover, the reduction of the nation in terms of the religion of the majority erases the presence of communities who belong to minority faiths and minority religious sectarian affiliations. Indeed, as Prashad states,

> There are forms of religious practice that borrow from every major tradition, there are enormous numbers of languages and dialects, [and] there is every kind of social custom and taboo. . . . Rendering this diversity into such terms as "Hindu" or "Muslim" tells us less about the people in question than about those over-determined categories. (2000: 137)

In Houston, through call-in segments on various Pakistani radio programs, listeners debated the issue of nuclear armament in India and

Pakistan. An invited panelist on a popular radio program attributed the nuclearization to the persistent absence of resolution of the "Kashmir issue." The on-air discussions, including input from listeners, appropriated Pakistan State's discourse on Pakistani nationhood centered on Pakistan's inherent entitlement to and "ownership" of the disputed territory of Kashmir, which both India and Pakistan claim as a part of their national territory, and positioned nuclear capabilities as being central to Pakistani Islamic nationalism. One male caller went so far as to congratulate Pakistan on its nuclear capabilities and suggested that Pakistan sell the technology to other Muslim countries (which, as it turns out, it actually had done). The interactive nature of radio and the ability of listeners to shape, redirect, and participate in the program's on-air production reiterated the uniqueness of radio a mass-mediated communicative practice that is always in the making.

The strategic appropriation of Pakistani State discourse by several of the Pakistani radio hosts/programmers in Houston extended well beyond mass-mediated and interactive discussions on politics and religion in South Asia. As I discussed in chapter 3, several Pakistani radio hosts/programmers advocated a boycott of local Indian businesses in Houston. The boycott extended to watching Indian films, a hugely popular leisure activity among middle-class Pakistanis in Houston.[14] Several Pakistani radio programs stopped airing Indian film music and songs and continued to do so through the 2000s. Instead, Pakistani radio programs began to vigorously promote Pakistani popular and film music and soundtracks.

The proposed boycott drew on long-distance nationalism but was only partially successful because of the value of Indian media and popular culture for Pakistani entrepreneurs and businesses. Most South Asian DVD and video sale and rental stores and the two multiplex cinemas that feature new Indian films several times daily, are owned and managed by Pakistani families and entrepreneurs. Thus, the protests demonstrated a precarious negotiation between affirming transnational belonging to Pakistan and Islam on the one hand and exigencies of the neoliberal market economy on the other. These negotiations were embodied by the pronouncements made by a Pakistani radio host who also owned one of the multiplex cinemas. As tensions escalated, he went on air with the following plea:

Music is a part of life. Music is the common ground between Indians and Pakistanis and all South Asians. Whenever there is tension in our [home] countries, I think it is our duty to encourage and arrange programs that promote harmony and friendship between our communities. For businessmen, religion is business. We are here for economic reasons. We did not come here to fight. It is our moral duty to stick together and promote each other's businesses and promote harmony.

By 2001, even though the boycott had been only a partial success, it transformed Pakistani radio from what had been a medium for developing a shared, united diasporic South Asian community in the 1970s and the 1980s into one that emphasized difference and separation on the basis of religion and national origin.

Conclusion

Pakistani radio programming in Houston provides an important case study of Pakistani mass-mediated engagements in the diaspora and the complex intertwining of transnational religious belonging with projects of long-distance nationalism, diasporic nationhood, and neoliberalism. Pakistani radio programming first emerged in the 1970s as a community-based initiative on a nonprofit radio station in the United States. Through its programming, the first Pakistani radio program emphasized the postcolonial and diasporic convergences between South Asian nationality communities, notably Indians and Pakistanis, in Houston, and focused on airing Pakistani and Indian songs and music, and dramatic productions in Urdu. Structured around aurality, the first radio program drew on familiar genres of radio broadcasting and enabled the construction of associative memories, nostalgia, and imagination among listeners. In spite of the goal of transcending differences of national origin and religion, the use of Urdu as the broadcasting language suggests an intertwining of homeland politics and histories with mass-mediated cultural production in the diaspora.

By the 1990s, the rapid increase in the Pakistani immigrant population in Houston, and the increase to fifteen regularly scheduled programs democratized the production of Pakistani radio programs, as evidenced by the entry of a cross-section of Pakistani Americans representing a range of socioeconomic backgrounds, Islamic religious sectarian affiliations, and generations. Pakistani radio in Houston was also transformed from a community-centered initiative into a business enterprise. Pakistani radio programmers, often entrepreneurs in the transnational Muslim heritage economy, created radio programs as vehicles to market their business and services. As business ventures, these radio programs depend on sponsorship from other businesses, and the intense competition for sponsorship has led to the airing of grievances between radio hosts. Rather than locate these conflicts solely within the domain of financial imperatives, I have argued that these arguments also represent the desire for voice and agency and mark a discursive response to the experience of Muslim marginality, alienation, and racism in mainstream U.S. society, especially following 9/11.

The desire to be heard extends to the coverage of politics and current affairs in South Asia, thereby recasting Pakistani radio as a practice of long-distance nationalism, diasporic nationhood, and transnational religious belonging. The on-air discussion of political tensions and militaristic conflicts between India and Pakistan since the 1990s offers an exemplary case study of diasporic engagements with Islam and Pakistani nationhood. Radio, an understudied facet of transnationality and of the circulation of Islamic ideologies in the West, represents an important and mass-mediated site through which identities are generated and a sense of diasporic nationhood and transnational belonging produced among new immigrant communities in the United States of the early twenty-first century.

Table 6.1. Pakistani Radio Programs, KILE 1560 AM Frequency

Name	Genre	Program segments
1. Radio Naya Andaaz	Variety	• Pakistani contemporary pop music and songs • Interactive listeners call-in segments, quizzes, and contests; song requests; request for information regarding businesses and events advertised on the program • Purana Andaaz: Old Pakistani songs • News broadcasts in English and Urdu (re-broadcasts of BBC Radio Service and Radio Pakistan news broadcasts) via the Internet • Special religious programming during Moharram and Ramadan *Program sponsors*: Pakistani and Indian businesses and professional services
2. Radio Sangeet Simultaneous broadcast on KGOL 1180 AM frequency	Variety	• Pakistani and Indian contemporary pop music and songs • Interactive listeners call-in segments, quizzes, and contests; song requests; request for information regarding businesses and events advertised on the program • Pakistani and international news broadcasts in English and Urdu • Literature and Urdu poetry segment • Immigration segment • Special religious programming during Moharram and Ramadan *Program sponsors*: Pakistani and Indian businesses and professional services
3. Iqra (Radio Haya-lal-fallah)	Religious, Islam	• Panel discussions on Islam, and current affairs from a Muslim religious perspective *Program sponsors*: Islamic Circle of North America (ICNA), Houston
4. Radio Shalimar	Infomercial for real estate; talk show / political discussion	• On-air live discussions on real-estate-related issues in Houston • Live panel discussions on Pakistani ethnic and mainstream American politics from a Pakistani perspective *Program sponsors*: Pakistani businesses and professional services
5. Baseerat	Religious, Islam	• Panel discussions on Islam and current affairs from a Muslim religious perspective *Program sponsors*: Al-Noor Masjid, Houston
6. Punjab Rang	Variety, Pakistani regional	• Pakistani regional songs and music in Punjabi • Interactive listener call-in segments: song requests, quizzes, and games *Program sponsors*: Pakistani businesses and professional services

Table 6.2. Pakistani Radio Programs, KGOL 1180 AM Frequency

Name	Genre	Program segments
1. Agahi	Variety	• On-air live discussions on Pakistani social and cultural issues • Pakistani and Indian songs • Interactive listener call-in segments
2. Ahmadiya Radio	Religious, Ahmadiya Islam	• Panel discussions on Islam and current affairs from an Ahmadiya Islamic religious perspective *Program sponsors*: Ahmadiya Jamat Khaana, Houston
3. Kahkashan	Talk show / variety	• On-air live discussions on Pakistani social and cultural issues • Pakistani and Indian songs • Interactive listener call-in segments *Program sponsors*: Pakistani and Indian businesses and professional services
4. Radio Pehli Dhadkan	Infomercial for the West Bellfort Cinema, southwest Houston; Indian film songs	• Pakistani and Indian songs • Detailed information and songs of Indian movies playing at the West Bellfort Cinema *Program sponsors*: Pakistani and Indian ethnic businesses and professional services providers, and the West Bellfort Cinema
5. Radio Young Tarang	Variety	• Pakistani songs • Original news broadcasts in Urdu and regional languages *Program sponsors*: Pakistani ethnic businesses and professional services providers
6. Music Marathon	Variety	• Pakistani songs • Dramatic skits *Program sponsors: Pakistan Chronicle* newspaper, and Pakistani ethnic businesses and professional services providers
7. Radio Sub-Rang	Pakistani and Indian film songs; Urdu poetry	• Pakistani and Indian songs • Live and prerecorded Urdu poetry recitals *Program sponsors*: Pakistani and Indian ethnic businesses and professional services providers
8. Geetmala	Pakistani and Indian film songs	• Pakistani and Indian film songs *Program sponsors*: Pakistani and Indian ethnic businesses and professional services providers

Table 6.3. Pakistani Radio Program, KCHN 1050 AM

Name	Genre	Program segments
1. Radio Young Tarang Simultaneous broadcast on KGOL 1180 AM frequency	Variety	• Pakistani songs • Original news broadcasts in Urdu and regional languages *Program sponsors*: Pakistani ethnic businesses and professional services providers

Conclusion

On a late summer Sunday afternoon in 2005, over a leisurely lunch of delicious chicken shawarma and hummus sandwiches at a halal Lebanese restaurant and supermarket on Hillcroft Avenue, I met with Tariq. Tariq is a middle-aged Pakistani American engineer who is actively involved in one of the major Sunni Muslim community centers in Houston. I had first met Tariq during the course of my initial fieldwork in 2001–2002, and we were meeting on this day to catch up. The conversation turned to the challenges that continued to face Muslim Americans. About one thing, Tariq was clear: the need for the second-generation Muslims to forge alliances with non-Muslim Americans and to participate in the larger political society. As Tariq said to me:

> On the one hand we have to keep our fundamentals intact. On the other, we have to keep open, all [of] the avenues of interactions with Americans from all religions. We cannot remain isolated. We need to hold on to our fundamentals, our culture and our traditions but we also need to interact [with non-Muslims] at the same time.

We were interrupted as Tariq got up to greet some of his friends who were shopping at the super market. As Tariq sat down, he continued:

> This is a very difficult time for Muslims. . . . The second generation, the children of the immigrants, need to stay committed to their religious beliefs and culture . . . at the same time, they are the best people to communicate with the [U.S.] society. They are more familiar with the politics of this society.

As if to emphasize the point, Tariq repeated:

They are more familiar with this culture . . . but that does not mean that they need to adopt everything in this culture. . . . They are a part of this culture . . . but September 11. . . it has been a setback for us.

Given the surveillance of, and racism toward, Muslim Americans following 9/11, community activists and leaders like Mohammad Omar and Tariq feared that their efforts to situate themselves within the fabric of a pluralistic U.S. society as Americans had been severely undermined. Tariq's words, "This is a difficult time for Muslims," echoed those of Omar, who had said to me: "It is almost as if we have to start all over again. It is just very sad." For both men, the severe public backlash and hostilities indexed a major "setback." Muslim community leaders responded with strategically driven and multivaried engagements in mainstream political society and interfaith engagements and alliance building.

Following 9/11, there has been an emergence and consolidation of a discourse within Muslim American communities. It is centered on the mediating leadership and public involvement of second-generation Pakistani Muslim American men and women. In Houston, this discourse, as articulated by community elders and activists, targets upwardly mobile Pakistani Muslim men and women who have been born and/or raised in the United States, educated in English-medium schools and colleges, and employed in the corporate sectors. Tariq asserted that "the second generation is more familiar with the politics of this country [and] the culture of this country." In his assessment, it is this familiarity that endows second-generation Muslims with the cultural capital with which to mediate the exclusionary discourses and practices of citizenship that had made Muslims the objects of heightened state and public scrutiny and surveillance. Omar had similarly believed that the second generation was the single most important bridge between Pakistani Muslims and mainstream U.S. political society. Recall that Omar had insisted to me that in spite of his involvement in interfaith activities in Houston and his many appearances on radio and public television, overcoming the setbacks following 9/11 required the leadership and political involvement by second-generation Muslim Americans.

The sustained involvement of the second-generation in transnational communities, notably communities of ancestral and religious affilia-tions, makes them uniquely positioned as post-9/11 cultural brokers. In spite of individual specificities in appropriations of Islam and the heterogeneity of the Muslim American experience, it is the perceived embodied religiosity of the second-generation that have made them central to the discourses on future Muslim American leadership and cultural brokerage. Recall Tariq's statement: "The second generation . . . needs to stay committed to their beliefs and culture . . . at the same time they are the best people to communicate with the [U.S.] society."

This discourse has intersected with multiethnic and multireligious alliances and activism that are centered on protesting U.S. economic and militaristic engagements globally and especially in the Muslim world and regimes of surveillance, oppression, and racism domestically, in the United States. The call for greater engagement in mainstream U.S. society speaks to what anthropologist Richard Parker has termed the "politics of solidarity" that is, "a politics capable of hearing not only our own pain and suffering, but also the pain and suffering of others, sub-ject to the multiple forms of oppression, exploitation, and injustice that have been produced by the contemporary world system" (1999: 231). The importance of alliance building notwithstanding, such notions of solidarity risk an oversimplification, as they persist in variously leav-ing intact hegemonic notions and boundaries of religion, race, ethnic-ity, class, gender, and sexuality. These projects of alliance building can also overlook specificities of historical experience and the imbalance of power within and between ethnic and racial groups and communities that undermine solidarities. The marginality we have seen of Pakistani gay Muslim men within the Muslim ummah as well as in seemingly inclusive but ultimately exclusionary projects of U.S. nationalism, and South Asian diasporic nationhood and community, for example, sug-gests the complexities in productively and meaningfully building soli-darities toward the goals of political action, inclusion, and equality without effacing specificities of a group's historical experience, strug-gles, and oppression. Within the larger U.S. context, different experi-ences on the axis of religion, race, class, ethnicity, gender, and sexuality require creating a space for working through of differences. As post-Marxist philosophers Michael Hardt and Antonio Negri (2000) have argued in the context of proletarian solidarity and militancy:

The figure of an international cycle of desires based on the communication and translation of the common desires of labor in revolt seems no
longer to exist. The fact that the cycle as the specific form of the assemblage of struggles has vanished, however, does not simply open up to an
abyss. On the contrary, we can recognize powerful events on the world
scene that reveal the trace of the multitude's refusal of exploitation and
that signal a new kind of proletarian solidarity and militancy. (54)

The heterogeneity of the Muslim American experience in the early
twenty-first century explored in this book also provides entryways
for identifying spaces for building alliances and solidarity not only
within proletarian and classed identifications but also across class. The
sometimes mundane and sometimes dramatic fragments of everyday
life gleaned from the narratives suggest relatable ordinariness as well
as compelling specificity. These fragments also show how the Muslim
American experience is shaped by class as well as by sectarian affiliations, profession, gender, and sexuality, and through participation in
diasporic public cultures such as cultural celebrations and mass media.
The emphasis in this book on unpacking the heterogeneity of the Pakistani American and Pakistani immigrant experience is important not
only in making visible spaces for building alliances and collaborations
but also in pointing to the value of disavowing the representational
impulse to homogenize any group or community in scholarly studies
and public policy. The negotiation of religious belonging among Muslim American gay men of Pakistani descent and the experience of marginality, vulnerability, and abjection of the Pakistani working class and
the working poor employed in the ethnic businesses discussed in this
book, for instance, resonate with similar historical and contemporary
experiences within Latino, African American, and Asian communities.
A deeper understanding of these experiences then may productively
enable alliance building and solidarities.

The cultural analysis of Pakistani radio in Houston in this book
demonstrates a pattern of growth and commercial vitality as evidenced
by the ever increasing number of radio programs entering the market,
and it may appear to be an unusual site for discussions of solidarity in
the post-9/11 world. Yet Pakistani radio provides important insight into
the complexities of solidarities that are relevant to the discussion here.

During the course of my fieldwork at the Pakistani radio programs, I spent time with the personnel at the radio station studios from where these programs are broadcast. On one occasion, I was sitting with the manager of a radio station, Elizabeth Melendez, a second-generation Mexican American woman in her late forties. As we sat in her office chatting over coffee, our conversation was often interrupted by Pakistani radio programmers/hosts who stopped by the office. Sohail, a second-generation Pakistani American radio programmer, had brought his two young children with him to the studios. As Sohail spoke with Elizabeth about a technical problem with the equipment in the recording studio, his children kept running around and making noise. Sohail, embarrassed, apologized for his children. As Sohail left, Elizabeth smiled with understanding, turned to me and said:

> You know, this reminds [me] of when I was a child in the 1970s. My father was a Mexican immigrant, and he started his radio program in this studio as a hobby, as a way for him to feel connected to his culture. He would bring us to the studios, and we would always be running around, just like Sohail's children. . . . When I see these kids, it reminds me of how my father got involved in Spanish-language radio [in Houston]. That is how I became interested in radio. This is how we got started, and now Spanish-language radio is everywhere [in the United States].

I recall this conversation as one of the "light bulb" revelatory moments in my research that enabled me to imagine the possibility of Pakistani radio as a site of convergence between Pakistani immigrants and earlier waves of immigrants in Texas and elsewhere in the United States. Indeed, histories of non-English-language radio programming in the United States show how immigrant communities have utilized radio as a vehicle for negotiating experiences of marginality and racism in mainstream American media industries. Moreover, Spanish-language radio programming in Texas during the twentieth century and Pakistani radio today reflect similar genealogies and progressions: from community-based nonprofit initiatives to marketing tools for businesses, and as spaces of commerce that reach audiences locally, regionally, and nationally. This growth in Spanish-language radio programming has required alliance building and ongoing accommodations of difference among the varied South American and Central American nationality communities in media production and consumption in Houston.

The convergences between Pakistani and Spanish-language radio suggest not only models of growth for Pakistani radio in Houston but also potentialities for greater solidarities between South Asian radio programmers across religion and nations of ancestral affiliations. Alas, my discussion about this issue with several different Pakistani radio programmers was met with pointed reservation. When I mentioned my conversation with Elizabeth to Shahzad, a Pakistani radio host/programmer, and asked if he anticipated that Pakistani radio in Houston might follow a trajectory similar to that of Spanish-language radio, he was silent for a moment before he said:

> Maybe it will be down the road. I think a lot of it has to do with the advertising money. It is scarce. We [Indian and Pakistani radio hosts] are all fighting for that dollar so sometimes that brings a little bit of bitterness. I hope that we will get over it and realize that if we can co-exist, we will all do a little bit better. Most of the squabbles that I have seen have to do with the competition over the advertising dollar.

My interlocutor's misgivings were based on the recurrence of tensions between South Asian radio hosts/programmers as well as between Pakistani and Indians on the issue of sponsorship. These fissures within the South Asian diaspora stand to limit a strategic broadening of consumer base and sponsorship and growth potential. Indeed, this construction of difference and antagonism has undermined the ability of Pakistani radio to collaborate and build alliances. Collaboration and alliance building might allow South Asian radio to develop in ways similar to Spanish-language programming in the United States but would require solidarities that do not render invisible as much as work through historically contingent postcolonial and diasporic differences and antagonism.

The Pakistan Independence Day Festival represents another site or entryway into building alliances. In spite of the specificities of historical and cultural contexts that have shaped the Festival, the analysis converges with cultural celebrations in Asian and Latino communities that may also be positioned as practices of long-distance nationalism, transnational religious belonging, and cultural citizenship. For example, in the early decades of the twentieth century, Chinese New Year celebrations in San Francisco emphasized U.S. patriotism and the anti-communist convictions of Chinese Americans as a strategy to publicly contest the public perception of Chinese Americans as "virtual enemies of the state" (Yeh 2004: 395–396) in ways that are similar to the reframing of the Pakistan Independence Day Festival as a "Houston tradition." In spite of the naturalization of Chinese immigrants as U.S. citizens in 1943, "legal citizenship did not free [Chinese-Americans] from being [perceived as] perpetual foreigners. They remained vulnerable under Cold War politics, which threatened to make them "enemies" from within" (ibid.: 397). As a result of the hostility that prevailed toward Communist nations and Chinese nationality groups in the United States during the Cold War, a group of Chinese American male leaders in San Francisco "orientalized" the Chinese New Year Festival by underplaying religious rituals and highlighting exotic cultural characteristics that were not threatening to Americans. Instead, the celebrations showcased Chinese American loyalty to the United States, and the attempts of Chinese Americans to reach out to mainstream American society (Yeh 2004; 2008). According to historian Chiou-ling Yeh:

> [These leaders] understood that only by appealing to the American Orientalist imagination could they distinguish themselves from the 'Red' Chinese. Only by turning Chinatown into an Orientalist space could they lure more tourists, as tourism was the mainstay of Chinatown's economy. . . . They rooted ethnic cultural preservation in the Cold War rhetoric of "freedom" and "democracy" and actively chose certain "Chinese" and "American" cultural attributes to construct a Chinese American identity that was not threatening to the United States. Ethnicity became capital for them to counter prejudices and create business opportunities. (2004: 397)

The origins of the Japanese Nisei Week Festival and the Mexican American Festival of Cinco de Mayo provide additional examples of the strategic use of festivals as a collective response in face of the vulnerabilities experienced by minority communities in the United States. The Nisei Week Festival organized by Japanese Americans in California materialized as a practice of cultural citizenship intended to mediate the fears and the vulnerabilities associated with racial conflicts and tensions between Japanese Americans and other Americans. According to historian Lon Kurashige (2002), in spite of the dramatic decline in anti-Japanese discrimination and persecution since Japanese internment during World War II, the organizers of the Festival continued to deploy the celebratory event for "racial rearticulations" (Omi and Winant 1986) by defusing threatening racialized images of Japanese as foreigners and as threats to the United States. In terms of the Cinco de Mayo celebrations, during periods of institutionalized racial segregation, antimiscegenation laws, and limited economic opportunities for Mexican Americans, the event provided Mexican Americans communities an opportunity to protest discriminatory governmental policies and build community.

Cultural performances not only contest dominant racial hierarchies of American society but also symbolize protest based on gender, sexuality, and religion. For example, anthropologist Jack Kugelmass (1991) examines the Greenwich Village Halloween Parade and shows that the lesbian and gay participants in the parade use the occasion as a Bakhtinian carnival to raise questions regarding the legitimacy of the heterosexual and homophobic social and cultural order. The annual gay pride parade that now takes place in several cities in the United States as well as globally similarly contests dominant ideologies of citizenship and belonging that exclude nonheteronormative histories and experiences. Similarly, in an incisive essay on the Muslim World Day Parade that took place in New York City in the year 1990, anthropologist Susan Slyomovics states that the Parade was a "self assertion of a religious grouping" (1995) that reclassified distinctive ethnic groups as a pan-ethnic religious community.

* * *

As an intellectual project, the community-intensive study of Pakistani Americans and immigrants in Houston bridges Asian American studies, South Asian American studies, and Muslim American studies. Moreover, in spite of the growing scholarship on Muslim Americans and South Asian American communities, the South Asian Muslim

American experience in southern states has received little scholarly attention. Given the increase in the South Asian and Muslim immigration to southern states like Texas, this volume has provided insights into the ways in which locality and racialized geographies in the southern and southwestern United States shape the new immigrant experience.

The case studies discussed in this book have revealed the embeddedness and appropriations of transnational Islam in everyday life as well practices of place making. As embodied in the institutional space of the oldest Pakistani community organization in Houston, as performed at cultural events such as the annual Pakistan Independence Day Festival, as materially commodified through a Muslim heritage economy, and as expressed in everyday life, Islam emerges as a contemporary, early-twenty-first-century discursive tradition that is creatively and variously deployed in transnational projects of subjectification and belonging. Indeed, religious histories, heritage, and ideologies have provided the capital with which Pakistani Americans and immigrants can negotiate and claim space, rights, and privileges within the dominant racial, ethnic, and religious hierarchies of U.S. society and situate themselves within overlapping transnational religious and ethnic communities. In the post-9/11 epoch marked by intensified racism against Muslims and regimes of surveillance such as special security and background checks required of Muslim immigrants in issuance of visas or immigration benefits, the need for alliance building and solidarities becomes recast as an urgent and politically expedient project.

NOTES

NOTES TO THE INTRODUCTION

1. For exemplary post-9/11 analyses of Muslim Americans, see: Abu-Lughod 2002; Ahmed 2002; Bakalian and Bozorgmehr 2009; Cainkar 2009; Ewing 2008; W. Haddad 2002; Y. Haddad 2002; 2004; 2011; Hing 2006; Howell and Shryock 2003; Jamal and Naber 2008; Kane 2011; Kibria 2011; Leonard 2005; Maira 2009; Naber 2012; Prashad 2012; Puar 2007; Rana 2011; Reddy 2011; Schmidt 2004. Studies have focused on cultural citizenship and subjectification of South Asian youth in a medium-size New England city (Maira 2009), the Arab American experience in Chicago (Cainkar 2009), Sierra Leonean Muslims and place making in Washington, DC (D'Alisera 2004), Arab American communities in Detroit (Detroit Arab American Study Group 2009), Middle Eastern and Muslim American organizations and individuals in Washington, DC (Bakalian and Bozorgmehr 2009), and Pakistani transmigrants, race and representation in multiple sites (Rana 2011).

2. U.S. regimes of surveillance display "unrestrained pseudo patriotic narcissism" (Said 1988) and pathologize the Muslim as terrorist as a body without history and political context, who only acquires a history after 9/11 (Butler 2004). According to Judith Butler, the liberal secularist interpretation "works as a plausible and engaging narrative in part because it resituates agency in terms of a subject, something we can understand, [and] something that accords with our idea of personal responsibility" (5). In this pseudo-narcissism, the discourse around trauma commemorates and remembers the victims of 9/11 but denies the same to those who have experienced loss, trauma, and injustice as a result of U.S. foreign policy globally (Bacchetta 2002).

3. In using "governmentality" in this chapter and elsewhere in the manuscript, I invoke Michael Foucault's (1991) use of the term and refer to the art and idea of a government that is not limited to state politics alone but includes a wide range of control and regulatory techniques and applies to a wide variety of objects, ranging from one's control of the self to the "biopolitical" control of populations. In Foucault's writings, governmentality is linked to other concepts such as biopolitics and power-knowledge. For a detailed discussion of the term, see Foucault 1991 and Lemke 2001.

4. On May 26, 2011, President Barack Obama signed a four-year extension of three

key provisions in the USA Patriot Act: roving wiretaps, searches of business records, and surveillance of individuals suspected of terrorist-related activities not linked to terrorist groups. Representatives of the U.S. government argue that these practices and public policy (notably the USA Patriot Act) form an integral part of the U.S.-led global war against terrorism and are intended to keep the United States safe.

5. For a detailed news story about Pakistani immigrants and hate crimes following the terrorist attacks of September 11, see: "'A Regular Day' at Store Despite Protest Threats: Workers at Pakistani Convenience Store Rumored to Support Terrorism," *Houston Chronicle*, September 22, 2001. For a detailed feature story, see: "A Year Later, Many Muslims Still Shackled by 9/11," *Houston Chronicle*, September 8, 2002.

6. See Jess Spross, "Hate Crimes against Muslims Remain Near Decade High," *Think Progress*, December 12, 2012. http://thinkprogress.org/security/2012/12/10/1312341/hate-crimes-against-muslims-remain-near-decade-high, accessed August 15, 2013.

7. For analyses of Muslim sectarian communities in the West, see Fisher and Abedi 2002; Haddad and Smith 1993; Kane 2011; Mir and Hasan 2013; Werbner 2002; 2003; Williams 1988.

8. For cultural analyses of globalization, see Appadurai 1996; A. Gupta and Ferguson 1997; Habermas 1998; Hannerz 1996; Sassen 1996.

9. For analyses, see Appadurai 1996; Glick Schiller, Basch, and Blanc-Szanton 1992; A. Gupta and Ferguson 1997; Habermas 1998; Hannerz 1996.

10. See Appadurai 1996; A. Gupta and Ferguson 1997; Hannerz 1996.

11. See Glick Schiller, Basch, and Blanc Szanton 1992; 1994; Glick Schiller and Fouron 1999; Itzigsohn 2000; Laguerre 1998.

12. The staged performance of Pag-big sa Tinubuang Lupa among the Filipinos in Hawaii is yet another case in point. Pag-big sa Tinubuang Lupa celebrates the centennial anniversary of Philippine independence from Spain and "dramatizes cultural and ethnic identity claims, constructing and enacting what it means to be "Filipino" and at the same time addressing issues of power, voice and visibility" (Labrador 2002: 287). According to Roderick Labrador (2002), the cultural performance served as an important occasion for Filipinos in Hawaii to confront issues of power and marginality in mainstream American society, and also masked internal tensions and differences within Filipino American communities in Hawaii.

13. See Abelman and Lie 1995; Glick Schiller, Basch, and Blanc-Szanton 1992 and1994; Clarke 2004; D'Alisera 2004; Kane 2011; Kibria 2011; Kwong 1997; Lessinger 1995; Maira 2002; 2009; Ong 1999; Rana 2011; Rangaswamy 2000; R. Rouse 1995; Shukla 1997; 2003.

14. See Das Gupta 2006; Grewal 2005; Reddy 2011.

15. See Agnew 1999; Anderson 1983; Darien-Smith 1995; Jacobson 1996; Mandaville 1999; Maira 2009; Sassen 1996; Soysal 1996.

16. See Glenn 2000; Das Gupta 2006; Lowe 1996; Maher 2002; Yuval-Davis 1997.

17. For exemplary analyses of transmigrants see: Abelman and Lie 1995; Clarke 2004; Davila 2004; Duany 2000; Glick Schiller, Basch, and Blanc-Szanton 1994; Hirsh 2003; Kwong 1997; Laguerre 1998; Leonard 2007; Lessinger 1996; Sassen 1996; 1998; Shukla 2003; Smith 2005; Stepick et al. 2003; Yeh 2008.

18. Studies have noted the transnational flows of financial capital between the diaspora and the homeland to support the creation of religious infrastructure and institutions in both sites. In the diaspora, religious institutions serve vital functions, even for secularized Muslims, who participate in Islamic rituals "at crisis points, life cycle changes, annual reaffirmations of communal solidarity (e.g., at the fast of Ramadan), or occasional individual reaffirmations of spiritual strength" (Fischer and Abedi 2002: 268). As R. Stephen Warner notes, religious institutions "become worlds unto themselves, 'congregations,' where new relations among the members of the community—among men and women, parents and children, recent arrivals and those settled—are forged" (1998: 3). See also: Baumann 1998; Clarke 2004; Glick Schiller Basch, and Blanc-Szanton 1992 and 1994; Kane 2011; Kibria 2011; Lessinger 1995; Prashad 2000.

19. See Sutton and Vertigans 2005.

20. As Vijay Prashad (2000) argues, "In recent years, the most significant element of "national culture" among Indian Americans has been the turn to religion, especially a syndicated form of Hinduism. Today, most community gatherings feel emboldened to relate themselves in some way to religion, either by holding these events at one of the many temples, by celebrating more and more religious festivals, or by token gestures of solicitude to a faith whose intricacies are forgotten" (2000: 134). Moreover, Prashad states, "In its early years the VHPA worked through the good graces of those few committed ideologues who migrated for technical-professional work as well as the slowly growing community of petty-bourgeois merchants. These people gave their time to the erection of centers of worship, took crucial positions in the boards of religious organizations, and started to offer themselves as the translators of a homogenized Hindu culture into what they considered the wasteland of U.S. society. The VHPA fed off the energy of the VHP and related organizations in India, so it was not until those groups came close to power that the VHPA exerted its power in the United States" (ibid.: 135). See also Mathew and Prashad 2000; Mathew 2000.

21. See D'Alisera 2004; Ebaugh and Chafetz 2002; Kibria 2011; Kurein 2001; Metcalf 1996; D. Miller and Slater 2000; Vertovec 2009; Williams 2000.

22. See Cainkar 2009; Cesari 2009; Ewing 2008; Leonard 2003; Maira 2009; Peek 2010; Rana 2011.

23. See D'Alisera 2004; Kibria 2011.

24. See Kurashige 2002; Yeh 2004; 2008.

25. See Flores and Benmayor 1997; Maira 2009.

26. In a scathing critique of multiculturalism and cultural pluralism in *Latino Cultural Citizenship: Claiming Identity, Space and Rights* (1997), William B. Flores and

Rina Benmayor utilize the notion of cultural citizenship to refer to the multivaried participation of Latino communities in "practices that organize the daily life of individuals, families, and the community" (6), which, taken together, claim and establish a distinct social and cultural space. As Flores and Benmayor argue, cultural citizenship is fundamentally a concept about empowerment and agency.

27. See Kibria 2011; Mandaville 2001; Sutton and Vertigans 2005.

28. See Appadurai 1996; Featherstone, Lash, and Robertson 1995.

29. See Abu-Lughod 2005; Appadurai 1996; all essays in Ginsburg, Abu-Lughod, and Larkin 2002; Maira 2002; Mankekar 1999.

30. See Askew and Wilk 2002; Fabian 1983; Ginsburg, Abu-Lughod, and Larkin 2002.

31. See Bessire and Fisher 2012; Keith 2008; Kane 2011; Naficy 1993; Walker 1999.

32. See D'Alisera 2004; Haddad and Lummis 1987; Haddad and Smith 1994; Slyomovics 1995; Werbner 1996; Werbner and Basu 1998.

33. See I. A. Adams 2011; Chua 2010; J. Fischer 2005; James 2004; C. Rouse and Hoskins 2004; Saha 2012.

34. See Abelman and Lie 1995; Hondagneu-Sotelo 2007; Kang 2010; Kwong 1997.

35. See Dhingra 2012; Das Gupta 2006; Rana 2011. This is not to argue that there is a complete absence of scholarship on working poor ethnic immigrants, but rather that the working poor are often treated as an aside to the main story—that of the managerial elite and entrepreneurial success in America. Some recent scholarship provides important directions in the study of working-class immigrants in America. For exemplary studies, see: Bourgois 2002; Kwong 1997; Ong 2005; R. Rouse 1995.

36. For a comprehensive analysis of ideologies of the American dream, see Hochschild 1995.

37. See Abelmann and Lie 1995; Afzal 2005b; Davila 2004; Dhingra 2007; 2012; Kwong 1997; Shankar 2008.

38. See Maira 2009; Rana 2011; Reddy 2011.

39. The gay liberalist understandings of persecution of gays and lesbians in the Muslim world constructs Muslim nationhood as a threat to LGBTIQ "persons, organizations, communities, and spaces of congregation" (Puar 2007: xxiv). The discourses around such persecutions construct whiteness as queer norm. Indeed, as documented in the U.K.-based gay rights organization OutRage!, Puar notes a highly problematic oppositional positioning of gay rights and Muslims in the production of homonormative Islamophobia, in spite of other efforts at "inclusion and acknowledgment of multicultural diversity" (ibid.: 19).

40. In spite of the proliferation of ethnographic studies of transnational communities in the United States, there has been relatively little research on nonheteronormative transnational sexual cultural and community formations in the United States. Martin Manalansan's (2003) ethnographic study of "global divas," Filipino gay men in New York City, is one of the few book-length monographs that focus on the lived and embodied experience of transnationality and the

formation of nonheteronormative sexual cultures. Carlos Ulises Decena's (2011) study of same-sex desire among Dominican men in New York City is another significant ethnographic study that explores race, class, and cultural formations in the context of gay immigrant men of color. My analysis follows Manalansan and Decena in choosing to focus on moments in narrative through which queer immigrants evoke multiple registers in constructions of transnational sexual and gendered subjectivities. In the case of Decana's interlocutors, these registers include Dominican, heterosexual, gay and bisexual, and family. According to Decena, these registers are central in constructions of masculinity, sexual practices, and in strategies for cultural border crossings in the United States.

41. See Calhoun 2003; Cheah and Robbins 1998; Mignolo 2000.

42. See Abelman and Lie 1995; Clarke 2004; Dhingra 2012; Freeman 1989; Johnson 2004; Kwong 1997; Rangaswamy 2000; Takaki 2000.

43. See Lessinger 1996; Leonard 1992; 1997; 2007; Rangaswamy 2000.

44. See Clifford and Marcus 1986; M. Fischer and Abedi 2002; Marcus and Cushman 1982; Marcus and Fischer 1986; Narayan 1993.

NOTES TO CHAPTER 1

1. Although Pakistani communities are dispersed throughout Texas, especially in Dallas and Austin, the largest concentration of Pakistanis in Texas is in Houston (Najam 2006).

2. Almost 75 percent of Pakistanis in the United States have immigrated since 1987, and only 10 percent immigrated prior to 1978.

3. These figures are based on estimates by the Pakistan Embassy, Washington, DC, and analyzed in Najam (2006). The data does not account for interstate relocations, especially for jobs or education. Numerical differences are explained by conservative estimates provided in official statistics that undercount interstate immigrants who move to Houston from other cities throughout the United States for jobs, to rejoin family, kin, and *biradaris* networks, as well the undocumented and overstays. Since the total number of a nationality group can confer power, visibility, and access to resources and privileges from the state, it is in the interest of the local community organizations to overstate the total numbers in order to assert greater clout in negotiations and demands for rights, privileges, and entitlements from the state. For this reason, the total number, as Najam (2006) suggests, "can sometimes lead to heated discussion within the Pakistani-American community" (56).

4. Here I refer to the Pakistan Embassy, Washington, DC, rather than census data because these estimates are more reliable than the census data, which do not break down South Asian immigration data by nationality/country of origin. The Pakistani Embassy figures are based on data from U.S. immigration and the Embassy's own consular records. Moreover, according to Adil Najim (2006), this data is further corroborated by the percentage share of Pakistanis in the American Muslim population, estimated at approximately 3 million. 27 percent of all

Muslim immigrants hail from South Asia, including 15 percent from Pakistan, placing the total population at 525,000, a number that is close to the Pakistan Embassy's estimates of half a million. See Najam (2006) for a detailed quantitative analysis of the Pakistani American population in the United States.

5. See http://www.houstontx.gov/abouthouston/houstonfacts.html, accesed August 20, 2013.

6. Studies of pre-1965 immigration focus primarily on Punjabi farmers, who settled in Canada, Washington, Oregon, and California in the nineteenth century, provided labor on rural farms, and created a remarkably distinctive Mexican Punjabi community (see Leonard 1992). South Asian immigration, such as the travel of Pakistani students during the 1950s and the early 1960s, is missed almost entirely in historiographies of South Asian immigrants in the United States (see Najam 2006). A recent historical study elaborates concurrent waves of South Asian immigration, notably the lives of Bengali Muslims, who settled in the northeastern states and the industrial Midwest during late nineteenth century (see Bald 2013).

7. For a discussion of U.S. immigration and Asian Americans, see Hutchinson 1981; Lowe 1996; Ong and Liu 2000.

8. See Carlson 1994; Chan 1991; Portes and Rumbaut 1996; Reimers 1985.

9. See Abraham 2000; Leonard 1997; Lessinger 1995; Prashad 2000; Rangaswamy 2000.

10. See Dhingra 2012; Prashad 2000; Rana 2011; Shankar 2008.

11. See Vojnovic 2003a; 2003b; Shelton et al. 1989.

12. http://www.portofhouston.com/about-us/history/, accessed September 10, 2013.

13. For a discussion of the exclusion of African Americans from the aviation industry during the 1960s, see Northrup (1968).

14. See National Science Foundation (NSF), *Science and Engineering Degrees by Race and Ethnicity (and Gender) of Recipients* (Arlington, VA: NSF, 2000.)

15. See Bullard 1987, 1990; Cohn and Fossett 1996.

16. See Bullard 1987; Meeks 2011.

17. http://www.houstontx.gov/planning/Demographics/demog_links.html, accessed August 20, 2013.

18. See Feagin 1985; 1988; Vojnovic 2003a; 2003b.

19. See Shelton et al. 1989; Steptoe 2008; Tischauser 2012.

20. See Bullard 2002; 2005; Westra and Lawson 2001.

21. http://www.houstontx.gov/planning/Demographics/docs_pdfs/SN/sn_coh_race_ethn.pdf, accessed August 20, 2013

22. http://www.houstontx.gov/health/UT-executive.html, accessed August 20, 2013.

23. http://www.houstontx.gov/abouthouston/houstonfacts.html, accessed August 20, 2013.

24. In this chapter and elsewhere in the book, I follow the categorizations used in the U.S. census and use "Latino" to refer to any ethnic group that may be of any race, as one category, and all persons of non-Latin ancestry as non-Latino racial

categories: non-Latino whites, non-Latino blacks, and non-Latino Asians. This is significant because white, African Americans, and Asian communities can be found throughout South and Central America, and as such certain member of these groups may well claim Latino racial and ethnic identity.

25. See Emerson et al. 2013; Frey 2000.

26. See Lin 1995; Shelton et al. 1989.

27. See Waldinger 1989; Ebaugh and Chafetz 2000; Portes and Rumbaut 2001; Yang and Ebaugh 2001.

28. See McIntosh (2008) for a statistical analysis of changes to job market and opportunities for evacuees and native labor, when controlled for race, gender, educational level, and type of industry.

29. For example, Mexican churches in Houston have historically been central to practices of cultural production, community building, political activism, and social reform. Equally significant, Mexican churches have represented "ethno-Catholicism" that incorporated faith healing practices, saint veneration, home alter worship, and religious-cultural celebrations that placed such appropriations of religion at the margins of the institutional Catholic Church in the United States (Trevino 2006). For Asian populations, including Chinese laborers, who had contributed projects of urban development in Houston in the early twentieth century (von der Mehden 1984), and new immigrants like Koreans, establishing religious places of worship has been central in how immigrant communities have reshaped cityscapes through practices of cultural production and place making (for example, Belden 1997; Yang and Ebaugh 2001; Kwon, Ebaugh, and Hagan 1997).

30. http://www.islamicdawahcenter.org/html/history.html, accessed August 20, 2013.

31. http://faithcommunitiestoday.org/sites/faithcommunitiestoday.org/files/The%20 American%20Mosque%202011%20web.pdf, accessed August 20, 2013.

32. http://www.chron.com/life/houston-belief/article/Masked-men-try-to-burn -Houston-mosque-HFD-1682665.php, accessed August 20, 2013.

33. The Houston Galleria provides an exemplary case study of an edge city in Houston. See Garreau (1992) for a discussion of edge cities in Texas in general and the Galleria in particular.

34. http://www.chron.com/news/houston-texas/article/Houston-community -celebrates-district-named-for-1613050.php, accessed August 25, 2013.

35. http://www.allianceontheweb.org/, accessed August 1, 2013.

36. Matt Woolsey, "Top Suburbs to Live Well," Forbes.com, March 26, 2008, http:// www.forbes.com/2008/03/25/suburbs-quality-lifestyle-forbeslife-cx_mw_0326 realestate.html, accessed August 10, 2013.

NOTES TO CHAPTER 2

1. For in-depth scholarly studies of Enron, see, Bradley 2009; Fox 2003; Healy and Palepu 2003; Salter 2008.

2. For analyses of neoliberalism, see Harvey 2005; A. Ong 2006; Salter 2008.

3. For discussions of Houston's energy sector, see Feagin 1985; 1988; Garreau 1992.

4. For studies of South Asian skilled labor flows, see Dhingra 2012; Khandelwal 2002; Maira 2002; Shankar 2008; Rangaswamy 2000.

5. Most recently, African American American women have been recast as a model minority, expanding the racial contours associated with model minorities beyond East and South Asian immigrants. Data indicating high college enrollment and degree attainment levels for African American women, and low instances of criminality, among others factors, are used to construct black American women as model minority citizens, especially in light of the historical experience of slavery, racism, and gender discrimination. See Kaba 2008.

6. For critical studies of the model minority concept and Chinese and Japanese communities, see, for example, Waters and Eschbach 1995; Xie and Goyette 2004.

7. According to Pierre Bourdieu (1984), cultural capital draws on social knowledge and resources that are passed from one generation to the next within the context of kinship based intergenerational relationships.

8. For critiques of the model minority and South Asian communities, see Bald et al. 2013; Bhatia 2007; Dhingra 2007; Das Gupta 2006; Okihiro 1994; Shankar 2008.

9. For discussions of South Asian ideologies of nation building and education in the hard sciences, see Bald et al. 2013; Prashad 2000.

10. For insightful ethnographic case studies of the myth of the American dream, see Abelmann and Lie 1995; Dhingra 2012; Hochschild 1995; Shankar 2008.

    In particular, note Hochschild's discussion of the American dream as the nation's very soul, even though society has denied it to millions of African Americans. Hochschild combines data from opinion surveys with chilling personal stories, both ironic and prophetic. Individual views of the American dream divide along lines of race and class. White Americans are convinced that African Americans have more opportunities than ever before. African Americans, on the other hand, argue that racial discrimination persists in spite of advancement. According to Hochschild, middle-class blacks, despite their achievements and growing numbers, have much less faith in the American dream than poor blacks do. Middle-class blacks see other blacks in poverty and feel bitter. Hochschild also suggests that those who grew up in the afterglow of the civil rights movement expect more from the dream than they have been able to achieve.

11. For analyses of the impact of these legislations on Asian communities, see Hutchinson 1981; Lowe 1996; Ong and Liu 2000.

12. See Carlson 1994; Chan 1991; Portes and Rumbaut 1996; Reimers 1985.

13. See Abraham 2000; Leonard 1997; Lessinger 1996; Prashad 2000; Rangaswamy 2000.

14. See Das Gupta 2006; Leonard 1997; Lessinger 1996; Prashad 2000; Rangaswamy 2000; Williams 1988.

15. Operations of race and class in transnational contexts involve what Koshy (2001)

describes as "class fraction projected as the model minority produced through changed demographics, class stratifications, new immigrations, and a global econom . . . thereby enabling opportunistic alliances between whites and different minority groups as circumstances warrant . . . project[ing] a simulacrum of inclusiveness even as it advances a political culture of market individualism that has legitimized the gutting of social services to disadvantaged minorities in the name of the necessities of the global economy" (156).

16. For critiques of the model minority, see Cheng and Yang 2000; Osajima 2000; Prashad 2000.

17. See Maira 2009; Ong 1999.

18. See Bhatia 2007; Dhingra 2008; Shankar 2008.

19. For analyses of Enron, see Henderson, Oakes and Smith 2009; Sims and Brinkmann 2003.

20. See Ernst 1994; Ima 1995; J. Lee and Zhou 2004; S. J. Lee 1996; Lew 2006.

21. Shankar (2008) states that high tech industry has typically drawn from highly educated and technologically trained individuals "who are well poised to succeed. Many desis in Silicon Valley have the cultural capital to succeed in this process and inculcate in their children the need to develop similar skills. Such a disposition, however, speaks more to the type of professional immigration the United States sought rather than an innate aptitude in Desis" (145).

22. See Lowe 1996; Mathew 2004; Okhirio 1994; Prashad 2000; Zhou 1997.

23. For the model minority and the undermining of interethnic and interracial alliance building, see S. J. Lee 1996; Omatsu 1994; Reyes 2002; Tuan 1998.

24. In the opinion of Vijay Prashad, the model minority stereotype is "a godsend for desis. It provided them with an avenue toward advancement, despite its negative impact on blacks and its strengthening of white supremacy. In the throes of an intensified Black Liberation movement, the white establishment pointed to its civil rights legislation as the ceiling for state action. The rest, they said, was to come from the initiative of the oppressed themselves. This implied that the oppressed did not take initiative, a notion as condescending as it was erroneous" (2000: 170).

25. For analyses of racialization of Asian Americans, see Bald 2013; Bhatia 2007; Leonard 1992; Prashad 2002; Sharma 2004.

26. See Agarwal 1991; Bacon 1996; Dasgupta 1998; Helweg and Helweg 1990; Leonard 1997; Rangaswamy 2000; Saran 1985; Sheth 2001.

27. See Kibria 1998; Prashad 2000; Visweswaran 1994.

28. For discussion of these court rulings, see Hess 1976; Leonard 1992.

29. In addition to the extensive writings on Ismaili ideologies, history, and experiences by Farhad Daftary 1990; 1998, also see Hafizullah Emadi 1998 for a succinct but important discussion of Ismaili history.

30. The Aga Khan IV currently supports a network of some 300 educational institutions and programs in India, Pakistan, Kenya, Tanzania and elsewhere, ranging from day care centers and elementary schools to specialized projects. . . . In

1983, the Aga Khan University, with a medical college and a nursing school, was founded in Pakistan. The Aga Khan's health and education services are available to all people regardless of their race or religion (Daftary 1990: 527–528).

31. I suggest that the reason for the elision of this period in historiographies of South Asian immigration is a result of the dominant classificatory schemes that label a law by the year of its passage into law. Thus, the normalizing of "post-1965" as a descriptive marker in South Asian historiographies perpetuates the positioning of 1965 as a definitive and totalizing year marking the start of contemporary immigration from Asia rather than a moment in twentieth-century immigration history.

32. See Jalal 1995; Malik 1997.

33. For historical analyses of national building and education in South Asia, see Burki 1999; Jalal 1995; Toor 2005.

34. For analyses of the U.S.-Pakistan alliances historically, see Ayoob 1969; Brodkin 1967; S. I. Khan 1972; Malik 1988b; Slonim 1972; Talbot 1970; Waterston 1963.

35. For twentieth-century historical studies of Ismailis, see B. Adams 1974; Kaiser 1996; Kadende-Kaiser and Kaiser 1998; Morris 1957; Nanji 1974.

36. See Espiritu 2003; Kim 2004.

NOTES TO CHAPTER 3

1. For cultural analyses of Islam and consumption patterns, see I. A. Adams 2011; Chua 2010; J. Fischer 2005; James 2004; Rouse and Hoskins 2004; Saha 2012.

2. For cultural analyses of the barriers to integration in U.S. economic society, see Das Gupta 2006; Kang 2010; Kwong 1997.

3. Ethnic businesses are perceived as providing a route to upward mobility (see for example, Assudani 2009; Light and Roach 1996; Portes and Bach 1985) and making traditional products and services available to immigrants. Ethnic businesses enable entrepreneurs to build "successful businesses without large sums of capital because their specialized niche protects them from competition in the wider market" (McDaniel and Drever 2009: 4). The success of these businesses is based in part on a fragmented demand because these businesses fill a market niche that is not served by mainstream firms or native middle-class entrepreneurs (see, for example, Razin 1993; Yoon 1991). Historically, ethnic businesses have also drawn on social capital (see, for example, Adler and Kwon 2002; Bourdieu 1984; Coleman 1990; Valdez 2008), such as culture or specifically shared values and beliefs, as capital and resources in the formation of credit associations, coethnic labor force, and enclave economies (see, for example, Marger and Hoffman 1992; Min and Bozorgmehr 2000).

4. For discussion of contextual categorizations of classed identities in South Asian immigrant communities, see Kibria 2011; Shankar 2008.

5. For discussions of the ethnic economy, see Light 1972; Portes and Rumbaut 1996; Rath 2000; Zhou 2004.

6. For discussion of the growth and globalization of the halal industry, see, for

example, I. A. Adams 2011; Chua 2010; J. Fischer 2005; James 2004; C. Rouse and Hoskins 2004; Saha 2012.

7. In a sophisticated ethnographic study of transnational Sierra Leonean Muslim cab drivers and food-vending-stand owners in Washington, DC, anthropologist JoAnn D'Alisera (2004) examines the display of religious objects in the work place, here cabs and vending stands. D'Alisera argues that these religious objects are sites for construction of transnational communities and spaces in which Sierra Leonean Muslim refugees are embedded. The display of religious commodities throughout the cab, for example, has the effect of marking the work space as Muslim and the display as belonging to a transnational Muslim community. For cultural analyses of transformations in the practice of Islam, see D'Alisera 2004; M. Fischer and Abedi 2002; Starret 1995.

8. For analyses of the complexities of working in ethnic businesses, see Das Gupta 2006; Kang 2010; Kwong 1997; Ong, Bonacich, and Cheng 1994.

9. For a detailed ethnographic and historical analysis of contestations over ethnicity in Karachi, see, Ahmar 1996; Haq 1995; Verkaaik 2004; Wright 1991.

10. For analyses of Muslims as terrorist, see M. Ahmed 2002; Cainkar 2009; Maira 2009; Puar 2007; Rana 2011; Reddy 2011.

NOTES TO CHAPTER 4

1. Avtar Brah (1996) offers a framework to understand the multiplicity of positions of South Asian young Muslim women in the labor market in England to show how "structure, culture and agency are conceptualized as inextricably linked, mutually inscribing formations" (442). Brah focuses on the everyday life of these women to show how social lives are fashioned "in and through matrices of power embedded in intersecting discourses and material practices" (ibid.: 449).

2. For gendered discussions of South Asian diasporic nationalist projects, see Gopinath 2005; Das Gupta 2006; Mankekar 1999; Ratti 1993; Thangaraj 2010.

3. Throughout the discussion, I use "gay" and "queer" interchangeably. There is a considerable body of literature on the specificities and varied contexts for the usage of the two words. Certainly, there are benefits and drawbacks to using either term without qualification. In an excellent discussion on the subject, anthropologist Kath Weston writes: "If lesbian and gay take a fixed sexual identity, or at least a "thing" called homosexuality, as their starting point, queer defines itself by its difference from hegemonic ideologies of gender and sexuality" (1998: 159). To qualify, I use the term "queer" in the context of contestations over religion and ethnicity and to highlight the tensions between Pakistani homosexual men and such hegemonic ideologies. I use the word "gay" in discussions of narratives of selfhoods and social identities. For an insightful discussion in the subject, see Weston 1998.

4. See Maira 2009; Rana 2011; Reddy 2011; Thangaraj 2012.

5. For critical analyses of Western human rights activism in the non-West, see Grewal 2005 and Puar 2007.

6. For studies of transnational sexualities, see Barnard 2004; Brady 2002; Cantu and Luibheid 2005; Cruz-Malave and Manalansan 2002; Eng, Halberstam, and Munoz 2005; Gopinath 2005; Leap and Motschenbacher 2012; Luibheid 2002; Manalansan 2003; Patton and Sanchez-Eppler 2000; Rodriguez 2003.

7. For analyses of the conception of diasporic nation in terms of heterosexuality, see Gopinath 2005; Maira 2002; Mankekar 1999; Shukla 2003.

8. For more information on the Montrose District, and its emergence as a queer space in Houston, please visit: http://www.montrose.com. For a description of the Museum District, see Scardino, Stern, and Webb 2003.

9. Although research (Breakwell 1986; Jaspal and Siraj 2011) has discussed the derogatory categorizations of men who have sex with men in India and Pakistan through words such as *gandu* or *bund-marao*, for example, I do not discuss these scripts in this chapter, primarily because these words were not invoked in self-identifications among my interlocutors. It is outside the scope of the research in this chapter to fully interrogate the uses of these words, except to suggest the need for ethnographically grounded research to fully and more complexly understand vocabulary such as *gandu* and *bund-marao*. Breakwell (1986) and Jaspal and Siraj (2011) persist in perpetuating problematic and literalist readings of these words, using the lens of Western epistemologies of sexuality and resulting notions of homophobia that elide the cultural and contextual specificities within which these words are used.

10. For studies of same-sex sexual intimacies between men and between women in South Asia, see Afzal 2005a; Dasgupta 1998; Dave 2006; 2012; S. Gupta 1999; B. Khan 1997.

11. For discussions of homosociality and potential for locating same-sex sexual eroticism and relationships in Indian popular culture, especially Indian cinema, see Chakravarty 1993; Derne 2000; Dissanayake and Sahai 1992; Gopinath 2005; Holtzman 2011; Rao 2001; Thomas 1985;Vanita 2001.

12. An anthropologist who lived with a Tamil family in southern India during the 1980s suggests that such themes in Bollywood cinema were continually reproduced in the social relations and vice versa (Trawick 1992). In a book-length ethnographic reception study of film going in India, Steve Derne states that "for many young (single) men, film-going with their male friends is a practice that celebrates their bonds with each other. Physical closeness between men is an important component of the film-going experience. Film-going is an arena in which male friends can joke, dance, and roughhouse together" (2000: 159).

13. Martin Manalansan makes a similar argument in his discussion of the uses of drag within gay Filipino communities in New York City, saying that drag evokes "the image and memory of the Filipino homeland while at the same time acknowledging being settled in a 'new home' here in the U.S" (2003: 136).

14. According to Gaytri Gopinath (2005): "The song and dance sequence is also the most transnational of all the various components that make up the Bollywood film: often a particular sequence travels across national borders independently

from the film in which it originally appeared. We can therefore understand the song and dance sequence as a peculiarly queer form: because it falls outside the exigencies of narrative coherence and closure, it can function as a space from which to critique the unrelenting heteronormativity that this narrative presents" (101).

15. For ethnographic studies of honor among Pathan men, see Ahmed 1976; Asad 1972; Barth 1959; Lindholm 1982; Meeker 1980.

16. Benedicte Grima (1991) identifies a genre of narrating life stories in which narrative focuses on a woman's honor, which is expressed through personal experiences of suffering, sacrifice, hardship, and endurance. Grima also considers the subgenre of personal experience tales that typically relate to illness, catastrophe, and misfortune and externalized in narrative in the context of "formal emotion rituals called tapos, i.e. ... "visitation by women to the homes of other women to share sadness over their misfortune" (79). According to Grima, "the display, or performance of emotion, in this case of loss and suffering, is related to identity: Pathan, Muslim and feminine" (79–80).

17. It was only in 2001 that the NFIA reluctantly allowed organizations such as SALGA and Sakhi, a South Asian progressive women's' organization, to march in the India Day Parade (Das Gupta 2006). SALGA continues to be denied permission to march alongside other, more "authentic" Pakistani groups at the Pakistan Day Parade in New York City. See also Gopinath 2005; Mathew and Prashad 2000; Mathew 2000; Prashad 2000.

18. The fear of physical violence, rather than being an exception, also appears as one of the major themes in the coming-out narratives of British Muslim gay men of Pakistani descent (see, for example, Jaspal and Siraj 2011) and underlies anxieties around queer Muslim organizing in the United States as well.

19. During the last decade and a half, several ethnographic studies and cultural analyses have documented the formation of the South Asian Lesbian and Gay Association (SALGA) in New York and the ensuing protests over its exclusion from the India Day and the Pakistan Day Parades in the 1990s. Some of the major studies include: Das Gupta 2006; Gopinath 2005; Khandelwal 2002; Lessinger 1995; Mukhi 2000.

20. For discussions of Islamic revivalism, see Asad 2003; D'Alisera 2004; Kibria 2011.

21. Writing about the experience of being Muslim and gay, Shahid Dossani states: "I find it hard to imagine being able to live a mentally peaceful life, content with one's gay nature, in a Muslim country" (1997: 236). Significantly however, in Dossani's assessment: "Overall there does not seem to be as much fear and hatred of homosexuality in the Qur'an as gay Muslims and others generally tend to think there is" (ibid.).

22. Murray and Roscoe (1997), in one of the only cross-cultural analyses of mostly Orientalist historical, anthropological, and literary texts produced in the Muslim world, make visible the occurrence of same-sex sexual eroticism, love, and relationships and belie literalist interpretations of Islam and Muslim societies.

23. For exemplary discussions of accommodations of homosexuality in Islam, see Kugle 2003; 2014; Rowson 1991.
24. See Doi 1984; Duran 1993; Jamal 2001; Yahya 2000; Yip 2004.
25. See Duran 1993; Jamal 2001.
26. See Jung and Smith 1993; Kahn 1989.
27. As noted by Monisha Das Gupta, "South Asian queer organizations mount a critique of racism, transnational capital, and hetero-sexist U.S., Indian, and Pakistani nationalisms" (2006: 9).
28. Here I invoke Jose Munoz's (1999) notion of counterpublics as "communities and relational chains of resistance that contest the dominant public sphere" (5).

NOTES TO CHAPTER 5

1. This is a pseudonym for the Pakistani organization in Houston. The names of interlocutors quoted in this chapter have also been changed.
2. Victor Turner, in his classic ethnographic studies (1967; 1969; 1974), analyzes ceremony, celebration, and spectacle as externalized reflections on daily existence that are "anti-structural, creative, often carnivalesque and playful" (1974: 7). Genres of cultural performances, such as festivals, consist of distinctive elements, for example, costumes, music, and floats, that distinguish the performance from the everyday moment yet remain comprehensible to spectators. Turner conceptualized ceremony, celebrations and spectacle as "social drama" in which social conflicts are dramatized through ritual performance.

Moreover, cultural performances did not merely reflect or express the social system but also created a space of liminality, that is, a release from the constraints of prescribed social roles. The shared liminality induced what Turner termed "communitas." Cultural performances are also a part of an ongoing social process, rather than a break from social processes.

Milton Singer (1972) makes a similar argument regarding the continuities between everyday life and cultural performances, based on his field research in Madras, India. According to Singer, cultural performances, which are central features of the social lives of Indians in Madras, were not limited to plays or concerts but included prayers, rituals, readings and recitations, rites and ceremonies, and festivals, and could be classified as cultural and artistic performances rather than as religion and rituals. For an in-depth discussion, see Singer 1972.
3. See Das Gupta 2006; Khandelwal 2002; Lessinger 1995; Rangaswamy 2000.
4. See also Kurashige 2002; Yeh 2008.
5. For an exemplary analysis of Mohammad Ali Jinnah as a Muslim nationalist leader who spearheaded the demand for a separate nation for the Muslims of the Indian-subcontinent, see Jalal 1985. Jalal's study offers insight into the aims and strategy of Jinnah and the All India Muslim League and reveals the divergences in the interests of Muslims in majority and minority Muslim provinces of colonial India.

6. For exemplary historical analyses see Bose and Jalal 1996; Butalia 2000; Menon 1998; Pandey 2002.

7. For a historiographical discussions and analyses of the formation of Pakistan, see Bray 1997; Jalal 1985; 1995; Malik 1997.

8. See Kane 2011; Kibria 2011: Kurein 2001.

9. In the 1990s, several specific events in India found resonance within the Indian immigrant population and led to a strengthening of religious infrastructure in cities with large Indian populations in North America and Europe. These events—watershed moments—propelled the right-wing Bharatiya Janata Party and its allies to power and included the demolition of a sixteenth-century mosque in North India in 1992 by Hindutva supporters and the resulting Hindu-Muslim riots in cities throughout India, Pakistan, and Bangladesh.

    For a discussion of the growing importance of Hindu and Muslim religious institutions in the United States, see Coward, Hinnells, and Williams 2000; Kurein 2001.

10. For a complete coverage of the Pakistan Independence Day celebrations in Houston in 2001, see "Special Edition," *Weekly Pakistan Chronicle*, August 10, 2001. Select articles and photographs from the celebrations are available online at http://www.pakistanchronicle.com.

11. Carlson (1998) argues that the transformation of Cinco de Mayo reflects a marke-driven demographic reality. Because Latinos are the largest ethnic group in the United States, the capitalist economy targeted and mobilized Latino festive culture as a strategy to enter a lucrative consumer market. The Pakistan Independence Day Festival reveals a similar potential, especially as it repositions itself as a broader South Asian festival, even as the boundaries of inclusion remain premised on a shared religion.

12. July 4 Independence Day celebrations are a significant case in point, revealing the commodification of American nationhood. In the weeks leading to the July 4 celebrations, a wide variety of businesses offer special sales and discounts, and mass media enterprises air special news reports, documentaries, and shows on various aspects of American history.

13. For an in-depth discussion of the objectification and commodification of culture and nationality, see Silverman 1986.

14. See Rouse and Hoskins 2004; Seremetakis 1996.

15. A collection of essays on contemporary food-related practices in the Australasian-Pacific region similarly emphasize the importance of ethnic cuisine in processes and practices of transnational cultural production, notably in "the reproduction of social forms via sociality's relating to food and commensality" (James 2004: 1). According to James, food serves as an important vehicle for the production of ethnic authenticity and "a clear sensory cultural order" (ibid.: 3). In the same volume, Charon Cardona notes that for Cubans in the United States, "maintaining Cuban food culture and its socialities are central to defining and

expressing Cuban identity in diaspora. Cuban tastes are a critical modality of Cuban identity-making anywhere" (Cardona 2004: 4).

16. For a discussion of postcolonial subjectivity and cuisine, see Appadurai 1988.

17. Interview, president of the Pakistan Organization of Greater Houston, November 2001.

18. For analyses of cultural citizenship, see Flores and Benmayor 1997; Maira 2009; T. Miller 1997; Ong 1996; Siu 2001.

19. http://www.pakistandayparadehouston.com/organiser_message, accessed May 11, 2011.

20. http://www.pakistandayparadehouston.com/parade_route, accessed May 11, 2011.

NOTES TO CHAPTER 6

1. Ousmane Oumar Kane (2011) makes a similar assessment of the uses of radio among Senegalese Muslim immigrant communities in New York City.

2. Religious radio programs are generally characterized as proselytizing and missionary projects (see, for example, Capa 1956; Gray and Murphy 2000); however, the production of Islam and religious identity in relation to transnationality on Pakistani radio transcends this characterization.

3. See Bauman and Briggs 2003; Fisher 2012; Kunreuther 2006; 2012.

4. For a detailed historical discussion of Pakistani Radio, see Ahmad 2005; Hasan 2000; Page and Crawley 2001; Siddiqui 1991.

5. See Bolton 1999; Hadlow 2004; Mrazek 2002.

6. See Metcalf 2003; Mitra 1995.

7. As discussed in chapter 5, the years preceding and following the formation of Pakistan witnessed the forced migration of millions of South Asians and a violent transition into the postcolonial epoch. In the present day, the ogoing dispute over the territory of Kashmir, which both India and Pakistan claim as part of their nation-state, further sustains government-sponsored militaristic action, diplomatic impasse, and distrust on both sides of the India-Pakistan border.

8. See Browne 2008; Roche 1982; Seaman 1972.

9. For ethnographic studies of community-based radio in the United States, see Dagron and Cajias 1989; Fraser and Restrepo-Estrada 1998; Shields and Ogles 1995.

10. Much like the use of native languages on minority and indigenous radio (see, for example, Browne 1998; 2008; Cormack 2000; Eisenlohr 2004), the use of regional Pakistani languages and the Pakistani national language of Urdu positions radio as a forum for valuing non-English language practices. Radio therefore offers linguistic resources that engage speakers in the production of difference and "locate such media practices within a wider set of social, political, and economic conditions" (Bessire and Fisher 2012: 19).

11. The competition for sponsorship and finances among immigrant radio programs in the same language also recurs as an issue during the early period of programming (Steffanides 1974).

12. Denigration of radio programming is not limited to South Asian communities; it is a pervasive discourse that recurs in reception analyses of ethnic radio programming in the United States. See Gurza 2004; Lopata 1976; Migala 1987.

13. Zafar Bangash, "Pakistan's Nuclear Prowess Boosts Morale of Muslims Worldwide," *Crescent International*, September 2009, http://www.crescent-online.net/2009/09/pakistans-nuclear-prowess-boosts-morale-of-muslims-worldwide-zafar-bangash-2181-articles.html, accessed August 15, 2013.

14. During the 2000s, segments of the Pakistani population in Houston as well as some radio hosts have protested the scathing and caricatured portrayal of Pakistan and Muslims as "villains" and nefarious enemies in mainstream Indian Hindi language films such as *Border* (1997), *Sarfarosh* (1999), *Mission Kashmir* (2000), *Pukar* (2000), *Gadar: Ek Prem Katha* (2001), *The Hero: Love Story of a Spy* (2003), *Indian* (2001), *Maa Tujhe Salaam* (2002), *Khakee* (2004), and *Deewar: Let's Bring Our Heroes Home* (2004). Several of these movies were blockbuster hits in India. These movies consolidated the genre of "patriotic" films and participated in the growing anti-Pakistan-centered Indian nationalism that transcended the borders of the Indian nation-state and was appropriated among segments of the Indian communities in the diaspora.

For a discussion of the cultural politics of Bollywood in Pakistan, see Chopra 2010.

BIBLIOGRAPHY

Abelman, Nancy, and John Lie. 1995. Blue Dreams: Korean Americans and the Los Angeles Riots. Cambridge, MA: Harvard University Press.

Abraham, Margaret. 2000. Speaking the Unspeakable: Marital Violence among South Asian Immigrants in the United States. New Brunswick, NJ: Rutgers University Press.

Abu-Lughod, Lila. 2002. Do Muslim Women Really Need Saving? Anthropological Reflections on Cultural Relativism and Its Others. American Anthropologist 104 (3): 783–790.

———. 2005. Dramas of Nationhood: The Politics of Television in Egypt. Chicago: University of Chicago Press.

Adams, Bert N. 1974. Urban Skills and Religion: Mechanisms for Coping and Defense among the Ugandan Asians. Social Problems 22 (1): 28–42.

Adams, Isiaka Abiodun. 2011. Globalization: Explaining the Dynamics and Challenges of the Halal Food Surge. Intellectual Discourse 19: 123–145.

Adler, P. S., and S. W. Kwon. 2002. Social Capital: Prospects for a New Concept. Academy of Management Review 27: 17–40.

Afzal, Ahmed. 2005a. Family Planning and Male Friendships: Saathi Condom and Male Same-Sex Sexual Desire in Pakistan. In Culture and the Condom, edited by Karen Anijar and Thuy DaoJensen, 177–205. New York: Peter Lang.

———. 2005b. Islam and the Making of Transnational Citizenship: Pakistani Immigrants in Texas. PhD diss., Yale University.

———. 2009. "It's Allah's Will That I Am Here": State Surveillance and the Immigrant Experience of the Pakistani Muslim Working Poor. In Shifting Positionalities: The Local and Global Geopolitics of Surveillance and Policy, edited by Maria Viteri and Aaron Tobler, 184–203. Newcastle upon Tyne, UK: Cambridge Scholars.

———. 2010. From an Informal to a Transnational Muslim Heritage Economy: Transformations in the Pakistani Ethnic Economy in Houston, Texas. Urban Anthropology, Special Issue: Informal Economies 39 (4): 397–424.

Agamben, Giorgio. 1998. Homo Sacer: Sovereign Power and Bare Life. Translated by Daniel Heller-Roazen. Stanford, CA: Stanford University Press.

———. 2005. State of Exception, translated by Kevin Attell. Chicago: University of Chicago Press.

Agarwal, P. 1991. Passage from India: Post-1965 Indian Immigrants and their Children. Palos Verdes, CA: Yuvati.

Agnew, Robert. 1999. A General Strain Theory of Community Differences in Crime Rates. Journal of Research in Crime and Delinquency 36: 123–155.

Ahmad, Nihal. 2005. A History of Radio Pakistan. Oxford: Oxford University Press.

Ahmar, Moonis. 1996. Ethnicity and State Power in Pakistan: The Karachi Crisis. Asian Survey 36 (10): 1031–1048.

Ahmed, Akbar S. 1976. Millenium and Charisma among Pathans: A Critical Essay in Social Anthropology. London: Routledge & Kegan Paul.

Ahmed, Muneer. 2002. Homeland Insecurity: Racial Violence the Day after September 11. Social Text 20 (3): 101–115.

Altman, Dennis. 2001. Global Sex. Chicago: University of Chicago Press.

Anderson, Benedict. 1983. Imagined Communities: Reflections on the origins and spread of nationalism. London: Verso.

Appadurai, Arjun. 1988. How to Make a National Cuisine: Cookbooks in Contemporary India. Comparative Studies in Society and History 30 (1): 3–24.

———. 1996. Modernity at Large: Cultural dimensions of globalization. Minneapolis: University of Minnesota Press.

Asad, Talal. 1972. Market Model, Class Structure, and Consent: A Reconsideration of Swat Political Organization. Man 7 (1): 74–94.

———. 2003. Formations of the Secular: Christianity, Islam, Modernity. Stanford, CA: Stanford University Press.

Askew, Kelly, and Richard R. Wilk, eds. 2002. Anthropology of Media. Malden, MA: Blackwell.

Assudani, Rashmi H. 2009. Ethnic Entrepreneurship: The Distinct Role of Ties. Journal of Small Business and Entrepreneurship 22 (2): 197–206.

Ayoob, Mohammad. 1969. U.S.-Pakistan Economic Transaction Flows: A Case-Study in International Relations. India Quarterly 25 (1): 44–58.

Ayyar, Raj. 1993. Yaari. In A Lotus of Another Color: An Unfolding of the South Asian Gay and Lesbian Experience, ed. Rakesh Ratti, 167–174. Boston, MA: Alyson Publications.

Bacchetta, Paola. 2002. Rescaling Transnational "Queerdom": Lesbian and "Lesbian" Identitiary-Positionalities in Delhi in the 1980s. Antipode: A Radical Journal of Geography 34 (5): 94–73.

Bacon, Jean. 1996. Life Lines: Community, Family, and Assimilation among Asian Indian Immigrants. New York: Oxford University Press.

Bakalian, Amy, and Mehdi Bozorgmehr. 2009. Backlash 9/11: Middle Eastern and Muslim Americans Repond. Berkeley: University of California Press.

Bald, Vivek. 2013. Bengali Harlem and the Lost Histories of South Asian America. Cambridge, MA: Harvard University Press.

Bald, Vivek, Miabi Chatterji, Sujani Reddy, and Manu Vimalassery, eds. 2013. The Sun Never Sets: South Asian Migrants in an Age of U.S. Power. New York: New York University Press.

Bangash, Zafar. 2009. Pakistan's Nuclear Prowess Boosts Morale of Muslims World-wide. The Crescent International. http://www.crescent-online.net/2009/09/pakistans-nuclear-prowess-boosts-morale-of-muslims-worldwide-zafar-bangash-2181-articles.html. Accessed August 15, 2013.

Barnard, Ian. 2004. Queer Race: Cultural Interventions in the Racial Politics of Queer Theory. New York: Peter Lang.

Barnouw, Erik. 1968. The Golden Web: A History of Broadcasting in the United States. New York: Oxford University Press.

Barth, Fredrik. 1959. Political Leadership among the Swat Pathans. London: Athlone.

Bauman, Richard, and Charles L. Briggs. 2003. Voices of Modernity: Language Ideologies and the Politics of Inequality. New York: Cambridge University Press.

Baumann, M. 1998. Sustaining "Little India": Hindu Diasporas in Europe. In Strangers and Sojourners, edited by G. ter Haar, 95–132. Leuven, Netherlands: Peeters.

Belden, Elionne L. W. 1997. Claiming Chinese Identity. New York: Garland.

Bessire, Lucas, and Daniel Fisher, eds. 2012. Radio Fields: Anthropology and Wireless Sound in the 21st Century. New York: New York University Press.

Bhatia, Sunil. 2007. American Karma: Race, Culture, and Identity in the Indian Diaspora. New York: New York University Press.

Bocock, Robert J. 1971. The Ismailis in Tanzania: A Weberian Analysis. British Journal of Sociology 22 (4): 365–380.

Bolton, Lissant. 1999. Radio and the Redefinition of Kastom in Vanuatu. Contemporary Pacific 11 (2): 335–360.

Bonilla-Silva. 2006. Racism without Racists: Color-Blind Racism and the Persistence of Racial Inequality in America. New York: Rowman & Littlefield.

Bose, Sugata, and Ayesha Jalal. 1996. Modern South Asia: History, Culture, Political Economy. New York: Routledge.

Bourgois, Philippe. 2002. In Search of Respect: Selling Crack in El Barrio. Cambridge: Cambridge University Press.

Bourdieu, Pierre. 1977. Outline of a Theory of Practice. Cambridge: Cambridge University Press.

———. 1984. Distinction: A Social Critique of the Judgment of Taste. Cambridge, MA: Harvard University Press.

Bradley, Robert L. 2009a. Capitalism at Work: Business, Government and Energy. Salem, MA: M&M Scrivener.

———. 2009b. Enron and Ken Lay. MA: M&M Scrivener.

Brady, Mary Pat. 2002. Extinct Lands, Temporal Geographies: Chicana Literature and the Urgency of Space. Durham, NC: Duke University Press.

Brah, Avtar. 1996. Cartographies of Diaspora: Contesting Identities. New York: Routledge.

Bray, John. 1997. Pakistan at 50: A State in Decline? International Affairs 73 (2): 315–331.

Breakwell, G. M. 1986. Coping with Threatened Identities. London: Methuen.

Brodkin, E. I. 1967. United States Aid to India and Pakistan: The Attitudes of the Fifties. International Affairs 43 (4): 664–677.

Brooks, Allison, Fatimah L. C. Jackson, and Roy Richard Grinker. 2004. Race and Ethnicity. In Anthropology Explored, edited by Ruth O. Selig, Marilyn London, and R. Ann Kaupp., 155–170. Washington, DC: Smithsonian Institution.

Browne, Donald. 1998. Talking the Talk on Indigenous Radio. Cultural Survival Quarterly 22 (2): 53–59.

———. 2008. Speaking in Our Own Tongues: Linguistic Minority Radio in the United States. In Radio Cultures: The South Medium in American Life, edited by Michael Keith, 23–46. New York: Peter Lang.

Bullard, Robert 1990. Dumping in Dixie: Race, Class and Environmental Quality. Boulder, CO: Westview.

———. 2002. Confronting Environmental Racism in the Twenty-First Century, 4 (1). http://www.worlddialogue.org/content.php?id=179, accessed August 1, 2013.

———. 2005. The Quest for Environmental Justice: Human Rights and the Politics of Pollution. San Francisco: Sierra Club Books.

Burki, Shahid. 1999. Pakistan: Fifty Years of Nationhood. Boulder, CO: Westview.

Butalia, Urvashi. 2000. The Other Side of Silence: Voices from the Partition of India. Durham, NC: Duke University Press.

Butler, Judith. 2004. Precious Life: The Power of Mourning and Violence. New York: Verso.

Cainkar, Louise A. 2009. Homeland Insecurity: The Arab American and Muslim American Experience since 9/11. New York: Russell Sage Foundation.

Calhoun, Craig. 2003. "Belonging" in the Cosmopolitan Imaginary. Ethnicities 3 (4): 531–553.

Cantu, Jr., Lionel, and Eithne Luibheid, eds. 2005. Queer Migrations: Sexuality, U.S. Citizenship, and Border Crossings. Minneapolis: University of Minnesota Press.

Capa, Cornell. 1956. Martyrdom in Ecuador. Life, January 30.

Cardona, Euridice T. Charon. 2004. Re-encountering Cuban Tastes in Australia. The Australian Journal of Anthropology 15 (1): 40–53.

Carlson, Alvar W. 1994. Caribbean Immigration to the U.S. 1965–1989. Caribbean Affairs 7 (March–April): 142–160.

———. 1998. America's Growing Observance of Cinco de Mayo. Journal of American Culture 21 (2): 7–16.

Cesari, Jocelyne. 2009. Muslims in the West after 9/11: Religion, Politics and Law. New York: Routledge.

Chakravarty, Sumita. 1993. National Identity in Indian Popular Cinema, 1947–1987. Austin: University of Texas Press.

Chan, Sucheng. 1991. Asian Americans: An Interpretive History. New York: Twayne.

Cheah, Pheng, and Bruce Robbins, eds. 1998. Cosmopolitics: Thinking and Feeling Beyond the Nation. Minneapolis: University of Minnesota Press.

Cheng, Lucie, and Philip Yang. 2000. The "Model Minority" Deconstructed. In Contemporary Asian America: A Multidisciplinary Reader, edited by Min Zhou and James Gatewood, 459–482. New York: New York University Press.

Chopra, Anuj. 2010. How Pakistan Fell in Love with Bollywood: The History of a Culture Clash. Foreign Policy, March 15.

Chua, Rosalind. 2010. Halal: The Next Frontier. Penang Economic Quarterly, May, 8–12.

Clarke, Kamari M. 2004. Mapping Yoruba Networks: Power and Agency in the Making of Transnational Communities. Durham, NC: Duke University Press.

Clifford, James, and George E. Marcus. 1986. Writing Culture: The Poetics and Politics of Ethnography. Berkeley: University of California Press.

Cohen, Lawrence. 1995. Holi in Banaras and the Mahaland of Modernity. Gay and Lesbian Quarterly 2: 399–424.

Cohn, Samuel, and Mark Fossett. 1996. What Spatial Mismatch? The Proximity of Blacks to Employment in Boston and Houston. Social Forces 75 (2): 557–573.

Coleman, J. 1990. Foundations of Social Theory. Cambridge, MA: Harvard University Press.

Constitution of the Shia Imami Ismaili Muslims. 1987. London: Islamic Publications.

Cormack, Mike. 2000. Minority Languages, Nationalism and Broadcasting: The British and Irish Examples. Nations and Nationalism 6 (3): 383–398.

Coward, Harold, John R. Hinnells, and Raymond B. Williams. 2000. The South Asian Religious Diaspora in Britain, Canada, and the United States. Albany: State University of New York Press.

Cruz-Malave, Arnoldo, and Martin F. Manalansan IV, eds. 2002. Queer Globalizations: Citizenship and the Afterlife of Colonialism. New York: New York University Press.

D'Alisera, JoAnn. 2004. An Imagined Geography: Sierra Leonean Muslims in America. Philadelphia: University of Pennsylvania Press.

Daftary, Farhad. 1990. The Ismailis: Their History and Doctrine. Cambridge: Cambridge University Press.

———. 1998. A Short History of the Ismailis: Traditions of a Muslim Community. Edinburgh: Edinburgh University Press.

Dagron, Alfonso and and Lupe Cajias, eds. 1989. Las Radios Mineras de Bolivia. La Paz, Bolivia: Cimca-Unesco.

Darien-Smith, Eve. 1995. Law in Place: Legal Mediations of National Identity and State Territory in Europe. In Nationalism, Racism and the Rule of Law, edited by Peter Fitzpatrick, 27–44. Dartmouth, UK: Aldershot.

Das Gupta, Monisha. 2006. Unruly Immigrants: Rights, Activism and Transnational South Asian Politics in the United States. Durham, NC: Duke University Press.

Dasgupta, S. 1998. A Patchwork Shawl: Chronicles of South Asian Women in America. New Brunswick, NJ: Rutgers University Press.

Dave, Naisargi. 2006. Between Queer Ethics and Sexual Morality: Lesbian and Gay Activism in New Delhi, India. Ann Arbor: University of Michigan Press.

———. 2012. Queer Activism in India: A Story in the Anthropology of Ethics. Durham, NC: Duke University Press.

Davila, Arlene. 2004. Barrio Dreams: Puerto Ricans, Latinos and the Neoliberal City. Berkeley: University of California Press.

Decena, Carlos Ulises. 2011. Tacit Subjects: Belonging and Same-Sex Desire among Dominican Immigrant Men. Durham, NC: Duke University Press.

Derne, Steve. 2000. Movies, Masculinity, and Modernity: An Ethnography of Men's Filmgoing in India. Westport, CT: Greenwood.

Devji, Faisal. 2005. Landscapes of the Jihad: Militancy, Morality, Modernity. Ithaca, NY: Cornell University Press.

Dhaliwal, Spinder. 1998. Silent Contributors: Asian Female Entrepreneurs and Women in Business. Women's Studies International Forum 21 (5): 463–474.

Dhingra, Pawan. 2007. Managing Multicultural Lives: Asian American Professionals and the Challenge of Multiple Identities. Stanford, CA: Stanford University Press.

———. 2008. Committed to Ethnicity, Committed to America: How Second Generation Indian Americans' Ethnic Boundaries Further their Americanization. Journal of Intercultural Studies 29 (1): 41–63.

———. 2012. Life Beyond the Lobby: Indian American Motel Owners and the American Dream. Stanford, CA: Stanford University Press.

Dissanayake, Wimal, and Malti Sahai. 1992. Sholay: A Cultural Reading. New Delhi, India: Wiley Eastern.

Doi, A. R. I. 1984. Shari'ah: The Islamic Law. London: Ta-Ha.

Dossani, Shahid. 1997. Being Muslim and Gay. In Que(e)rying Religion: A Critical Anthology, edited by Gary David Comstock and Susan E. Henking, 236–237. New York: Continuum.

Douglas, Susan J. 2004. Listening In: Radio and the American Imagination. Minneapolis: University of Minnesota Press.

Duany, Jorge. 2000. Nation on the Move: The Construction of Cultural Identities in Puerto Rico and the Diaspora. American Ethnologist 27 (1): 5–30.

Duggan, Lisa. 2002. The New Normativity: The Sexual Politics of Neoliberalism. In Materializing Democracy: Towards a Revitalized Cultural Politics, edited by Russ Castronovo and Dana Nelson, 175–194. Durham, NC: Duke University Press.

———. 2003. The Twilight of Equality? Neoliberalism, Cultural Politics, and the Attack on Democracy. Boston: Beacon.

Duran, K. 1993. Homosexuality and Islam. In Homosexuality and World Religions, edited by A. Swidler, 181–197. Valley Forge, PA: Trinity.

Dynes, W., and S. Donaldson, eds. 1992. History of Homosexuality in Europe and America. New York: Garland.

Ebaugh, Helen and Janet S. Chafetz. 2002. Religion across Borders: Transnational Religious Networks. Lanham, MD AltaMira.

Eisenlohr, Patrick. 2004. Language Revitalization and New Technologies: Cultures of Electronic Mediation and the Refiguring of Communities. Annual Review of Anthropology 33: 21–45.

Emadi, Hafizullah. 1998. The End of Taqiyya: Reaffirming the Religious Identity of Ismailis in Shughnan, Badakhshan: Political Implications for Afghanistan. Middle Eastern Studies 34 (3): 103–120.

Emerson, Michael O., Jenifer Bratter, Junia Howell, P. Wilner Jeanty, and Mike Cline.

2013. Houston Region Grows More Racially/Ethnically Diverse, With Small Declines in Segregation. A Joint Report Analyzing Census Data from 1990, 2000, and 2010. Houston: Kinder Institute for Urban Research and the Hobby Center for the Study of Texas.

Eng, David L., Judith Halberstam, and Jose Esteban Munoz, eds. 2005. What's Queer about Queer Studies Now? Social Text 23 (3–4): 84–85.

Ernst, Gisela. 1994. Beyond Language: The Many Dimensions of an ESL Program. Anthropology and Education Quarterly 25: 317–335.

Espiritu, Yen Le. 2003. Home Bound: Filipino American Lives across Cultures, Communities, and Countries. Berkeley: University of California Press.

Ewing, Katherine Pratt, ed. 2008. Being and Becoming: Muslims in the United States since 9/11. New York: Russell Sage.

Fabian, Johannes. 1983. Time and the Other: How Anthropology Makes Its Object. New York: Columbia University Press.

Faye Ginsberg, Lila Abu-Lughod, and Brian Larkin, eds. 2002. Media Worlds: Anthropology on a New Terrain. Berkeley: University of California Press.

Feagin, J. R. 1988. Free Enterprise City: Houston in Political-Economic Perspective. New Brunswick, NJ: Rutgers University Press.

———. 1985. The Global Context of Metropolitan Growth: Houston and the Oil Industry. American Journal of Sociology 90 (6): 1204–1230.

Featherstone, Mike, Scott Lash, and Roland Robertson, eds. 1995. Global Modernities. London: Sage Publications.

Fischer, Johan. 2005. Feeding Secularism: Consuming Halal among the Malays in London. Diaspora 14 (2/3): 275–297.

Fischer, Michael M. J., and Mehdi Abedi. 2002. Debating Muslims: Cultural Dialogues in Postmodernity and Tradition. Madison: University of Wisconsin Press.

Fisher, Daniel. 2012. From the Studio to the Street: Producing the Voice in Indigenous Australia. In Radio Fields: Anthropology and Wireless Sound in the 21st Century, edited by Lucas Bessire and Daniel Fisher, 69–88. New York: New York University Press.

Fix, Michael, and Wendy Zimmermann. 1993. Educating Immigrant Children: Chapter 1 in the Changing City. Washington, DC: Urban Institute Press.

Flores, William V., and Rina Benmayor, eds.1997. Latino Cultural Citizenship: Claiming Identity, Space, and Rights. Boston: Beacon.

Foucault, M. 1991. Governmentality. Translated by Rosi Braidotti and revised by Colin Gordon. In The Foucault Effect: Studies in Governmentality, edited by Graham Burchell, Colin Gordon, and Peter Miller, 87–104. Chicago: University of Chicago Press.

Fox, Lauren. 2003. Enron: The Rise and Fall. Hoboken, NJ: John Wiley.

Fraser, Colin, and Sonia Restrepo-Estrada. 1998. Communicating for Development: Human Change for Survival. London: Tauris.

Freeman, James. 1989. Hearts of Sorrow: Vietnamese-American Lives. Stanford, CA: Stanford University Press.

Frey, William H. 2000. The New Urban Demographics: Race Space and Boomer Aging. Brookings Review 18 (3): 20–23.

Garreau, Joel. 1992. Edge City: Life on the New Frontier. New York: Doubleday.

George, Annie. 2002. Review: Same-Sex Love in India: Readings from Literature and History. International Journal of Sociology of the Family 20 (1): 91–93.

Ginsburg, Faye D., Lila Abu-Lughod, and Brian Larkin, eds. 2002. Media Worlds: Anthropology on a New Terrain. Berkeley: University of California Press.

Glenn, Evelyn Nakano. 2002. Unequal Freedom: How Race and Gender Shaped American Citizenship and Labor. Cambridge, MA: Harvard University Press.

Glick Schiller, Nina, Linda Basch, and Cristina Blanc Szanton, eds. 1992. Towards a Transnational Perspective on Migration: Race, Class, Ethnicity and Nationalism Reconsidered. New York: New York Academy of Sciences.

———. 1994. Nations Unbound: Transnational Projects, Postcolonial Predicaments, and Deterritorialized Nation-States. London: Gordon and Breach Science.

Glick Schiller, Nina, and Georges Fouron. 1999. Terrains of Blood and Nation: Haitian Transnational Social Fields. Ethnic and Racial Studies 22 (2): 340–366.

Gole, Nilufer. 2002. Islam in Public: New Visibilities and New Imaginaries. Public Culture 14 (1): 173–190.

Gopinath, Gayatri. 1997. South Asian Sexualities in Motion. Positions: Journal of East Asia Critique 5 (2): 467–489.

———. 2005. Impossible Desires: Queer Diasporas and South Asian Public Cultures. Durham, NC: Duke University Press.

Gray, Frank, and Eila Murphy. 2000. The Unlikely Missionary: Radio Rises to the Challenge of the Unreached Peoples Groups. Posted on MissionFrontiers, November 1. http://www.missionfrontiers.org/issue/article/the-unlikely-missionary.

Greene, P.G. 1997. A Resource-Based Approach to Ethnic Business Sponsorship: A Consideration of Ismaili-Pakistani Immigrants. Journal of Small Business Management 35 (4): 58–71.

Greiner, Clemens, and Patrick Sakdapolrak. 2013. Translocality: Concepts, Applications and Emerging Research Perspectives. Geography Compass 7 (5): 373–384.

Grewal, Inderpal. 2005. Transnational America: Feminisms, Diasporas, Neoliberalisms. Durham, NC: Duke University Press.

Grima, Benedicte. 1991. The Role of Suffering in Women's Performance of Paxto. In Gender, Genre and Power in South Asian Expressive Traditions, edited by Arjun Appadurai, Margaret A. Mills, and Frank J. Korom, 78–101. Philadelphia: University of Pennsylvania Press.

Gupta, Akhil, and James Ferguson. 1997. Culture, Power, Place: Ethnography at the End of an Era. In Culture, Power, Place: Explorations in Critical Anthropology, edited by Akhil Gupta and James Ferguson, 1–32. Durham, NC: Duke University Press.

Gupta, Sangeeta R. 1999. Emerging Voices: South Asian American Women Redefine Self, Family and Community. New York: Sage.

Gurza, Agustin. 2004. Ay, Caramba! Spanish-Lanugage Radio Stations Filled with

Raunch. Alemeda Times-Star, August 30. Retrieved from http://www.freerepublic
.com/focus/fr/1203373/posts, July 21, 2013.

Habermas, Jurgen. 1998. The Inclusion of the Other. Studies in Political Theory. Cambridge, MA: MIT Press.

Haddad, William J. 2002. White Paper: Preliminary Report on Hate Crimes against
Arabs and Muslims in the United States. Chicago: Arab-American Bar Association
of Illinois.

Haddad, Yvonne, ed. 2002. Muslims in the West: From Sojourners to Citizens. Oxford:
Oxford University Press.

———. 2004. Not Quite American? The Shaping of Arab and Muslim Identity in the
United States. Edmonson Historical Lecture. Waco, TX: Baylor University Press.

———. 2011. Becoming American? The Forging of Arab and Muslim Identity in Pluralist America, Becoming American? The Forging of Arab and Muslim Identity in
Pluralist America. Waco, TX: Baylor University Press.

Haddad, Yvonne, and Adair T. Lummis. 1987. Islamic Values in the United States: A
Comparative Study. New York: Oxford University Press.

Haddad, Yvonne, and Jane Smith, eds. 1993. Mission to America: Five Islamic Sectarian
Movements in North America. Gainesville: University Press of Florida.

Haddad, Yvonne, Jane Smith, and John Esposito, eds. 2003. Religion and Immigration: Christian, Jewish, and Muslim Experiences in the United States. New York:
AltaMira.

Hadlow, Martin. 2004. The Mosquito Network: American Military Radio in the Solo-
mon Islands during World War II. Journal of Radio and Audio Media 11 (1): 73–86.

Halberstam, Judith. 2005. In a Queer Time and Place: Transgender Bodies, Subcultural
Lives. New York: New York University Press.

Hall, Stuart, ed. 1997. Representation: Cultural Representations and Signifying Practices. London: Sage.

Hannerz, Ulf. 1996. Transnational Connections: Culture, People, Places. New York:
Routledge.

Hansen, Thomas Blom, and Finn Stepputat. 2005. Sovereign Bodies: Citizens,
Migrants, and States in the Postcolonial World. Princeton, NJ: Princeton University
Press.

Haq Farhat. 1995. Rise of the MQM in Pakistan: Politics of Ethnic Mobilization. Asian
Survey 35 (11): 990–1004.

Hardt, Michael, and Antonio Negri. 2000. Empire. Cambridge, MA: Harvard University Press.

Harvey, David. 1989. The Condition of Post-Modernity: An Enquiry into the Origins of
Cultural Change. Cambridge, MA: Blackwell.

Harvey, David. 2005. A Brief History of Neoliberalism. Oxford: Oxford University
Press.

Hasan, Burhanuddin. 2000. Uncensored: An Eyewitness Account of Abuse of Power
and Media in Pakistan. Islamabad, Pakistan: Royal Book Company.

Healy, Paul M., and Krishna G. Palepu. 2003. The Fall of Enron. The Journal of Economic Perspectives 17 (2): 3–26.

Helweg, Arthur, and Usha Helweg. 1990. An Immigrant Success Story: East Indians in America. Philadelphia: University of Pennsylvania Press.

Henderson, M. C., M. G. Oakes, M. G., and M. Smith. 2009. What Plato knew about Enron. Journal of Business Ethics 86: 463–471.

Hess, Gary. 1976. The Forgotten Asian Americans: The East Indian Community in the United States. In The Asian American: The Historical Experience, edited by N. Hundley Jr., 157–177. Santa Barbara, CA: Clio Books.

Hing, Bill. 2006. Deporting Our Souls: Values, Morality, and Immigration Policy. Cambridge: Cambridge University Press.

Hinkson, Melinda. 2012. The Cultural Politics of Radio: Two Views from the Warlpiri Public Sphere. In Radio Fields: Anthropology and Wireless Sound in the 21st Century, edited by Lucas Bessire and Daniel Fisher, 142–159. New York: New York University Press.

Hirsh, J. S. 2003. A Courtship After Marriage: Sexuality and Love in Mexican Transnational Families. Berkeley: University of California Press.

Hochschild, J. 1995. Facing Up to the American Dream: Race, Class, and the Soul of the Nation. Princeton, NJ: Princeton University Press.

Holtzman, Dinah. 2011. Between Yaars: The Queering of Dosti in Contemporary Bollywood Films. In Bollywood and Globalization: Indian Popular Cinema, Nation, and Diaspora, edited by Rini Bhattacharya Mehta and Rajeshwari V. Pandharipande, 111–128. London: Anthem.

Hondagneu-Sotelo, P. 2001. Domestica: Immigrant Workers Cleaning and Caring in the Shadows of Affluence. Berkeley: University of California Press.

Howell, Sally, and Amaney Jamal. 2008. Detroit Exceptionalism and the Limits of Political Incorporation. In Being and Becoming: Muslims in the United States since 9/11, edited by Katherine Pratt Ewing, 47–79. New York: Russell Sage.

Houston Chronicle. 2001. "A Regular Day" at Store Despite Protest Threats: Workers at Pakistani Convenience Store Rumored to Support Terrorism. September 22.

Houston Chronicle. 2002. A Year Later, Many Muslims Still Shackled by 9/11. September 8.

Howell, Sally, and Andrew Shryock. 2003. Cracking Down on Diaspora: Arab Detriot and America's "War on Terror." Anthropological Quarterly 76 (3): 443–462.

Hutchby, Ian. 1999. Frame Attunement and Footing in the Organization of Talk Radio Openings. Journal of Sociolinguistics 3 (1): 41–64.

Hutchinson, E. P. 1981. Legislative History of American Immigration Policy, 1798–1965. Philadelphia: University of Pennsylvania Press.

Huxtable, Ada Louise. 1976. Kicked a Building Lately? San Francisco: University of California Press.

Ima, Kenji. 1995. Testing the American Dream: At-Risk Southeast Asian Refugee Students in Secondary Schools. In California's Immigrant Children: Theory, Research, and Implications for Educational Policy, edited by Ruben Rumbaut and Wayne Cornelius, 191–209. San Diego: University of California, Center for U.S.-Mexican Studies.

Inoue, Miyako. 2003. Gender, Language, and Modernity: Toward an Effective History of Japanese Women's Language. American Ethnologist 29 (2): 392–422.

Itzigsohn, Jose. 2000. Developing Poverty: The State, Labor Market Deregulation, and the Informal Economy in Costa Rica and the Dominican Republic. University Park: Pennsylvania State University Press.

Jacobson, David. 1996. Rights across Borders: Immigration and the Decline of Citizenship. Baltimore, MD: Johns Hopkins University Press.

Jalal, Ayesha. 1985. The Sole Spokesman: Jinnah, the Muslim League, and the Demand for Pakistan. Cambridge: Cambridge University Press.

———. 1995. Democracy and Authoritarianism in South Asia: A Comparative and Historical Perspective. Cambridge: Cambridge University Press.

Jamal, Amaney, and Nadine Naber. 2008. Race and Arab Americans Before and After 9/11: From Invisible Citizens to Visible Subjects. Syracuse, NY: Syracuse University Press.

Jamal, Amreen. 2001. The Story of Lot and the Qur'an's Perception of the Morality of Same-Sex Sexuality. Journal of Homosexuality 41 (1): 1–88.

James, Roberta. 2004. Halal Pizza: Food and Culture in a Busy World. Australian Journal of Anthropology April 15 (1): 1–11.

Jaspal, Rusi, and Siraj, Asifa. 2011. Perceptions of Coming Out Among British Muslim Gay Men. Psychology and Sexuality 2 (3): 183–197.

Johnson, Chalmers. 2004. The Sorrows of Empire: Militarism, Secrecy, and the End of the Republic. New York: Metropolitan Books / Henry Holt.

Jung, P., and R. Smith. 1993. Heterosexism: An Ethical Challenge. Albany: State University of New York Press.

Kaba, Amadu Jacky. 2008. Race, Gender and Progress: Are Black American Women the New Model Minority? Journal of African American Studies 12 (4): 309–335.

Kadende-Kaiser, Rose M., and Paul Kaiser. 1998. Identity, Citizenship, and Transnationalism: Ismailis in Tanzania and Burundians in the Diaspora. Africa Today 45 (3/4): 461–480.

Kahn, R. Y. H. 1989. Judaism and Homosexuality: The Traditionalist/Progressive Debate. Journal of Homosexuality 18: 47–82.

Kaiser, Paul J. 1996. Culture, Transnationalism, and Civil Society: Aga Khan Social Service Initiatives in Tanzania. Westport, CT: Praeger.

Kane, Ousmane Oumar. 2011. The Homeland Is the Arena: Religion, Transnationalism, and the Integration of Senegalese Immigrants in America. Oxford: Oxford University Press.

Kang, Miliann. 2010. The Managed Hand: Race, Gender, and the Body in Beauty Service Work. Berkeley: University of California Press.

Keith, Michael C. 2008. Radio Cultures: The South Medium in American Life. New York: Peter Lang.

Khan, Badruddin. 1992. Not-So-Gay Life in Karachi: A View of a Pakistani Living in Toronto. In Sexuality and Eroticism among Males in Moslem Societies, edited by Arno Schmitt and Jehoeda Sofer, 275–296. New York: Haworth.

———. 1997. Sex Longing and Not Belonging: A Gay Muslim's Quest for Love and Meaning. Oakland, CA: Floating Lotus.

Khan, Shaheen Irshad. 1972. Rejection Alliance? A Case Study of US–Pakistan Relations, 1947–1967. Lahore, Pakistan: Feroz Sons Ltd.

Khan, Shivananda. 1997. Perspectives on Males Who Have Sex with Males in India and Bangladesh. London: Naz Foundation.

Khandelwal, Madhulika S. 2002. Becoming American, Being Indian: An Immigrant Community in New York City. Ithaca, NY: Cornell University Press.

Kibria, Nazli. 1998. The Racial Gap: South Asian American Racial Identity and the Asian American Movement. In A Part, Yet Apart: South Asians in Asian America, edited by Lavina Shankar and Rajini Srikant, 69–78. Philadelphia: Temple University Press.

———. 2011. Muslims in Motion: Islam and National Identity in the Bangladeshi Diaspora. New Brunswick, NJ: Rutgers University Press.

Kim, Claire Jean. 2004. Unyielding Positions: A Critique of the "Race" Debate. Ethnicities 4 (3): 337–355.

Klineberg, Stephen. 2008. The Houston Area Survey, 1982–2008. Data and codebook available at www.houstonareasurvey.org.

Koshy, Susan. 2001. Morphing Race into Ethnicity: Asian Americans and Critical Transformations of Whiteness. Boundaries 2, 28 (1): 153–194.

Kreneck, Thomas H. 1985. Documenting a Mexican-American Community: The Houston Example. The American Archivist 48 (3): 272–285.

Kugelmass, Jack. 1991. Wishes Come True: Designing the Greenwich Village Halloween Parade. The Journal of American Folklore 104 (414): 443–465.

Kugle, Scott Siraj al-Haqq. 2003. Sexuality, Diversity, and Ethics in the Agenda of Progressive Muslims. In Progressive Muslims: On Justice, Gender and Pluralism, edited by Omid Safi, 190–234. Oxford: One World.

———. 2014. Living Out Islam: Voices of Gay, Lesbian, and Transgender Muslims. New York: New York University Press.

Kunreuther, Laura. 2006. Technologies of the Voice: FM Radio, Telephone, and the Nepali Diaspora in Kathmandu. Cultural Anthropology 21 (3): 323–353.

———. 2012. Aurality under Democracy: Cultural History of FM Radio and Ideologies of Voice in Nepal. In Radio Fields: Anthropology and Wireless Sound in the 21st Century, edited by Lucas Bessire and Daniel Fisher, 48–68. New York: New York University Press.

Kurashige, Lon. 2002. Japanese American Celebration and Conflict: A History of Ethnic Identity and Festival, 1034–1990. Berkeley: University of California Press.

Kurein, Prema. 2001. Religion, Ethnicity and Politics: Hindu and Muslim Indian Immigrants in the United States. Ethnic and Racial Studies 24 (2): 263–293.

Kwon, V.H., Helen Rose Ebaugh, and J. Hagan. 1997. The Structure and Function of

Cell Group Ministry in a Korean Christian Church. Journal for the Scientific Study of Religion 36: 247–256.

Kwong, Peter. 1997. Forbidden Workers: Illegal Chinese Immigrants and American Labor. New York: New Press.

Labrador, Roderick. 2002. Performing Identity: The Public Presentation of Culture and Ethnicity among Filipinos in Hawai'i. Journal for Cultural Research 6 (3): 287–307.

Laguerre, Michael. 1998. Diasporic Citizenship: Haitian Americans in Transnational America. New York: Palgrave Macmillan.

Leap, William L., and Heiko Motschenbacher. 2012. Launching a New Phase in Language and Sexuality Sudies. Journal of Language and Sexuality 1 (1): 1–14.

Lee, Jennifer, and Min Zhou, eds. 2004. Asian American Youth: Culture, Identity, and. Ethnicity. New York: Routledge.

Lee, S. J. 1996. Unraveling the Model Minority Stereotype: Listening to Asian American Youth. New York: Teachers College Press.

———. 2005. Up Against Whiteness: Race, School, and Immigrant Youth. New York: Teachers College Press.

Leichty, Mark. 1996. Katmandu as a Translocality: Multiple Places in a Nepali Space. In The Geography of Identity, edited by Patricia Yaeger. Ann Arbor: University of Michigan Press.

Lemke, T. 2001. The Birth of Bio-Politics: Michael Foucault's Lectures at the College de France on Neo-Liberal Governmentality. Economy and Society 30 (2): 190–207.

Leonard, Karen. 1992. Making Ethnic Choices: California's Punjabi Mexican Americans. Philadelphia: Temple University Press.

———. 1997. The South Asian Americans. Westport, CT: Greenwood.

———. 2000. State, Culture and Politics: Political Action and Representation among South Asians in North America. Diaspora: 9 (1): 21–38.

———. 2003. Muslims in the United States: The State of Research. New York: Russell Sage Foundation.

———. 2005. American Muslims and Authority: Competing Discourses in a Non-Muslim State. Journal of American Ethnic History (Fall): 5–30.

———. 2007. Locating Home: India's Hyderabadis Abroad. New Delhi, India: Oxford University Press.

Lessinger, Joanna. 1995. From the Ganges to the Hudson: Indian Immigrants in New York City. Boston: Allyn and Bacon.

Lew, J. 2006. Burden of Acting Neither White nor Black: Asian American Identities and Achievement in Urban School. Urban Review 38 (5): 335–352.

Li, Wei. 1998. Anatomy of a New Ethnic Settlement: The Chinese Ethnoburb in Los Angeles. Urban Studies 35 (3): 479–501.

———. 2009. Ethnoburn: The New Ethnic Community in North America. Honolulu: University of Hawaii Press.

Light, Ivan. 1972. Ethnic Enterprise in America: Business and Welfare among Chinese, Japanese, and Blacks. Berkeley: University of California Press.

Light, Ivan, and Elizabeth Roach. 1996. Self-Employment: Mobility Ladder or

Economic Lifeboat? In Ethnic Los Angeles, edited by Roger Waldinger and Mehdi Bozorgmehr. New York: Russell Sage Foundation.

Light, Ivan, Georges Sabagh, Mehdi Bozorgmehr and Claudia Der-Martirosian. 1994. Beyond the Ethnic Enclave Economy. Social Problems 41 (1): 65–80.

Lin, Jan. 1995. Ethnic Places, Postmodernism, and Urban Change in Houston. Sociological Quarterly 36 (4): 629–647.

Lindholm, Charles. 1982. Generosity and Jealousy: The Swat Pukhtun of Northern Pakistan. New York: Columbia University Press.

Lopata, Helena Znaniecki. 1976. Polish Americans: Status Competition in an Ethnic Community. Upper Saddle River, NJ: Prentice-Hall.

Lowe, Lisa. 1996. Immigrant Acts: On Asian American Cultural Politics. Durham, NC: Duke University Press.

Ludden, David. 1996. Contesting the Nation: Religion, Community, and the Politics of Democracy in India. Philadelphia: University of Pennsylvania Press.

Luibheid, Eithne. 2002. Entry Denied: Controlling Sexuality at the Border. Minneapolis: University of Minnesota Press.

Maher, Kristen H. 2002. Who Has a Right to Rights? Citizenship's Exclusions in an Age of Migration. In Globalization and Human Rights, edited by A. Brysk. Berkeley: University of California Press.

Maira, Sunaina. 2002. Desis in the House: Indian Youth Cultures in New York City. Philadelphia: Temple University Press.

———. 2009. Missing: Youth, Citizenship and Empire after 9/11. Durham, NC: Duke University Press.

Malick, Jayanti. 2010. Racial Triangulation of Latino/a Workers by Agricultural Employers. Human Organization 65 (4): 353–61.

Malik, Iftikhar. 1988a. Pakistanis in Michigan: A Study of Third Culture and Acculturation. New York: AMS.

———. 1988b. U.S.-South Asian Relations, 1940–47: American Attitudes towards the Pakistan Movement. New York: Macmillan.

———. 1997. State and Civil Society in Pakistan: Politics of Authority, Ideology and Ethnicity. New York: Macmillan.

Manalansan, Martin. 2003. Global Divas: Filipino Gay Men in the Diaspora. Durham, NC: Duke University Press.

Mandaville, Peter. 1999. Territory and Translocality: Discrepant Idioms of Political Identity. Millennium: Journal of International Studies 28 (3): 653–73.

———. 2001. Transnational Muslim Politics. London: Routledge.

Mankekar, Purnima. 1999. Screening Culture, Viewing Politics: An Ethnography of Television, Womanhood and Nation in Post-Colonial India. Durham, NC: Duke University Press.

Marcus, George E. and Michael F. Fischer. 1986. Anthropology as Cultural Critique. Chicago: University of Chicago Press.

Marcus, George, and Dick Cushman. 1982. Ethnographies as Texts. Annual Review of Anthropology 11: 25–69.

Marcus, George. 1995. Ethnography in/of the World System: The Emergence of Multi-Sited Ethnography. Annual Review of Anthropology 24: 95–117.

Marger, M., and C. Hoffman. 1992. Ethnic Enterprise in Ontario: Immigrant Participation in the Small Business Sector. International Migration Review 26: 968–981.

Massad, Joseph. 2008. Desiring Arabs. Chicago: University of Chicago Press.

Mathew, Biju. 2000. Byte-Sized Nationalism: Mapping the Hindu Right in the United States. Rethinking Marxism 12 (3): 108–128.

———. 2004. Taxi! Cabs and Capitalism in New York City. New York: New Press.

Mathew, Biju, and Vijay Prashad. 2000. The Protean Forms of Yankee Hindutva. Ethnic and Racial Studies 23 (3): 516–35.

Mayer, Vicki. 2000. Capturing Cultural Identity/Creating Community: A Grassroots Video Project in San Antonio, Texas. International Journal of Cultural Studies 3 (1): 57–78.

McComb, David G. 1981. Houston: A History. Austin: University of Texas Press.

McDaniel, Paul N., and Anita I. Drever. 2009. Ethnic Enclave or International Corridor? Immigrant Businesses in a New South City. Southeastern Geographer 49 (1): 3–23.

McDonald, John F. 1995. Houston Remains Unzoned. Land Economics 71 (1): 137–140.

McQuaid, Kim. 2007. Race, Gender, and Space Exploration: A Chapter in the Social History of the Space Age. Journal of American Studies 41 (2): 405–434.

McIntosh, Molly Fifer. 2008. Measuring the Labor Market Impacts of Hurricane Katrina Migration: Evidence from Houston, Texas. American Economic Review: Papers and Proceedings 98 (2): 54–57.

Medina, Jose. 2012. The Epistemology of Resistance: Gender and Racial Oppression, Epistemic Injustice, and Resistant Imaginations. Oxford: Oxford University Press.

Meeker, Michael E. 1980. The Twilight of a South Asian Heroic Age: A Re-reading of Barth's Study of Swat. Man 15: 682–701.

Meeks, Tomiko. 2011. Freedmen's Town, Texas: A Lesson in the Failure of Historic Preservation. Houston History 8 (2): 42–44.

Melkote, Srinivas, and H. L. Steeves. 2001. Communication for Development in the Third World. 2nd ed. London: Sage.

Memon, Muhammad Umar. 1983. Pakistani Urdu Creative Writing on National Disintegration: The Case of Bangladesh. Journal of Asian Studies 43 (1): 105–127.

Menon, Ritu. 1998. Borders and Boundaries: How Women Experienced the Partition of India. New Brunswick, NJ: Rutgers University Press.

Merchant, Hoshang, ed. 2011. Yaraana: Gay Writings from South Asia. New York: Penguin Books.

Metcalf, Barbara, ed. 1996. Making Muslim Space in North America and Europe. Berkeley: University of California Press.

———. 2003. Urdu in India in the 21st Century: A Historian's Perspective. Social Scientist 31(5/6): 29–37.

Migala, Jozef. 1987. Polish Radio Broadcasting in the United States. Boulder, CO: East European Monographs.

Mignolo, Walter. 2000. The Many Faces of Cosmo-polis: Border Thinking and Critical Cosmopolitanism. Public Culture 12 (3): 721–748.

Miguel, Guadalope San. 2005. The Impact of Brown on Mexican American Desegregation Litigation, 1950s to 1980s. Journal of Latinos and Education 4 (4): 221–236.

Miller, Daniel, and Slater, Don. 2000. The Internet: An Ethnographic Approach. Oxford, UK: Berg.

Miller, Toby. 1997. Technologies of Truth: Cultural Citizenship and the Popular Media. Minneapolis: University of Minnesota Press.

Min, Pyong Gap, and Mehdi Bozorgmehr. 2000. Immigrant Entrepreneurship and Business Patterns: A Comparison of Koreans and Iranians in Los Angeles. International Migration Review 34 (3): 707–38.

Minwalla, Omar, B. R. Simon Rosser, Jamie Feldman, and Christine Varga. 2005. Identity Experience among Progressive Gay Muslims in North America: A Qualitative Study within Al-Fatiha. Culture, Health and Sexuality 7 (2): 113–128.

Mir, Raza, and Farah Hasan. 2013. Awaiting the Twelfth Imam in the United States: South Asian Shia Immigrants and the Fragmented American Dream. In The Sun Never Sets: South Asian Migrants in an Age of U.S. Power, edited by Vivek Bald, Miabi Chatterji, Sujani Reddy, and Manu Vimalassery, 301–324. New York: New York University Press.

Mitra, Subrata K. 1995. The Rational Politics of Cultural Nationalism: Subnational Movements of South Asia in Comparative Perspective. British Journal of Political Science 25 (1): 57–77.

Modell, John. 1977. The Economics and Politics of Racial Accommodation: The Japanese of Los Angeles, 1900–42. Urbana: University of Illinois Press.

Mohanty, Chandra Talpade. 1988. Under Western Eyes: Feminist Scholarship and Colonial Discourse. Feminist Review 3: 61–88.

———. 1991. Under Western Eyes: Feminist Scholarship and Colonial Discourses. In Third World Women and the Politics of Feminism, edited by Chandra Talpade Mohanty, Ann Russo, and Lourdes Torres, 51–80. Bloomington: Indiana University Press.

Morris, H. S. 1956. Indians in East Africa: A Study in a Plural Society. British Journal of Sociology 7 (3): 194–211.

———. 1957. Factions in Indian and Overseas Indian Societies, Part 3: Communal Rivalry among Indians in Uganda. British Journal of Sociology 8 (4): 306–317.

———. 1958. The Divine Kingship of the Aga Khan: A Study of Theocracy in East Africa. Southwestern Journal of Anthropology 14 (4): 454–472.

Mrazek, Rudolf. 2002. Engineers of Happy Land: Technology and Nationalism in a Colony. Princeton, NJ: Princeton University Press.

Mukhi, S. M. 2000. Doing the Desi Thing: Performing Indiannes in New York City. New York: Garland.

Munoz, Jose Esteban. 1999. Disidentifications: Queers of Color and the Performance of Politics. Minneapolis: University of Minnesota Press.

Naber, Nadine. 2012. Arab America: Gender, Cultural Politics, and Activism. New York: New York University Press.

Naficy, Hamid. 1993. The Making of Exile Cultures: Iranian Television in Los Angeles. Minneapolis: University of Minnesota Press.

Najam, Adil. 2006. Portrait of a Giving Community: Philanthropy by the Pakistani-American Diaspora. Cambridge, MA: Harvard University Press.

Nanji, Azim. 1974. Modernization and Change in the Nizari Ismaili Community in East Africa: A Perspective. Journal of Religion in Africa 6 (2): 123–139.

Narayan, Kirin. 1993. How Native is a "Native" Anthropologist? American Anthropologist 95 (3): 671–686.

Northrup, Herbert. 1968. In-Plant Movement of Negroes in the Aerospace Industry. Monthly Labor Review 91 (2): 22–25.

Okihiro, Gary Y. 1994. Margins and Mainstreams: Asians in American History and Culture. Seattle: University of Washington Press.

Omatsu, Greg. 1994. The "Four Prisons" and the Movements of Liberation: Asian American Activism from the 1960s to the 1990s. In The State of Asian America, edited by Karin Aguilar-San Juan, 19–70. Boston: South End.

Omi, Michael, and Howard Winant. 1986. Racial Formation in the United States. New York: Routledge.

Ong, Aihwa. 1996. Cultural Citizenship as Subject-Making: Immigrants Negotiate Racial and Cultural Boundaries in the United States. Current Anthropology 37 (5): 737–751.

———. 1999. Flexible Citizenship: The Cultural Logic of Transnationality. Durham, NC: Duke University Press.

———. 2005. Splintering Cosmopolitanism: Asian Immigrants and Zones of Autonomy in the American West. In Sovereign Bodies: Citizens, Migrants, and States in the Post-Colonial World, edited by Thomas Blom Hansen and Finn Stepputat, 257–275. Princeton, NJ: Princeton University Press.

———. 2006. Neoliberalism as Exception: Mutations in Citizenship and Sovereignty. Durham, NC: Duke University Press.

Ong, Paul, Edna Bonacich, and Lucie Cheng. 1994. The New Asian Immigration in Los Angeles and Global Restructuring. Philadelphia: Temple University Press.

Ong, Paul, and John M. Liu. 2000. U.S. Immigration Policies and Asian Migration. In Contemporary Asian America: A Multidisciplinary Reader, edited by Min Zhou and James Gatewood, 155–174. New York: New York University Press.

Osajima, Keith. 2000. Asian Americans as the Model Minority: An Analysis of the Popular Press Image in the 1960s and 1980s. In Contemporary Asian America: A Multidisciplinary Reader, edited by Min Zhou and James Gatewood, 449–458. New York: New York University Press.

Osella, Caroline, and Osella, F. 2008. Nuancing the Migrant Experience: Perspectives from Kerala, South India. In Transnational South Asians: The Making of a Neo-Diaspora, edited by S. Koshy and R. Radhakrishnan, 146–178. New Delhi, India: Oxford University Press.

Page, David, and William Crawley. 2001.Satellites over South Asia: Broadcasting, Culture and the Public Interest. Oxford: Oxford University Press.

Pandey, Gyanendra. 2002. Remembering Partition: Violence, Nationalism and History in India. Cambridge: Cambridge University Press.

Parker, Richard. 1999. Beneath the Equator: Cultures of Desire, Male Homosexuality, and Emerging Gay Communities in Brazil. New York: Routledge.

Patton, Cindy, and Benigno Sanchez-Eppler, eds. 2000. Queer Diasporas. Durham, NC: Duke University Press.

Peek, Lori. 2010. Behind the Backlash: Muslim Americans after 9/11. Philadelphia: Temple University Press.

Peterson, Ruth, and Lauren Krivo. 2009. Segregated Spatial Locations, Race-Ethnic Composition, and Neighborhood Violent Crime. Annals of the American Academy of Political and Social Science 623: 93–107.

Pinto, Paulo G. 2007. Pilgrimage, Commodities, and Religious Objectification: The Making of Transnational Shiism between Iran and Syria. Comparative Studies of South Asia, Africa and the Middle East 27 (1): 109–125.

Portes, Alejandro, and Robert L. Bach. 1985. Latin Journey: Cuban and Mexican Immigrants in the United States. Berkeley: University of California Press.

Portes, Alejandro, and Ruben Rumbaut. 1996. Immigrant America: A Portrait. Berkeley: University of California Press.

———. 2001. Legacies: The Story of the Immigrant Second Generation. Berkeley: University of California Press.

Prasad, Madhava. 1998. Ideology of the Hindi Film: A Historical Construction. New Delhi, India: Oxford University Press.

Prashad, Vijay. 2000. Karma of Brown Folk. Minneapolis: University of Minnesota Press.

———. 2002. Everybody Was Kung Fu Fighting: Afro-Asian Connections and the Myth of Cultural Purity. Boston: Beacon.

———. 2012. South Asians in America Today. New York: New Press.

Puar, Jabir. 2007. Terrorist Assemblages: Homonationalism in Queer Times. Durham, NC: Duke University Press.

Puar, Jasbir, and Amit Rai. 2002. Monster, Terrorist, Fag: The War on Terrorism and the Production of Docile Patriots. Social Text 20 (3): 117–148.

———. 2004. The Remaking of a Model Minority: Perverse Projectiles Under the Spectre of Counter-Terrorism. Social Text 22 (3): 75–104.

Pugh, Clifford. 2001. Pakistani-Americans at Home in Houston. Houston Chronicle. October 28.

Pyne, Solana. 2003. Making Enemies: Post–9-11 Crackdowns Spurring Prejudice. Village Voice. July 8.

Rahman, Momin. 2010. Queer as Intersectionality: Theorizing Gay Muslim Identities. Sociology 44 (5): 944–61.

Rai, Amit. 2009. Untimely Bollywood: Globalization and India's New Media Assemblage. Durham, NC: Duke University Press.

Ramakrishnan. 1996. Bisexuality: Identities, behaviors and politics. Trikone. April.

Rana, Junaid. 2011. Terrifying Muslims: Race and Labor in the South Asian Diaspora. Durham, NC: Duke University Press.

Rangaswamy, Padma. 2000. Namaste America: Indian Immigrants in an American Metropolis. University Park: Pennsylvania State University Press.

Rao, R. Raj. 2000. Memories Pierce the Heart: Homoeroticism, Bollywood-Style. Journal of Homosexuality 39 (3/4): 299–306.

Rath, Jan. 2000. Immigrant Business: The Economic, Political and Social Environment. New York: St. Martin's.

Rathore, Naeem. 1957. The Pakistani Student. New York: American Friends of the Middle East.

Ratti, Rakesh, ed. 1993. A Lotus of Another Color: An Unfolding of the South Asian Gay and Lesbian Experience. New York: Alyson Books.

Razin, Eran. 1993. Immigrant Entrepreneurs in Israel, Canada and California. In Immigration and Entrepreneurship: Culture, Capital, and Ethnic Networks, edited by Ivan Light and Parminder Bhachu, 97–124. New Brunswick, NJ: Transaction Books.

Reddy, Chandan. 2011. Freedom with Violence: Race, Sexuality, and the US State. Durham, NC: Duke University Press.

Reimers, David M. 1985. Still the Golden Door: The Third World Comes to America. New York: Columbia University Press.

Reitz, Jeffrey. 1980. The Survival of Ethnic Groups. Toronto: McGraw-Hill.

Reyes, Angela. 2002. Are You Losing Your Culture? Poetics, Indexicality, and Asian American Identity. Discourse Studies 4 (2): 183–99.

Roche, John. 1982. Suburban Ethnicity: Ethnic Attitudes and Behavior among Italian Americans in Two Suburban Communities. Social Science Quarterly 63 (1): 295–303.

Rodriquez, Juana Maria. 2003. Queer Latinidad: Identity Practices, Discursive Spaces. New York: New York University Press.

Roscoe, W. and Stephen D. Murray. 1997. Islamic Homosexualities: Culture, History, and Literature. New York: New York University Press.

Rouse, Carolyn, and Janet Hoskins. 2004. Purity, Soul Food, and Sunni Islam: Explorations at the Intersection of Consumption and Resistance. Cultural Anthropology 19 (2): 226–249.

Rouse, Roger. 1995. Thinking through Transnationalism: Notes on the Cultural Politics of Class Relations in the Contemporary United States. Public Culture 7: 353–402.

Rowson, Everett. 1991. The Effeminates of Early Medina. Journal of the American Oriental Society 111: 671–693.

Saha, Anamik. 2012. "Beards, Scarves, Halal Meat, Terrorists, Forced Marriage": Television Industries and the Production of "Race." Media, Culture, Society 34: 424–438.

Sahlins, Marshall. 1981. Historical Metaphors and Mythical Realities: Structure in the Early History of the Sandwich Islands Kingdom. Ann Arbor: University of Michigan Press.

Said, Edward. 1988. The Essential Terrorist. In Blaming the Victims: Spurious Scholarship and the Palestine Question, edited by Edward Said and Christopher Hitchens, 149–158. New York: Verso.

Salter, Malcolm S. 2008. Innovation Corrupted: The Origins and Legacy of Enron's Collapse. Cambridge, MA: Harvard University Press.

Saran, P. 1985. The Asian Indian Experience in the United States. Cambridge, MA: Schenkman.

Sassen, Saskia. 1996. Losing Control? Sovereignty in an Age of Globalization. New York: Columbia University Press.

———. 1998. Globalization and Its Discontents. Essays on the New Mobility of People and Money. New York: New Press.

Scardino, Barrie, William F. Stern, and Bruce C. Webb, eds. 2003. Ephemeral City: Cite Looks at Houston. Austin: University of Texas Press.

Schmidt, Garbi. 2004. Islam in Urban America: Sunni Muslims in Chicago. Philadelphia: Temple University Press.

Seaman, P. David. 1972. Modern Greek and American English in Contact. The Hague, Netherlands: Mouton.

Seremetakis, C. Nadia. 1996. The Senses Still. Chicago: University of Chicago Press.

Shah, Nayan. 1993. Sexuality, Identity, and the Uses of History. In A Lotus of Another Color: An Unfolding of the South Asian Gay and Lesbian Experience, edited by Rakesh Ratti, 113–132. Boston, MA: Alyson.

———. 2001. Contagious Divides: Epidemics and Race in San Francisco's Chinatown. Berkeley: University of California Press.

———. 2011. Stranger Intimacy: Contesting Race, Sexuality and the Law in the North American West. Berkeley: University of California Press.

Shankar, Shalini. 2008. Desi Land: Teen Culture, Class, and Success in Silicon Valley. Durham, NC: Duke University Press.

Sharma, Nitasha. 2004. Claiming Space, Making Race: Second Generation South Asian American Hip Hop Artists. PhD diss., University of California at Santa Barbara.

Shelton, Beth Anne, Nestor Rodriguez, Joe Feagin, Robert Bullard, and Robert Thomas. 1989. Houston: Growth and Decline in a Sunbelt Boomtown. Philadelphia: Temple University Press.

Shelton, Jason, and M. Nicole Coleman. 2009. After the Storm: How Race, Class, and Immigration Concerns Influenced Beliefs About the Katrina Evacuees. Social Science Quarterly 90 (3): 480–496.

Sheth, Pravin. 2001. Indians in America: One Stream, Two Waves, Three Generations. Jaipur, India: Rawat Publications.

Shields, Steven, and Robert Ogles. 1995. Black Liberation Radio: A Case Study of Free Radio Micro-Broadcasting. Howard Journal of Communications 5: 173–183.

Shukla, Sandhya. 1997. Building Diaspora and Nation: The 1991 Cultural Festival of India. European Journal of Cultural Studies 11(2): 296–315.

———. 2003. India Abroad: Diasporic Cultures of Postwar America and England. Princeton, NJ: Princeton University Press.

Siddiqui, Idrees. 1991. Radio Journalism in Pakistan. Lahore, Pakistan: Feroz Sons.

Silverman, D. 1986. Selling Culture: Bloomingdale's, Diana Vreeland, and the New Aristocracy of Taste in Reagan's America. New York: Pantheon.

Silverstone, Roger. 1994. Television and Everyday Life. London: Routledge.

Sims, Rondal R., and Johannes Brinkmann. 2003. Enron Ethics: Culture Matters More than Codes. Journal of Business Ethics 45 (3): 243–256.

Singer, Milton. 1972. When a Great Tradition Modernizes. New York: Praeger.

Siu, Lok. 2001. Diasporic Cultural Citizenship: Chineseness and Belonging in Central America and Panama. Social Text 19: 7–28.

Skitka, L. J. 2006. Patriotism or Nationalism? Understanding Post-September 11, 2001 Flag Display Behavior. Journal of Applied Social Psychology 25: 1995–2011.

Slonim, Shlomo. 1972. The Indian-Pakistani War and the Middle East. Midstream 18 (3): 3–7.

Slyomovics, Susan. 1995. New York City's Muslim World Day Parade. In Nation and Migration: The Politics of Space in the South Asian Diaspora, edited by Peter van der Veer, 157–176. Philadelphia: University of Pennsylvania Press.

Smith, Robert C. 2005. Mexican New York: Transnational Lives of New Immigrants. Berkeley: University of California Press.

Song, Min. 1998. Pahkar Singh's Argument with Asian America: Color and the Structure of Race Formation. In A Part, Yet Apart: South Asians in Asian America, edited by Lavina Shankar and Rajini Srikant, 79–104. Philadelphia: Temple University Press.

Soysal, Yasemin N. 1996. Changing Citizenship in Europe: Remarks on Post-national Membership and the Nation State. In Citizenship, Nationality, and Migration in Europe, edited by David Cesarani and Mary Fulbrook, 17–29. London: Routledge.

Spitulnik, Debra. 2002. Mobile Machines and Fluid Audiences: Rethinking Reception through Zambian Radio Culture. In Media Worlds: Anthropology on a New Terrain, edited by Faye Ginsberg, Lila Abu-Lughod, and Brian Larkin, 337–354. Berkeley: University of California Press.

Spross, Jess. 2012. Hate Crimes against Muslims Remain Near Decade High. Think Progress. December 12. http://thinkprogress.org/security/2012/12/10/1312341/hate-crimes-against-muslims-remain-near-decade-high/. Accessed August 15, 2013.

Starret, Gregory. 1995. The Political Economy of Religious Commodities in Cairo. American Anthropologist 97: 51–58.

Steffanides, George. 1974. America the Land of My Dreams: The Odyssey of a Green Immigrant. Fitchburg, MA: Self-published.

Stepick, Alex, Guillermo Grenier, Max Castro, and Marvin Dunn. 2003. This Land Is Our Land: Immigrants and Power in Miami. Berkeley: University of California Press.

Steptoe, Tyina Leaneice. 2008. Dixie West: Race, Migration, and the Color Lines in Jim Crow Houston. PhD diss., University of Wisconsin.

Sutton, Philip, and Stephen Vertigans 2005. Resurgent Islam: A Sociological Approach. Cambridge and Oxford, UK: Polity.

Takaki, Ronald. 2000. Iron Cages: Race and Culture in 19th-Century America. Cambridge. New York: Oxford University Press.

Talbot, Phillips. 1970. The American Posture Toward India and Pakistan. Annals of the American Academy of Political and Social Science 390: 87–97.

Thangaraj, Stanley. 2010. Liting it Up: Popular Culture, Indo-Pak Basketball, and South Asian American Institutions. Cosmopolitan Civil Societies: An Interdisciplinary Journal 2 (2): 71–91.

———. 2012. Playing through Difference: The Black-White Racial Logic and Interrogating South Asian American Identity. Journal of Ethnic and Racial Studies 35 (6): 988–1006.

Thomas, Pradip. 2009. Selling God/Saving Souls: Religious Commodities, Spiritual Markets and the Media. Global Media and Communication 5 (1): 57–76.

Tischauser, Leslie V. 2012. Jim Crow Laws. Santa Barbara, CA: Greenwood.

Toor, Saadia. 2005. A National Culture for Pakistan: The Political Economy of a Debate. Inter-Asia Cultural Studies 6 (3): 318–340.

Trawick, Margaret. 1992. Notes on Love in a Tamil Family. Berkeley: University of California Press.

Trevino, Roberto. 1994. In Their Own Way: Parish Funding and Mexican-American Ethnicity in Catholic Houston, 1911-1972. Latino Studies Journal 5 (3): 87–107.

———. 2003. Facing Jim Crow: Catholic Sisters and the "Mexican Problem" in Texas. Western Historical Quarterly 34 (2): 139–164.

———. 2006. The Church in the Barrio: Mexican American Ethno-Catholicism in Houston. Chapel Hill: University of North Carolina Press.

Tuan, Mnia. 1998. Forever Foreigners or Honorary Whites? The Asian Ethnic Experience Today. New Brunswick, NJ: Rutgers University Press.

Turner, Victor. 1967. The Forest of Symbols: Aspects of Ndembu Ritual. Ithaca, NY: Cornell University Press.

———. 1969. The Ritual Process: Structure and Anti-Structure. Lewis Henry Morgan Lectures. Chicago: Aldine Transaction.

———. 1974. Dramas, Fields, and Metaphors: Symbolic Action in Human Society. Symbol, Myth, and Ritual. Ithaca, NY: Cornell University Press.

———. 1985. The Anthropology of Performance. In On the Edge of the Bush, edited by Edith Turner, 177–204. Tucson: University of Arizona Press.

U.S. Congress, Senate Committee on Foreign Relations. 1959. Study of United States Foreign Policy: Summary of Views of Retired Foreign Service Officers, 86th Congress, 1st Session.

Valdez, Zulema. 2008. The Effect of Social Capital on White, Korean, Mexican and Black Business Owners' Earnings in the U.S. Journal of Ethnic and Migration Studies 34 (6): 955–973.

Vanita, Ruth. 2001. Same-Sex Love in India: Readings from Literature and History. New York: Palgrave Macmillan.

Verkaaik, Oskar. 2004. Migrants and Militants: Fun and Urban Violence in Pakistan. Princeton, NJ: Princeton University Press.

Vertovec, Steven. 2009. Transnationalism. New York: Routledge.

Visweswaran, Kamala. 1994. Fictions of Feminist Ethnography. Minneapolis: University of Minnesota.

Vojnovic, Igor. 2003a. Governance in Houston: Growth Theories and Urban Pressures. Journal of Urban Affairs 25 (4): 589–624.

———. 2003b. Laissez-Faire Governance and the Archetype Laissez-Faire City in the USA: Exploring Houston. Georgrafiska Annaler. Series B, Human Geography 85 (1): 19–38.

von der Mehden, Fred. 1984. The Ethnic Groups of Houston. Houston: Rice University.

Waldinger, Roger. 1989. Immigration and Urban Change. Annual Review of Sociology 15: 211–232.

Walker, Doug. 1999. The Media's Role in Immigrant Adaptation: How First-Year Haitians Use the Media. Journalism and Communication Monographs 1(3): 158–196.

Warner, R. S. 1998. Immigration and Religious Communities in the United States. In Gatherings in Diaspora, edited by R. S. Warner and J. G. Wittner. Philadelphia: Temple University Press, 3–34.

Waters, Mary C., and Karl Eschbach. 1995. Immigration and Ethnic and Racial Inequality in the United States. Annual Review of Sociology 21: 419–446.

Waterston, Albert. 1963. Planning in Pakistan. Baltimore, MD: Johns Hopkins University Press.

Waugh, Thomas. 2001. Queering Bollywood, or "I'm the Player, You're the Naïve One": Patterns of Sexual Subversion in Recent Indian Popular Cinema. In Keyframes: Popular Cinema and Cultural Studies, edited by Matthew Tinkcon and Amy Villarejo. New York: Routledge.

Weber, Max. 1905. The Protestant Ethic and the Spirit of Capitalism. New York: Penguin.

Weston, Kath. 1998. Long Slow Burn: Sexuality and Social Science. New York: Routledge.

Werbner, Pnina. 1996. Stamping the Earth in the Name of Allah: Zikr and the Sacralizing of Space Among British Muslims. Cultural Anthropology 11 (3): 309–338.

———. 2002. Imagined Diasporas among Manchester Muslims: The Public Performance of Pakistani Transnational Identity Politics. Santa Fe, NM: School of American Research Press.

———. 2003. Pilgrims of Love: The Anthropology of a Global Sufi Cult. Bloomington: Indiana University Press.

Werbner, Pnina, and Helene Basu, ed. 1998. Embodying Charisma: Modernity, Locality and the Performance of Emotion in Sufi Cults. New York: Rutledge.

Westra, Laura, and Bill E. Lawson. 2001. Faces of Environmental Racism: Confronting Issues of Global Justice. Lanham, MD: Rowman & Littlefield.

Williams, Raymond Brady. 1988. Religions of Immigrants from India and Pakistan: New Threads in the American Tapestry. Cambridge: Cambridge University Press.

———. 2000. The South Asian Religious Diaspora in Britain, Canada, and the United States. Albany: State University of New York Press.

Wright, Theodore P., Jr. 1991. Periphery–Periphery Relations and Ethnic Conflict in Pakistan: Sindhis, Muhajirs, and Punjabis. Comparative Studies in Society and History 22 (4): 576–596.

Xie, Yu, and Kimberly A. Goyette. 2004. Asian Americans' Earnings Disadvantage Reexamined: The Role of Place of Education. American Journal of Sociology 109: 1075–1108.

Yahya, H. 2000. Perished Nations. London: Ta-Ha.

Yanagisako, Sylvia Junko. 1995. Transforming Orientalism: Gender, Nationality and Class in Asian American Studies. In: Naturalizing Power: Essays in Feminist Cultural Analysis, edited by Sylvia Junko Yanagisako and Carol Lowery Delaney, 275–298. New York: Routledge.

Yang, Fenggang, and Helen Rose Ebaugh. 2001. Transformations in New Immigrant Religions and Their Global Implications. American Sociological Review 66 (2): 269–288.

Yeh, Chiou-Ling. 2004. "In the Traditions of China and in the Freedom of America": The Making of San Francisco's Chinese New Year Festivals. American Quarterly 56 (2): 395–420.

———. 2008. Making an American Festival: Chinese New Year in San Francisco's Chinatown. Berkeley: University of California Press.

Yip, A.K.-T. 2004. Embracing Allah and Sexuality? South Asian Non-Heterosexual Muslims in Britain. In South Asians in the Diaspora, edited by K.A. Jacobsen and P. Pratap Kumar, 294–310. Leiden, Netherlands: Brill.

Yoon, I. J. 1991. Changing Significance of Ethnic and Class Resources in Immigrant Business: The Case of Korean Businesses in Chicago. International Migration Review 25: 303–31.

Yuval-Davis, Nira. 1997. Gender and Nation. New York: Sage.

Zhou, Min. 1997. Segmented Assimilation: Issues, Controversies, and Recent Research on the New Second Generation. International Migration Review 31: 975–1008.

———. 2004. Revisiting Ethnic Entrepreneurship: Convergences, controversies, and conceptual advancements. International Migration Review 38: 1040–74.

Zoll, Rachel. 2010. Businesses Reaching out to U.S. Muslim community: Halal Industry is Tapping into an Expanding Market. Associated Press. December 26.

Ahmed Afzal received a BA in Third World Studies from Vassar College, an MSc in cultural geography from the London School of Economics, and a PhD in cultural anthropology from Yale University in 2005. He is Assistant Professor of Anthropology at Purchase College, State University of New York.